MICHIGAN SALVAGE

MICHIGAN SALVAGE

THE FICTION OF
Bonnie Jo Campbell

Edited by Lisa DuRose, Ross K. Tangedal, and Andy Oler

MICHIGAN STATE UNIVERSITY PRESS
East Lansing

Michigan State University Press
East Lansing, Michigan 48823-5245

Library of Congress Cataloging-in-Publication Data
Names: DuRose, Lisa, editor. | Tangedal, Ross K., 1986–, editor. | Oler, Andy, editor.
Title: Michigan salvage : the fiction of Bonnie Jo Campbell / edited by Lisa DuRose,
Ross K. Tangedal, and Andy Oler.
Description: East Lansing : Michigan State University Press, [2023] |
Includes bibliographical references.
Identifiers: LCCN 2022024189 | ISBN 978-1-61186-452-6 (paperback) |
ISBN 978-1-60917-727-0 (pdf) | ISBN 978-1-62895-495-1 (epub) |
ISBN 978-1-62896-489-9 (kindle)
Subjects: LCSH: Campbell, Bonnie Jo, 1962—Criticism and interpretation. |
Campbell, Bonnie Jo, 1962—Study and teaching. | LCGFT: Literary criticism. | Essays.
Classification: LCC PS3553.A43956 Z76 2023 | DDC 813/.54—dc23/eng/20220523
LC record available at https://lccn.loc.gov/2022024189

Book design by Shaun Allshouse, www.shaunallshouse.com
Cover design by Anastasia Wraight
Adobe Stock | Dump of rusty old vintage cars, retro autos collection, by DedMityay

Visit Michigan State University Press at www.msupress.org

Contents

Acknowledgments vii

Books by Bonnie Jo Campbell x

Introduction xi

PART 1. CRITICAL ESSAYS

Carp, Mud, Poison, and Stench;
or, Once Upon the Kalamazoo River
JEFFREY INSKO 3

Indigeneity in *Once Upon a River*
HEATHER A. HOWARD-BOBIWASH 15

The Radical Class Politics of *American Salvage*
CHARLES CUNNINGHAM 33

The Cultural Critique of American
Patriarchal Capitalism in *American Salvage*
ALEJANDRA ORTEGA 46

Power Tool Mishaps: Women and Alcohol in "Playhouse"
ELLEN LANSKY 59

Bonnie Jo Campbell's Millennium and the Infrastructure of Failure
GARTH SABO 72

Mothers, Daughters, and Rape Culture in
Mothers, Tell Your Daughters
LAURA FINE 86

Up the Road, Down the River:
The Novels of Bonnie Jo Campbell Side by Side
MONICA FRIEDMAN 99

PART 2. TEACHING ESSAYS

Kalamazoo County: Nurturing a Community of Readers
MARSHA MEYER   119

Entering the Current: Connecting High School Readers
with *Once Upon a River*
BECKY COOPER   125

Fiction Friction: Teaching Chronic and Acute Conflict in
Bonnie Jo Campbell's Short Fiction
RS DEEREN   143

The Expatriate Midwesterner: Teaching Bonnie Jo Campbell to
Second Language Writing Students
DOUG SHELDON   157

American Weirdos on Parade: Reader-Response Journals
and "The Smallest Man in the World"
JENNY ROBERTSON   171

APPENDIX. TEACHING ACTIVITIES   187

Contributors   213

Acknowledgments

In this first full-length study of Bonnie Jo Campbell's fiction, we were especially conscious of creating a diverse, usable collection for a wide range of readers. *Michigan Salvage* thus features the work of dedicated scholars and teachers, a graphic artist, and a public librarian. Becky Cooper, Charles Cunningham, RS Deeren, Laura Fine, Monica Friedman, Heather A. Howard-Bobiwash, Jeffrey Insko, Ellen Lansky, Marsha Meyer, Alejandra Ortega, Jenny Robertson, Garth Sabo, and Doug Sheldon deserve special mention for their patience and expertise, and for trusting us with their work.

We are thrilled that the first critical book on Campbell, a Michigan native, will be published by a Michigan-based press. The team at Michigan State University Press, under the direction of Gabriel Dotto and Catherine Cocks, shepherded the book from acquisition to release. We are glad that the book found a good, Michigan home. We would also like to thank the two anonymous reviewers for the time and care they took with the manuscript; their specific suggestions improved the strength and unity of this collection.

It is especially fitting that the press is housed in East Lansing, Michigan, where the Society for the Study of Midwestern Literature was founded in 1970. This collection was born from the organization's annual conference in May 2019, when Campbell received the Mark Twain Award for Distinguished Contributions to Midwestern Literature. We would like to thank Sara Kosiba and Laura Julier, especially, for their efforts to support the work of Midwestern writers. We also wish to thank our respective institutions for their support: Inver Hills Community College, the University of Wisconsin–Stevens Point, and Embry-Riddle Aeronautical University.

We are grateful to the following venues in which parts of particular essays appeared in earlier forms: portions of Ellen Lansky's "Power Tool Mishaps" appeared first in "Miss Amelia's Pharmacy: Carson McCullers and the Influence of Alcohol" in *Reflections in a Critical Eye: Essays on Carson McCullers*, edited by Jan Whitt, University Press of America, 2008, pp. 61–76; an earlier version of Garth Sabo's "Bonnie Jo Campbell's Millennium and the Infrastructure of Failure" appeared as "Retrospective Futurity: Bonnie Jo Campbell's Millennial Fiction" in *Midwestern Miscellany*, vol. 48, Spring 2020, pp. 18–29; and an earlier version of Becky Cooper's "Entering the Current" appeared as "An Invitation to Connect High School Readers Critically and Creatively with Bonnie Jo Campbell's *Once Upon a River*" in *Midwestern Miscellany*, vol. 48, Spring 2020, pp. 40–51. Thank you to the University Press of America and the Society for the Study of Midwestern Literature for permission to include parts of those essays in this collection.

As an editorial team, collaborating on the first book on Campbell's writing has been energizing. Especially considering that this book came together during the COVID-19 pandemic, working with each other has been both stabilizing and joyful. However, no book comes without the sacrifice of time, and our loved ones supported us by giving us the time we needed to bring the collection together. We thank our spouses and children for their support and love while we did this work: Lisa DuRose to Susan Peters and Chandler Peters-DuRose; Ross K. Tangedal to CJ, Adeline, Hazel, and Charlie Tangedal; and Andy Oler to Elin Grimes and Ada, Silas, and Miriam Oler.

BOOKS BY BONNIE JO CAMPBELL

Women & Other Animals (1999)

Our Working Lives: Short Stories of People and Work (2000),
coedited with Larry Smith

Q Road (2002)

American Salvage (2009)

Love Letters to Sons of Bitches (2009)

Once Upon a River (2011)

Mothers, Tell Your Daughters (2015)

Introduction

At the end of "Winter Life," a short story from Bonnie Jo Campbell's *American Salvage* (2009), Harold sits in his parked car outside of the home he shares with his wife Trisha. He looks over at his garden buried in another heavy snow, victim of a harsh Michigan winter, "assuring himself it was still there beneath the snow, fertile and quiescent" (91). Once Trisha pulls in behind him, he finally gets out of the car, resolute in his implied mission to fix his troubled marriage. Near the end of "The Yard Man," Jerry opens up to his neighbor Holroyd about his wife Natalie, who had recently moved out of their home. "It was more relaxing now, not having to worry about fixing everything up, but it didn't stop him from missing her. Jerry said, 'My wife said I was always staring at her and it made her nervous. I thought it was a normal thing to look at your wife all the time.' . . . Anything seemed possible now that Jerry's wife was gone, any kind of sadness" (31). Quiet scenes like this populate so much of Campbell's fiction, but there's an ache under that veneer of resilience.

Campbell's writing invites readers to consider the dimensions of their lives—their limits and possibilities. One way to help students engage with Campbell's work is to ask them to think about aspects of their own backgrounds. At the University of Wisconsin–Stevens Point, for example, most students come from blue-collar backgrounds. They know dairy cows and milk machines, the stench of a thriving paper mill, and the fortitude and frailty of family—in many ways, they come from the kinds of rural spaces that Campbell presents in her fiction. When asked to write papers about their hometowns, with particular focus on the people they know, it becomes clear that many grew up with a Harold and a Trisha, or a Jerry and a Holroyd. Their essays tell about diesel mechanics, VFW organizers, postal workers, basketball coaches, and town drunks. Students use their hearts and their heads to craft critical anecdotes about home and the complexity of living in the region that many feel is the simplest of all.

Campbell does not shy away from the struggles that drive her characters to love, to succumb to addiction, to give up, to triumph, to dance. She makes them people that we know, and because we know them, we can do a better job of knowing ourselves. "A lot of our realizations as writers are suddenly waking up and saying, 'Oh, you can do that. Oh, we can write about that,'" she told *Arkana*. "Most importantly, we wake up to the possibility of writing about the kind of people we know best" ("Interview").

Writing about the people she knows best—rural, working-class folks in Southwest Michigan—took Campbell some time. For decades, she documented her hometown of Comstock, Michigan, in a newsletter, the *Letter Parade*, an assembly of Campbell's astute and humorous observations on her neighborhood as well as letters from readers and writers around the country. But her journey to published author took several detours. She recalls in a 2018 interview with the *Lab Review*, "Because I knew that writing was a competitive, tough business and because I lacked confidence in my abilities, for most of my life I tried to do other things. I majored in Philosophy, ran bicycle tours in Russia and Eastern Europe, and went into a PhD program in mathematics. All the while, though, I kept writing, and finally, after decades, I got better at it" ("An Interview"). In her thirties, Campbell completed an MA in mathematics at Western Michigan University and was on her way to a PhD when she enrolled in a fiction-writing workshop taught by National Book Award winner Jaimy Gordon. Campbell soon left her math program and completed an MFA in fiction.

After obtaining her MFA, Campbell won the AWP prize in short fiction for her first collection of short stories, *Women & Other Animals*. When it was published in 1999, a *Publishers Weekly* review described the collection as a "bold and eloquent debut" featuring "women from Michigan's Lower Peninsula who bite, claw, flee from danger and follow their instincts, revealing their untamed inner selves." National accolades followed the 2009 publication of her second short-story collection, *American Salvage*, a finalist for both the National Book Award and the National Book Critics Circle Award. From these beginnings, Campbell has built a career (two novels, a book of poetry, and three short-story collections, at the time of this writing) founded on illuminating the hardships and tenacity of rural inhabitants often overlooked in mainstream narratives.

They were dirty and rusted from the slush and mud and road salt,
but each of their bodies contained a core of platinum.
— "King Cole's American Salvage"

Campbell embroils her characters in the fallout from Michigan's declining manufacturing economy, producing a sense of local economic hardship that makes her writing legible beyond its immediate Kalamazoo-area context. As she said in an address at the Library of Congress, comparing Midwestern to Southern writing, "I kind of wonder if the upper Midwest—the seat of American manufacturing, and trade unions, and that fabulous middle class we used to have—has had its own plunge and economic fall from grace" ("Literary"). Because of the structural challenges faced by Campbell's characters, critics often contextualize her writing within the genres of "country noir" or "grit lit," which Brian Carpenter defines through its focus on rural, working-class, occasionally violent subjects. While Carpenter labels grit lit a Southern genre, he notes that many non-Southerners are among its best practitioners, specifically mentioning Campbell, Ohioan Donald Ray Pollock, and Benjamin Percy, whose fiction ranges from Minnesota to Oregon to Alaska. We also read Campbell in conversation with recent award-winning rural crime writers such as Texan Attica Locke and Appalachia's Alison Stine.

Campbell is not exclusively a crime writer, however, and the range of her writing owes much to the competing sensibilities of the storytellers in her family. On one hand, Campbell describes how her mother, Susanna, told tales that felt far-fetched, fantastical, "stories of people drinking too much and dancing with lampshades on their heads, with somebody ending up in jail or at least asleep in the bathtub." On the other, her grandfather, Frank W. Herlihy, would recount "cute little misunderstandings" that were eventually resolved by reasonable people. In contrast to her grandfather's well-mannered, predictable cityscapes, her mother was drawn toward wild, unpredictable rural spaces, and Campbell began "to see how the different sensibilities created such different stories, and I had to come to understand my own sensibility, which is different from both of theirs" ("Survival"). Still, Campbell's style adopts aspects of her mother's and grandfather's approaches to storytelling, and as a result her stories and the characters within them move beyond urban/rural binaries and familiar tropes of the Midwest. She offers, instead, a nuanced version of the rural landscape, juxtaposing the pasture with the junkyard, the river with the paper mill.

Campbell's inclination toward diverse experiences appears in her life choices as well as her fiction. After a year at the University of Southern California, Campbell returned to the Midwest and, like her grandfather, attended the University of Chicago, where she majored in philosophy and lived with her grandparents in Hyde Park. After college, Campbell traveled widely: hitchhiking through Canada, running bike tours through the Baltics, and touring with the Ringling Bros. and Barnum & Bailey Circus (she sold snow cones). Campbell explained to the *Chicago Tribune* that abandoning a PhD in mathematics in favor of creative writing was driven, in part, by such multiplicity: "A mathematical proof is beautiful, but when you're finished, it's really only about one thing. A story can be about many things" (qtd. in Keller E2).

While Campbell's way of thinking about the world developed in Chicago and during her travels, her writing life didn't flourish until she returned home to Comstock, Michigan, where she lives just three miles from her childhood home, built by her grandfather. Tensions between those who left and those who stayed play out in a number of Campbell's stories. Estranged and educated daughters return to the farm where their mothers are struggling or dying, while other women attempt to navigate the violent and vicious world created by and for men. In her second collection, *American Salvage*, Campbell amplifies the hope necessary to bridge futility and fury: men prepare for Y2K, bemoan their lack of good union jobs, lament the loss of a simpler life, hold out for a better harvest, and contemplate a way out of who and what they are—a challenge, as so many of her characters are pulled between self-improvement and self-destruction. The nostalgic fiction of men providing the primary income has thus given way to women picking up the pieces of their American lives.

Campbell's characters live in the degraded post-industrial landscape of rural Michigan, which challenges them in different ways: how alcohol and drugs affect families and communities; how men hold much power over women and girls; what to do about the beauty and peril of place; and how to find hope in darkness. According to Sarah Shotland, creative writing students in prisons and rehab facilities connect with Campbell's fiction because even her most succinct stories find space for such complexity. The tangled uncertainty of promise and pain in ordinary lives fuels Campbell's examination of American exceptionalism in the post-industrial years of the late twentieth and early twenty-first centuries. In the introduction to *Our Working Lives* (2000), the collection she coedited with Larry Smith, Campbell articulates the value she places on telling the stories of working people: "characters struggle with the challenges and indignities of every sort of job and often found meaning there" (5). In *American Salvage*, she renders her characters as dormant but dreaming, their lives cobbled together by regret and repetition, yet she emphasizes equally their sincere search for meaning.

Her version of country noir, then, is distinctly centered around the working-class people of rural Michigan and the structural violence inherent in their lives. Accordingly, as Joseph Wydeven argues, country noir's emphasis on petty crime "and the constant stir of small-time pecuniary ambition" (48) distinguish it from earlier noir texts. Craig Fehrman situates Campbell among a specific Midwestern strain of country noir writers, and he defines the genre by quoting crime writer Dennis Lehane's contention that "in Greek tragedy they fall from great heights. In noir they fall from the curb." Fehrman differentiates country noir in that, in writing like Campbell's, "there are no curbs. The roads are gravel and dirt, but the people still find a way to fall." In Campbell's fiction, people fall for various reasons—poverty, addiction, the accumulation of daily indignities—and emphasizing the way that these become unmanageable demonstrates how Campbell challenges the prevailing expectations of rural working people. Scott D. Emmert argues that Midwestern country noir stories play on the expectation that country people hold "purer, simpler values" (29), arriving at a narrative in which the "denial of one's complex humanity in favor of a 'simple' view of the self can serve as a justification for our darkest deeds" (29–30).

Several essays in *Michigan Salvage* interrogate the simpler views and darker deeds of Campbell's characters. Garth Sabo argues that in a trio of stories about the millennium, Campbell's methods of negotiating futures that failed provide a valuable lens for looking at the Midwestern present in terms of what was imagined but never realized. RS Deeren approaches a similar question from a craft perspective, showing how Campbell intermingles plot and character development to complicate immediate conflicts through long-term struggles such as poverty and drug abuse. For Charles Cunningham, such complications demonstrate how *American Salvage* condemns the social order by way of negation and signals the necessity for a more just and humane society. Whether Campbell's characters are breaking the law or enduring everyday hardships, by examining the structural challenges they face, the essays in *Michigan Salvage* both acknowledge Campbell's scholarly and popular categorization as a country noir writer and show how she exceeds it.

I guess you never believed in them folk songs, how a man's love
was going to be a reward for all the hardship of a woman's life.
—"Mothers, Tell Your Daughters"

Campbell's representation of working-class life takes on special resonance in the experiences of women. Her working-class female protagonists must negotiate the intersections of poverty, addiction, and sexual violence that reside in the rural Midwest and beyond. In this representation of women's lives—particularly in the challenges they face and the spaces they inhabit—Campbell joins a lineage of celebrated American authors like Flannery O'Connor, Bobbie Ann Mason, and Dorothy Allison. And, like them, she does not shy away from the imperfections of her characters. Speaking at a celebration on what would have been O'Connor's ninety-first birthday, Campbell articulated what may well be her own approach to writing character: "Flannery shows us that the characters we love in fiction may be precisely the ones we would not want to spend time with in real life" ("Literary").

Such complexity was readily apparent in Campbell's mother, Susanna. Describing her as a powerful, unconventional role model, Campbell told Lisa DuRose: "I had someone worth watching as I was growing up" ("Personal"). As a young woman, Susanna left Chicago because she wished to live beyond the confines of the city and outside of the family's culture of conventional education (both her father and her sister graduated from the University of Chicago, as did Bonnie, her eldest daughter). Later, after ten years of marriage, when her eldest child was nine and her youngest a year, Susanna and her husband Rick divorced, and Susanna was left to feed her family on forty dollars a month child support. When the price of milk increased one cent a gallon (and the family was using four gallons a day), she decided to buy a cow. With the help of kind neighbors, Susanna learned how to milk the creature, and eventually all of her children learned to tend the animals. According to Susanna, the cow offered a path to sustainability: "I never looked back on the farming after that. Basically, I was farming to feed my kids" (S. Campbell, "Personal"). Susanna's efforts to live as free a life as possible explains Campbell's sustained interest in the lives of rural women, whose agency is too often contingent on the whims of men and weather.

Since her debut, *Women & Other Animals* (1999), Campbell's writing has highlighted the vulnerability and strength of women, a delicate balancing act that is a key feature of *Love Letters to Sons of Bitches* (2009), the only book of poetry Campbell has published. Campbell's focus on women's survival in an ecosystem often dominated by men appears most prominently in her collection *Mothers, Tell Your Daughters* (2015). In some cases, these women confront similar sexual threats as protagonist Margo Crane from *Once Upon a River* (2011), but in other circumstances these dangers come from less acknowledged sources—unwanted pregnancy, poverty, and parenting (too much or too little). Because Campbell's women and girls so often face a complex of cultural pressures and overt threats, their successes tend to be bounded by their circumstances. Still, Campbell strives to avoid limiting her characters to the experience of trauma. As she said in a 2015 interview, "Nobody considers Huck [Finn] a victim though he has been abandoned and abused by his family and society. I want my female characters to have the same chance Huck has to be the prime actors in their own stories, even when they are victims of rape and other abuse" ("Versions").

Writing women characters who are fully formed within their own narratives places Campbell within a long tradition of feminist authorship. Specifically, since Campbell sets much of her fiction in the rural Midwest, Judith Fetterley and Marjorie Pryse's regionalist framework suggests how to consider the contingencies of feminist stories outside the metropolis. Writing about the "landscapes of deprivation and blankness" of late-nineteenth- and early-twentieth-century regionalists Celia Thaxter and Mary Austin (38), Fetterley and Pryse offer one way to read Campbell's stories of women in the post-industrial Midwest. While they agree that "a feminist reader might read the landscapes themselves as a form of critique" (38), they center their analysis on the possibilities of representing such spaces: "The point of both Thaxter's and Austin's meticulous, loving, even obsessive observations of their respective topographies is to demonstrate how meaning can be constructed rather than discovered, how in environments of such apparent desolation a woman can in fact find a way not just to survive but to flourish" (38). Following this regionalist tradition, Campbell writes women who resist patriarchal expectations in rural Michigan, which takes many forms, from grinding in low-paying jobs to coping through substance abuse, from farming the land to running away from it. Her descriptions of their lives and surroundings—in Fetterley and Pryse's words, those "meticulous, loving, even obsessive observations"—show both how they are circumscribed as well as the ways they operate within that context.

The contributors in this collection consider how Campbell's female characters contend with social and economic forces as wide and varied as the landscapes they occupy. Laura Fine examines the way rape culture infects mother-daughter relationships in Campbell's work, exposing the difficulties mothers face in helping their daughters forge healthy and successful bonds with men. Ellen Lansky explores the influence alcohol has upon these relationships, as she places Campbell's "Playhouse" within the long tradition of works that consider the intersection of alcohol and women's disempowerment "masquerading as fun." In an effort to expose how American patriarchal capitalism leads to gendered violence, Alejandra Ortega situates Campbell's fiction in the rural noir genre as she considers the transgressions committed and endured by characters in "The Trespasser" and "The Solutions to Brian's Problem." Finally, Jenny Robertson articulates a classroom approach to "The Smallest Man in the World," showing how her students think through tropes of American exceptionalism, beauty, and spectacle as they both empathize with and critique the story's narrator, who describes herself as "the most beautiful woman in the bar" (*Women* 171).

> *The Stark River flowed around the oxbow at Murrayville*
> *the way blood flowed through Margo Crane's heart.*
> —*Once Upon a River*

In Campbell's most acclaimed novel, *Once Upon a River*, readers are introduced to a young protagonist, Margo Crane, whose very heart beats in sync with the river that surrounds her home. Margo is so much an embodiment of the river that when swimming, "she swallowed minnows alive and felt the Stark River move in her" (15). Margo's intimacy with the land around her owes much to Campbell's careful depiction of her own hometown, Comstock, and the economic and environmental histories of rural southwest Michigan. Like her protagonist, Campbell's knowledge of rural southwest Michigan stretches from the river to the land, from the farm to the mill. She knows where to forage chicken of the woods and puffball mushrooms, when to gather the pawpaw fruit that has fallen on the ground (the ones on trees do not ripen well), and how to quickly determine the difference between a dog tick and deer tick, pokeweed and ragweed. Growing up on a small family farm made Campbell profoundly aware of the richness and fragility of the natural world, and she has sustained a powerful curiosity in the people who inhabit it. In her 2015 essay "Cow-Milking Lessons from Mom," Campbell remembers why she needs to write about Michigan, especially those folks "who have special knowledge and skills that I know about, such as how to scrap out metal for money and steal railroad ties and castrate pigs. These are poor and working-class people and some farmers, people who fix their own cars and work low-paying jobs that aren't very satisfying, and maybe they drink too much, these people, and maybe they love uncarefully."

Telling those stories is part of what makes Campbell definitively a Michigan writer. While she participates in national conversations on gender, poverty, and American identity, she develops them within the context of the state's environment and economy. For instance, all three short story collections explore the byproducts of Michigan's long, slow economic downturn. And in an interview with *Arkana*, Campbell describes how southwest Michigan ecology influences her novels, as she imagined Rachel Crane in *Q Road* (2002) growing from the soil of Kalamazoo County and Margo Crane in *Once Upon a River* as the Kalamazoo River come to life in human form. Reviewing the novel for the *New York Times*, Jane Smiley observes the link between regional details and broader American stories, noting that Margo must navigate not only the Stark River but also "an ecosystem in which animals and humans, field and stream, purity and pollution, love and hate are tightly interconnected" (11). Michigan's environment and culture serve as foundational, as well as complicating, factors for characters and communities throughout Campbell's fiction, and the Library of Michigan has recognized the value of that approach by designating three of her works as Michigan Notable Books: *American Salvage, Once Upon a River,* and *Mothers, Tell Your Daughters.*

Such tight interconnections between Campbell's characters and their environs depend upon consistent attentiveness to the history of Michigan in the late twentieth century. For example, Lisa DuRose has shown elsewhere how Campbell represents the unseen dangers of rural life in the story "Mothers, Tell Your Daughters" through the characters' ingestion of PBB (polybrominated biphenyl), which according to Joyce Egginton was accidentally added to animal feed and poisoned upwards of nine million Michiganders in the early 1970s. Campbell also details the effects of recurrent experience, as each of her books includes the prospect or aftermath of annual river flooding—a history that Nancy Germano recounts in Kalamazoo, noting not only the ever-present risk but also that, "because of its unpredictability and irregularity, the threat was often forgotten in favor of more immediate or desirable economic concerns" (106).

More broadly, the region's long-term histories contribute to the ways that Campbell's characters build their identities, such as the tension in *Q Road* between settler colonialism and Native American removal. Rachel Crane learns that her father may have been a Potawatomi man, and she becomes fascinated with a story he told as well as the traces of Native garden plots around her land. These stories function much as described by Jill Doerfler, Niigaanwewidam James Sinclair, and Heidi Kiiwetinepi-nesiik: "Anishinaabeg stories are roots; they are both the origins and the imaginings of what it means to be a participant in an ever-changing and vibrant culture in humanity" (1). Still, despite these gestures toward the region's Anishinaabe history, *Q Road* focuses on a white farming commu-nity—a combination suggesting the opportunity for further scholarship and critique of Campbell's fiction. For example, recalling Liza Black's analysis of "the constant tension between white representations of Indi-ans, their erasure of Native presence, and the reality of Native survival" (12), it is notable that the story of present-day Greenland Township in *Q Road* includes the Potawatomi only through their material remains and Rachel's uncertain ancestry.

In this vein, Richard Hathaway describes Michigan history as "a series of continuing stress-lines or conflicting interests" (321). *Michigan Salvage* aims to show how such "stress-lines" emerge from Campbell's precise local story-telling. Beyond the essays exploring women's experiences and working-class life in rural Michigan, some authors explore longer histories of the Great Lakes State. Jeffrey Insko, for instance, demonstrates how the environmen-tal history of the Kalamazoo River—damaged by the short-sighted, unre-strained behavior of Michiganders, paired with multiple fraught attempts at regeneration—echoes Margo Crane's trajectory in *Once Upon a River*. That tension is on full display in Monica Friedman's literary-analytical comic, which compares *Q Road* and *Once Upon a River* through the his-tories that act on the novels' gun-toting teenage protagonists, Rachel and Margo. Heather A. Howard-Bobiwash explores one of those histories in detail—the evocation of the Potawatomi tribe in the novel and film versions of *Once Upon a River*—complicating their ambiguous Indigeneity through critical settler-colonial and Indigenist-feminist analytical perspectives. Sev-eral essays in this collection also show how to use these histories to help readers engage with Campbell's writing. For example, the teaching section opens with a public humanities perspective, as Kalamazoo-area librarian Marsha Meyer discusses how local authors can contribute to a community of readers through author visits, community programming, and in collaboration with libraries, schools, and bookstores. Becky Cooper demonstrates how Michigan high school students in particular can use Campbell's writing to consider their place in the world, then how they can express that through their own creative work. Considering this engagement from the perspective of students who have moved to the Midwest, Doug Sheldon assesses second-language learners' responses to Campbell's depictions of poverty, addiction, gender, and violence.

Bonnie Jo Campbell fixes her vision firmly on a rural Midwest that appears to be diminishing, and on lives that are too often discarded. She has published three short-story collections, two novels, an edited collection, a book of poetry, and more than one hundred pieces in other venues (Tangedal 463). The contributors to this collection make plain how Campbell centers the act of salvage, and as a whole they demonstrate growing interest in Campbell's writing among readers of all kinds. Because of the way teaching is entwined with critical reading both in the classroom as well as in Campbell's own practice as a frequent speaker and workshop participant, this collection is designed as a useful text for teachers, scholars, and readers. Part 1, "Critical Essays," begins with two chapters that provide compelling historical and cultural overviews, then shifts into essays examining the class and gender implications of Campbell's work. In Part 2, "Teaching Essays," practitioners articulate the possibilities and outcomes of teaching Campbell in a variety of pedagogical settings, from high school to the public library, from first-year composition to the creative-writing classroom. The appendix, "Teaching Activities," features classroom activities—designed by each contributor to correspond with their chapter—meant to spark discussion and encourage further investigation into these stories and novels.

From junkyard to farmyard, Campbell writes the American Midwest into all of her fiction. Her portrayal of economic hardship, however, and the social complications that go along with it resonate with readers of regional fiction from the Deep South to the Pacific Northwest. Her characters likewise feel familiar: struggling factory workers, neglected teenagers, battered wives and belligerent husbands, drug addicts and recovering alcoholics, blue-collar stiffs trying to make it in a landscape of change. Campbell makes their environments relevant and their narratives complex. So much of our understanding of the Midwest—not to mention rural life more broadly—is rooted in staid stereotypes of heartland and breadbasket, but Campbell's Michigan is enigmatic and alive, as bustling as a city and as complicated as a large family. Her writing is vital to the continued reappraisal of an America we think we know.

Works Cited

Black, Liza. *Picturing Indians: Native Americans in Film, 1941–1960*. U of Nebraska P, 2020.

Campbell, Bonnie Jo. *American Salvage*. Wayne State UP, 2009.

———. "Cow Milking Lessons from Mom: Life (and Writing) Skills from My Mother." *Salon*, 4 Oct. 2015.

———. "Literary Birthday Celebration: Flannery O'Connor." Library of Congress, 25 Mar. 2016.

———. "Interview: Bonnie Jo Campbell." Interview by Jack West and Liz Larson. *Arkana*, no. 6, 2019.

———. "An Interview with Bonnie Jo Campbell." Interview by Clayton Crook. *Lab Review*, 3 Dec. 2018.

———. "Introduction: Writing of Work Today." *Our Working Lives: Short Stories of People and Work*, edited by Bonnie Jo Campbell and Larry Smith. Bottom Dog Press, 2000, pp. 5–7.

———. *Mothers, Tell Your Daughters*. Norton, 2015.

———. *Once Upon a River*. Norton, 2011.

———. Personal interview by Lisa DuRose. 19–22 Aug. 2015.

———. "Survival Is Not Guaranteed." Interview by Christine Rice. *The Millions*, 25 Sept. 2015.

———. "Versions of Trouble." Interview by Polly Atwell. *Fiction Writers Review*, 5 Oct. 2015.

———. *Women & Other Animals*. Scribner's, 1999.

Campbell, Susanna. Personal interview by Lisa DuRose. 22 Aug. 2015.

Carpenter, Brian. "Introduction: Blood and Bone." *Grit Lit: A Rough South Reader*, edited by Brian Carpenter and Tom Franklin. U of South Carolina P, 2012.

Doerfler, Jill, et al., editors. *Centering Anishinaabeg Studies: Understanding the World through Stories.* Michigan State UP, 2013.

DuRose, Lisa. "Who Will Drown the Kittens? Bonnie Jo Campbell's Farm Women and the Burdens of Necessity." *Midwestern Miscellany*, vol. 48, 2020, pp. 52–64.

Egginton, Joyce. *The Poisoning of Michigan.* 1980., 2nd ed. Michigan State UP, 2009.

Emmert, Scott D. "The Horror of a Simple Man: Midwestern Evil in Scott Smith's *A Simple Plan.*" *Midwestern Miscellany*, vol. 42, Spring 2014, pp. 27–32.

Fehrman, Craig. "Country Noir: Frank Bill and the New Violent Midwestern Fiction." *American Prospect*, 23 Apr. 2013.

Fetterley, Judith, and Marjorie Pryse. *Writing out of Place: Regionalism, Women, and American Literary Culture.* U of Illinois P, 2003.

Germano, Nancy. "'A Flood of Problems' in Michigan: An Urban Environmental History." *Michigan Historical Review*, vol. 45, no. 1, 2019, pp. 81–107.

Hathaway, Richard J., editor. *Michigan: Visions of Our Past.* Michigan State UP, 1989.

Keller, Julia. "A Woman of True Grit: Ex-Chicagoan Bonnie Jo Campbell Tells It Straight." *Chicago Tribune*, 10 May 2009, p. E2.

Review of *Women & Other Animals*, by Bonnie Jo Campbell. *Publishers Weekly*, 1 Nov. 1999.

Shotland, Sarah. "The Solutions to Brian's Problem: Teaching Flash Fiction to Incarcerated Writers." *SmokeLong Quarterly*, 27 Jan. 2020.

Smiley, Jane. "Bonnie Jo Campbell's Rural Michigan Gothic." Review of *Once Upon a River*, by Bonnie Jo Campbell. *Sunday Book Review, New York Times*, 22 July 2011, p. 11.

Tangedal, Ross K. "Bonnie Jo Campbell (1962–): A Descriptive Bibliography." *Papers of the Bibliographical Society of America*, vol. 115, no. 4, 2021, pp. 463–506.

Wydeven, Joseph J. "Daniel Woodrell's New American Adam: Myth and Country Noir in *Winter's Bone.*" *Midwestern Miscellany*, vol. 42, Spring 2014, pp. 45–56.

PART 1
Critical Essays

Carp, Mud, Poison, and Stench; or, Once Upon the Kalamazoo River

JEFFREY INSKO

"Margo couldn't understand," says the narrator late in Bonnie Jo Campbell's *Once Upon a River*, "why people would let the river be treated so poorly" (302). The river in question here is not the Stark River, the "lively old river paradise" that Margo, her mother, and the Murrays "had once all been a part of" (180) and that provides the setting for the first half of the novel. Rather, Margo is reflecting upon the Kalamazoo River, where she has settled, living on a boat she purchased from her dying friend Smoke. The two rivers, distinct although conjoined, help signal key transformations in the novel's narrative arc and in Margo's life. But here I'm interested in another difference: the Stark River is Campbell's invention, while the Kalamazoo is very much real. In this essay, I want to underscore and examine how the history and condition of the "real" river—the Kalamazoo—can enrich our understanding of the novel.

The Kalamazoo River, near both Campbell's childhood and current homes, is a recurring feature in Campbell's fiction and poetry, appearing, for example, in the stories "King Cole's American Salvage" (2009) and "Mothers, Tell Your Daughters" (2015), in the novel *Q Road* (2002), and in the poem "The Fat White Woman Fails to Be Stoic When Her Lover Betrays Her" (2009). In these texts, responses to the river echo Margo's. In "Mothers, Tell Your Daughters," "fishermen troll for suckers and carp" (102). In *Q Road*, the river is "muddy [and] factory-poisoned" (26). And the speaker of "The Fat White Woman" calls it "the stinking Kalamazoo" (17). These characterizations gesture with piercing specificity toward the historical facts and, consequently, the notorious, decades-long reputation of the Kalamazoo River as a site of seemingly intractable environmental degradation and irremediable industrial pollution.

In a 2011 interview soon after the publication of *Once Upon a River*, Campbell described her protagonist as "an embodiment of a river," stating that "if the river became human, it might be like Margo" ("Trawling"). Yet because of Campbell's regional commitments, and her dedication to the lives of characters rooted in and shaped by specific locations and landscapes, it would be a mistake to think of Margo in terms of a decontextualized or metaphorized river—a river that symbolizes some abstract quality like freedom or fluidity or the passage of time. Instead, I'd like to consider what it might mean to think historically and materially about Margo not just as the embodiment of *a* river, but as the embodiment of the Kalamazoo River in particular. Tracing the river's blighted history—the two centuries or more of abuse and contamination that have characterized its settler-colonial life—I argue that Margo and the river struggle against and within similar masculinist extractive logics of domination and exploitation.

Ruin

Once Upon a River opens with a frontispiece: a hand-drawn map of the Kalamazoo River, reminiscent, self-consciously perhaps, of the maps William Faulkner drew of his fictional Yoknapatawpha County. But Campbell's map is comparatively sparse, a mostly blank landscape devoid of roads, streets, and interstates, or even of cities and towns (with only a few exceptions). The result is that the Kalamazoo is rendered as the most salient feature of the Michigan landscape, decluttered and, one might even say, cleaned up (a point to which I'll return). The map more or less accurately depicts the river's 130-mile route roughly from the meeting point of its north and south branches in the east (which are not pictured) to its termination in Lake Michigan just west of the city of Saugatuck. The confluence of the Kalamazoo and Campbell's Stark is situated in the general vicinity of what is the city of Battle Creek in Calhoun County (also not identified) just east of the city of Kalamazoo. The map also identifies key sites along the Stark, including the Murray Metal Fabricating Plant, the Murray and Crane houses on opposite sides of the river and, upriver to the southeast, Brian's house on stilts and Michael's cabin.

Aside from the map's obvious instrumentality—providing readers with a visual cartography of Margo's almost constant movement up and

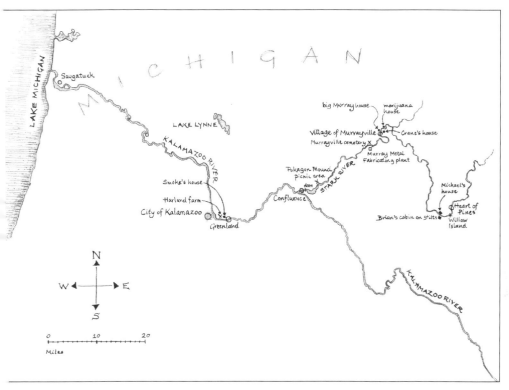

Map of Stark River, *Once Upon a River* (2011), by Adrian Kitzinger

down the river—the map serves an aesthetic function. For one thing, it insists upon geographical specificity, the particularity of place, and thus emphasizes Campbell's investment in the local. "MICHIGAN" spans the map in large block letters, and the two rivers as well as Lake Michigan highlight important features of the region's natural environment. Interestingly, the river itself splits the M from ICHIGAN, thus tripping up the name, perhaps as a subtle recognition of the artificiality of settler-colonial entities like states. This is reinforced by the map's absence of borders; its peripheral emptiness left open to the margins of the page suggests that the novel's local concerns aren't sequestered or sealed off from the wider world and, perhaps more importantly, identifies the land now called "Michigan" in bioregional (that is, according to its geomorphic and biotic features) rather than political terms. The map establishes the novel's initial refusal to accede to the logic of "coloniality"—the epistemological and material enterprise that Walter Mignolo calls the "hidden agenda (and darker side)" of modernity's promises of progress and freedom, in which "Western Christians asserted . . . control over knowledge about nature" and "engaged in an economy of brutal resource extraction" (9).

Mignolo helps make legible what Campbell's frontispiece does not, and perhaps cannot, convey: the map's emphasis on geography conceals the history of the river that Campbell's writings, as in the previous examples, so often gesture toward. Carp, mud, poison, and stench help index the noxious results of more than two centuries of extraction and industrial development, as well as environmental concern and mitigation efforts, on and along the Kalamazoo River system. The post-settler history of the Kalamazoo River thus echoes Margo's story in *Once Upon a River*: twin narratives of abuse, resilience, and dreams of regeneration.

The Kalamazoo River had a moment of national infamy in 1953, when *Life* magazine published a gruesome photo of Dumont Creek, a small tributary of the river. The photograph, captioned "Four Acres of Carp Corpses on the Kalamazoo," depicts a massive fish kill: hundreds of dead carp heaped upon one another, their floating corpses receding into the distance and "chok[ing] the waters in glistening, smelly death." Carp, like those Margo catches on the river, are a fish species "extraordinarily tenacious of life," as the magazine notes. Because they are hardy bottom-feeders able to thrive in conditions that other, more highly prized fish like trout and bass cannot, the mass death of large numbers of carp, in particular, provided a vivid and morbid indication of just how dire the state of the river had become by mid-century.

But local residents, and sportsmen in particular, had been concerned about the state of the Kalamazoo River well before then. Once known as a world-class bass fishery—one nineteenth-century account, "On the Kalamazoo," describes it as a "beautiful river, in whose limpid depths untold numbers of huge bass" could be found (133)—the river's desirable fish had all but disappeared by the second or third decade of the twentieth century, wiped out by decades of raw sewage dumped into the river and the discharge of industrial waste from the eighteen paper mills that populated the river and its tributaries. An article in the *Detroit Free Press* in 1939, for example, reported that the mills released some 60 million gallons of waste, and the city of Kalamazoo some 8 million gallons of sewage, every day ("Pollution" 6). Ten years later, another article explained that much of the waste resulted from "de-inking processes in which the fiber is reclaimed to make new paper." Ink and other substances were then dumped into the river, such that "oxygen in the river becomes so exhausted that fish no longer can live there" (Van Coevering B6).

The river suffered the effects of other industrial pollutants as well, as operations of all kinds used the river as a dump site, such as the "Murray Metal elimination pipe" Margo recalls at one point, "near which nobody fished" because it "spewed junk" (*Once* 266), or the "big blue fabricating plant" Margo sees "churning orange smoke across the river (198). In 1947, for instance, a plating company in Battle Creek released some four thousand gallons of zinc plating solution containing cyanide into the city's sewers. Eventually, the cyanide was carried into the river, killing thousands of fish. Later, in the 1960s, Michigan experienced a significant oil boom following the discovery of the Albion-Scipio trend near the meeting place of the north and south branches of the Kalamazoo. Drilling and development in the area yielded overnight riches for local farmers and provided sensational images of blazing gushers reminiscent of the oil excitement in Pennsylvania of the nineteenth century. But the absence of regulations or cautious containment practices by developers meant that for years, unquantified amounts of oil seeped into wetlands and streams, where it invariably found its way into the river. As a result of all of these practices, and others, the river seemed to many to be, as the character in *Once Upon a River* known simply as "the Indian" puts it, "polluted all to heck, polluted beyond any possibility of rejuvenation" (209). "The Indian" echoes the sentiment of a Michigan Department of Natural Resources official who, as the local historian Kit Lane has reported, proclaimed the river to be as "dead as a river can be," with the only living things in it "sow bugs, leeches, and a couple of trash algae species" along with "a few carp in backwater sloughs" (Lane 41).

This swampy characterization of the river echoes Margo's first impression upon reaching it in the company of "the Indian." She, too, notices its "brown" and "mucky" appearance (*Once* 218). The river's "muddy" reputation came from the toxic sludge it carried for decades, which observers have described in ghastly shades ranging from brown to white and even blueberry. (The journalist Mike VanBuren once joked that the river "has a colorful past. It used to be different colors on different days. Sometimes it was green, sometimes red and sometimes white—depending on which wastes were being dumped into the water.") The river was notorious for its thick consistency as much as for its unnatural polychromatic opacity. It has been described as having the viscous appearance of a milkshake; in the

Battle Creek Enquirer in 1959, one local famously described it as "a gravy river" ("Kalamazoo's" 7).

The river appeared gravy-like because of the materials swept along by its currents—not the ordinary clay and silt transported by rivers but an industrial mud comprised of waste and sediment laced with thousands of pounds of carcinogenic chemical pollutants like polychlorinated biphenyls (PCBs). Over many years, this sludge accumulated at dam sites along the river. Beginning in the first half of the nineteenth century, dozens of dams, like the one Campbell places at Confluence, were built in the Kalamazoo River watershed, disturbing aquatic communities and disrupting the spawning migrations of fish. Dams on the river and its tributaries also powered the paper mills and the sawmills and grist mills that preceded them. In the latter part of the century, hydroelectric development proliferated along the river. According to a federal report in 1932, seventeen dams along the river were producing power for industrial and municipal electricity; a few continue in operation today (Lane 26).

PCB contamination at a number of these damsites and elsewhere along the river was so severe that in 1990, the U.S. Environmental Protection Agency (EPA) designated an eighty-mile stretch of the river and a portion of Portage Creek, which feeds into the river, as a Superfund Site. Remediation activity, including containment measures and the removal of accumulated sediment containing the toxins, has been ongoing for more than thirty years. At present, the river remains an official EPA Area of Concern and a site of environmental contamination under the Michigan Natural Resources and Environmental Protection Act. Health and environmental agencies advise against the consumption of fish from the river owing to the bio-accumulation of poisonous PCBs in their tissue.

Fittingly, Margo notices the Kalamazoo River's "chemical smells . . . different from the chemical smells on the Stark." "There was," she thinks upon first noticing it, "a tinge of mold in the air" (*Once* 218). By the mid-twentieth century, the foul odor along the river had become legendary. At a campaign stop in Battle Creek in 1948, gubernatorial candidate and soon-to-be governor G. Mennen Williams told an audience that "you could tell which way the wind was blowing by the strength of the stench from the polluted Kalamazoo River" (qtd. in Noer 76). In a public hearing in 1950 held by the newly formed Water Resources Commission, residents lamented that "windows couldn't be opened in the summer because of the stench from the river water" (qtd. in Gilbert 184). In 1951, during a congressional debate over an appropriations bill, Michigan U.S. Representative Clare Hoffman railed about the state of Michigan's rivers. In Kalamazoo, he said, "the stench of the river made it almost impossible for people to sleep down there. It nauseated people who lived there—who drove through that part of our town" (8896). Almost a decade later, the city manager of Allegan, downriver from Kalamazoo, complained to the Water Resources Commission that "it will be impossible for the city of Allegan to live with the stench this summer" (Dempsey 148).

Still, the problem of industrial odor on and around the river has persisted for decades. In the 1960s, as a solution to the problem of waste from the paper mills, city engineers created sludge pits to gather the pulp. But the pits only exacerbated the problem. One resident recalled the "putrid odor" from the pits, an odor that "permeated the whole neighborhood" (Mann). Even in this century, foul odors emanating from one of Kalamazoo's remaining paper mills and a nearby wastewater management facility remain sources of controversy. In 2020, as reported by Garret Ellison, a group of residents filed a lawsuit against the company, and in 2021, the city formed an odor task force to investigate the problem.

Recovery

Yet the history of the Kalamazoo River, like Margo's, is not simply a story of disregard, degradation, and abuse. Rehearsals of the blighted state of the river have always been attended by hopes and plans for its restoration. In 1948, for example, researchers from the University of Michigan announced a pilot program to treat paper-mill waste with the hope that it would "restore" at least a portion of the river "to a satisfactory condition" (Van Coevering B6). And in 1955, the city of Kalamazoo built its first wastewater treatment plant. Upgrades and improvements to the handling of sewage were implemented in the 1960s. Additional improvements followed in the 1970s in response to increased national concern for environmental protections, which produced the modern environmental movement and led to the establishment of the Environmental Protection Agency in 1970, the passage of the Clean Water Act in 1972, and the Toxic Substances Control Act of 1976, which banned the discharge of dangerous chemicals like PCBs.

These developments yielded noticeable improvements to the river—improvements registered by Smoke in *Once Upon a River*, who tells Margo "about how dirty the river had been when he bought [his] property decades ago and how much cleaner it was now that the factories and cities upstream couldn't dump their waste and sewage into the water" (266). Accounts like Smoke's became commonplace in the later decades of the twentieth century. In 1989, the *Battle Creek Enquirer* ran a three-part series titled "The Kalamazoo River: From Sewer to Salvation," which sent a reporter and photographer on a canoe trip to document and interview locals about the renewed state of the river. The same year, the essayist and Kalamazoo native Bil Gilbert published a piece in *Sports Illustrated* documenting the river's restoration. Recounting a canoe trip with his wife, Gilbert reported that it "smelled like a regular river" and that it seemed, on the whole, "much more like the river my mother remembers from 1920 than the wretched mess Ann and I knew in 1950" (180). Such a dramatic transformation, Gilbert argues, made the river something of "a marvel of natural and social history" (180). These triumphal accounts of the river's resurrection from the dead are echoed in the title of Dave Dempsey's 2001 history of the conservation movement in Michigan (in which the history of the Kalamazoo River plays a significant role), *Ruin & Recovery*.

Margo's narrative unfolds according to a similar logic and follows a similar trajectory. On the one hand, settlers transformed, both materially and conceptually, features of the New World environment into natural resources or—to borrow Kathryn Yussof's phrase—"units of economic extraction" (2), making them available for the taking and licensing ecological degradation in the name of progress and civilization. These same (Western, masculinist) logics of power and domination, at a different scale, help account for Margo's sexual abuse by Cal and Paul. On the other hand, the novel is ultimately less about Margo's degradation than it is about her strength and resilience. In the same way, the history of the Kalamazoo River, while painful, has typically been told as a story of imminent "recovery," of a river on the verge of regeneration, its comeback always just around the bend.

Yet this is not exactly Campbell's ecological vision in *Once Upon a River*. While not despairing, the novel is also, I think, less sanguine about conventional possibilities for remediation and regeneration (whether ecological or social). Its vision, of both the present and the future, is both more sober and, I want to suggest in closing, more expansively radical. The limitations of what we might call the recovery narrative are evident in two recent incidents related to the Kalamazoo River that postdate the events and publication of the novel. In 2010, an oil pipeline ruptured near Marshall, Michigan, thirty miles upriver from Kalamazoo. For seventeen hours, oil gushed into Talmadge Creek, a small tributary of the river. Eventually, the oil made its way into the river, where it traveled another thirty miles toward Lake Michigan. By the time the rupture was finally stopped, over a million gallons of diluted bitumen had been released, much of which sank to the river bottom, making conventional containment and recovery strategies very difficult. As a result, it took more than five years and cost more than a billion dollars to clean it up, making it the costliest inland oil spill in U.S. history.[1]

By the end of the oil spill saga, proclamations of the river's recovery once again abounded. Politicians, some local residents, and, most of all, representatives from the pipeline company declared the river cleaner than ever—a claim that, given the scope and scale of the cleanup, is in all likelihood perversely true. Yet an estimated 80,000 gallons of oil remain in the riverbed, monitoring of wildlife continues, and the long-term health effects upon displaced residents remain unstudied and unknown.

What's more, good news about the river didn't last long. In October 2019, Eagle Creek Renewable Energy, the owner and operator of Morrow Dam, one of the remaining hydroelectric dams on the river, opened its spillway gates to perform emergency repairs. The action released hundreds of thousands of cubic yards of sediment, accumulated over decades at the dam, into the river. The sludge, deposited for a stretch of nearly forty miles down the river, as much as twelve feet deep in places, has smothered fish and wildlife habitats. According to Monica Auger, ecologists estimate that the effect it will have on populations of fish, mussels, invertebrates, insects, as well as plants and grasses, is likely to last for years, if not decades.

These two recent examples of ecological devastation on the Kalamazoo River, even in a period of heightened public concern for and legislative protection of the environment, reveal how the abuse and violence inflicted upon the natural world I have traced here is, to borrow a well-known phrase from Patrick Wolfe, "a structure, not an event" (163). That is to say, the cycle of ruin and recovery, ongoing now on the Kalamazoo River (and elsewhere across North America) for more than five decades, is a constitutive feature of extractive capitalism rather than a series of accidents and corrective actions. The decades-long accumulation of polychlorinated biphenyls and the hours-long discharge of diluted bitumen differ in scale and temporal extent, but neither is unique; they are, rather, instances in an ongoing process that is the result of what Naomi Klein has called Western capitalism's "nonreciprocal, dominance-based relationship with the earth" (169).

Margo embodies a different kind of relationship with the natural world, one that explicitly rejects the values and practices responsible for its defilement. Margo chafes against, for example, the logic of progress. When "the Indian" presses Margo about her education, saying, "you can't get ahead in this life if you don't finish school," Margo replies, "I don't want to get ahead. What's so great about getting ahead?" (*Once* 233). Similarly, Margo refuses romantic idealizations. When "the Indian" refers to Margo as "a river spirit," she becomes exasperated. "I'm not a river spirit. Why do guys always want to make a girl into something other than what she is?" (240). Even more powerfully, by the end of the novel, Margo repudiates masculine power entirely. When she meets the farmer, who grants Margo permission to continue to live on his land (in Smoke's riverboat), Margo is thankful but also announces, emphatically: "No men are welcome here" (316).

Hence, Margo neither recoils from the river and its degraded condition nor feels the impulse to save it, to clean it up; the novel neither harbors illusions about its recovery nor indulges in nostalgic dreams about it in some pristine pre-settler past (the latter a danger, which Campbell deftly avoids, posed by the introduction of "the Indian," whose appearance could easily have slipped into the kind of romanticization typical of too many U.S. cultural productions). Rather, Margo lives *with* the river; it is, she thinks upon first encountering it, a world "she understood" (226). And rather than humans, she identifies with rats. Unlike most people, who find no value in their "skins and meat," Margo sees them simply as "creatures getting by on the river as best they could" (310).

Thus the novel ends, appropriately, with images of what we might call Margo's kinship with the river, as she introduces her unborn child, who "had drifted fishlike within her, had swum her like a river" (330), to the Kalamazoo, Margo's own symbolic mother.[2] Wading into the river barefoot, Margo feels "the silt of the Kalamazoo squeeze through her toes," leaving "her footprints beside the four-toed signatures of the songbirds" (345). Then naked, she wades in further to feel "the river weeds brush against her like a mother's long hair." Saying "all right baby, welcome to the river," Margo then decides to swim and, after a brief moment of "uncertainty about her ability to swim," she remembers not to struggle against the river but "to relax in the current, let it flow around her" (345). It's a lovely, affecting moment in the novel (and what feels like Campbell's reworking of the famous conclusion of Kate Chopin's *The Awakening* rendered in a less despairing key) but also a fraught one in light of the history of the Kalamazoo River I've presented here. After all, the potential dangers to pregnant women of consuming fish from the river, and even of swimming in portions of the river, have been well documented.[3] But the power of the image lies in its insistence that a lasting recovery, true regeneration, requires the courage and the risk to imagine relations, human and nonhuman, otherwise, as trust.

Notes

1. For an account of the spill, see "The Dilbit Disaster," the Pulitzer Prize–winning series of reports by Elizabeth McGowan, Lisa Song, and David Hasemyer. For more on the aftermath of the spill, see Jeffrey Insko, "The 2010 Marshall, Michigan Tar Sands Oil Spill."
2. With "kinship," I have in mind here Donna Haraway's notion of "staying with the trouble" (1).
3. In 1998, for example, the Kalamazoo River Watershed Public Advisory Council published a report titled "The Kalamazoo River: Beauty and the Beast." The report lists "restrictions on body contact," including "swimming and other full body contact activities," as one of the Use Impairments in the Kalamazoo River Area of Concern (25).

Works Cited

Armstrong, Joe. "Four Acres of Carp Corpses on the Kalamazoo." *Life*, 5 Oct. 1953, p. 27.

Auger, Monica. "Ecological Disaster on the Kalamazoo River." *Flylords*, 29 Apr. 2021.

Campbell, Bonnie Jo. "The Fat White Woman Fails to Be Stoic When Her Lover Betrays Her." *Love Letters to Sons of Bitches*. Center for Book Arts, 2009, p. 17.

———. "Mothers, Tell Your Daughters." *Mothers, Tell Your Daughters*. Norton, 2015, pp. 85–104.

———. *Once Upon a River*. Norton, 2011.

———. *Q Road*. Scribner's, 2002.

———. "Trawling the River of Words: An Interview with Bonnie Jo Campbell." Interview by Alicia L. Conroy. Rain Taxi online edition, Fall 2011, www.raintaxi.com/trawling-the-river-of-words-an-interview-with-bonnie-jo-campbell/.

Dempsey, Dave. *Ruin & Recovery: Michigan's Rise as a Conservation Leader.* U of Michigan P, 2001.

Ellison, Garret. "Odor Violations Mount at Kalamazoo Paper Mill Seeking Major Tax Break," *MLive,* 20 Aug. 2020.

Gilbert, Bil. *Natural Coincidence: The Trip from Kalamazoo.* U of Michigan P, 2004.

Haraway, Donna. *Staying with the Trouble: Making Kin in the Chthulucene.* Duke UP, 2016.

Hoffman, Clare. Statement. *Congressional Record,* vol. 97, part 7, 25 July 1951, p. 8896.

Insko, Jeffrey. "The 2010 Marshall, Michigan Tar Sands Oil Spill." *Encyclopedia of Water, Science, and Technology,* edited by Patricia Maurice. Wiley, 2020, pp. 2679–2684.

"Kalamazoo's Paper Mills Report Pollution Progress." *Battle Creek Enquirer,* 25 Sept. 1959, p. 7.

"The Kalamazoo River: Beauty and the Beast." Kalamazoo River Watershed Public Advisory Council, 1998.

Klein, Naomi. *This Changes Everything: Capitalism and the Climate.* Simon & Schuster, 2014.

Lane, Kit. *The Kalamazoo.* Pavilion, 2006.

Mann, Sehvilla. "Why's That: Kalamazoo's Notorious Sludge Pits." WMUK Radio, 13 Feb. 2020, www.wmuk.org/post/whys-kalamazoos -notorious-sludge-pits#stream/0.

McGowan, Elizabeth, et al. "The Dilbit Disaster." *Inside Climate News,* 2012.

Mignolo, Walter. *The Darker Side of Western Modernity: Global Futures, Decolonial Options.* Duke UP, 2011.

Noer, Thomas J. *Soapy: A Biography of G. Mennen Williams.* U of Michigan P, 2005.

"On the Kalamazoo." *Forest and Stream: A Journal of Outdoor Life, Travel, Nature Study, Shooting, Fishing, Yachting,* 4 Sept. 1890, p. 133.

"Pollution Still Big Headache." *Detroit Free Press,* 9 Apr. 1939, p. 6.

VanBuren, Mike. "Commentary: Healing Rivers." *Michigan Radio Environment Report,* 19 February 2001.

Van Coevering, Jack. "Way Opened to Cleanse Kalamazoo River." *Detroit Free Press,* 18 Jan. 1948, p. B6.

Wolfe, Patrick. *Settler Colonialism and the Transformation of Anthropology.* Cassel, 1999.

Yusoff, Kathryn. *A Billion Black Anthropocenes or None.* U of Minnesota P, 2019.

Indigeneity in *Once Upon a River*

HEATHER A. HOWARD-BOBIWASH

This chapter examines transformations in the tropes of Indigeneity in Bonnie Jo Campbell's *Once Upon a River* (2011), from the novel to the feature film version of the book, directed by Haroula Rose and released in 2019. The role of fiction in the production of knowledge about Indigenous peoples is explored through questions of representation and the intersections of race, gender, identity, and landscape. The chapter explains why depictions of Indigenous peoples have real and powerful implications for Indigenous persons, communities, and Tribes in the United States, and why they are important for everyone to know and understand. To do this, the chapter utilizes the anthropological method described by Pauline Turner Strong as the ethnography of representational practices. In so doing, it studies the social and political processes produced by and through portrayals of Indigenous peoples, which can both "work to establish and maintain colonial dominance [and] challenge dominant power structures" (4). The basic premise of this approach draws on Todorov's idea that "the discovery of self makes of the other" (3), in that American identities are created against and in relationship to constructed Indigenous others. Particularly relevant to understanding the representations of Indigeneity in *Once Upon a River* are the ways in which its simultaneous absence and presence underpin the story's key themes of gendered self-determination and the embodiment of nature.

When asked by radio host Alison Stewart in a 2020 interview about Native Americans in the film *Once Upon a River*, both Rose and lead actor Kenadi DelaCerna answered that they were attracted to the project because it is not an "issues" film. Rose said, "it is representative of people without making it overtly an issue film," and DelaCerna stated that "One of my favorite things about this film is that it's not an issue film." Indeed, the film departs not only from stereotypical Hollywood renderings of Indigenous peoples that, as Diamond shows, dominate the American imaginary, but also from the overtly decolonizing portrayals that Knopf, Hearne, and Robinson each find in the growing Indigenous filmmaking industry. And yet, the representational practices of *Once Upon a River* point to a multitude of Native American issues. Even as Rose's and DelaCerna's statements directly counter this notion, they also invite potential engagement with audiences who might subconsciously or overtly choose to not see a Native American issues film.

DelaCerna identifies as Indigenous Hawaiian, and her other fellow Indigenous cast members are well-known actors Tatanka Means (Oglala/Omaha/Dine) and Ajuawak Kapashesit (Anishinaabe/Cree). Kapashesit is notably recognizable for his performance in the 2017 film adaptation of Ojibway writer Richard Wagamese's *Indian Horse* (2012). According to Miroux, the film about the systematic terror and painful impacts of the Indian boarding school system has had a pivotal effect in Indigenous communities across North America. In her interview with Stewart, DelaCerna adds that *Once Upon a River* "just happens to be a story about a young girl, a family, and some of them happen to be Indigenous." Yet, there are significant differences in the representation of Indigenous people in Campbell's novel and in Rose's film that complicate this statement. Few reviewers of the novel note the Indigeneity of the lead character Margo Crane as enduringly relevant throughout the book, but according to Golus, Haroula Rose did, which is why she centered it in the film. And yet paradoxically, as this chapter will show, despite the film's direct Indigenous presence through its casting, the book speaks more profoundly to Indigenous experience even as it hardly mentions it.

Naming Indigeneity and Representational Practices

In *American Indians: Stereotypes and Realities*, aimed at helping teachers counter the misrepresentation of Indigenous peoples, Choctaw scholar Devon Mihesuah takes on two dozen persistent distortions, several of which are signaled in *Once Upon a River*. Some examples that will be discussed here include the idea of the "vanished Indian," which holds that Indigenous peoples were conquered and no "real" ones live today—that they are against science and schooling, are innately in tune with nature, and have a tendency toward alcoholism. Mihesuah writes about the actual harmful effects racist representational practices that derive from these distortions have on Indigenous peoples. These range from emotional distress and a sense of worthlessness to discriminatory employment and housing experiences, to health disparities, including disproportionate suicide rates.[1] Systemically, these stereotypes sustain the original belief that it is America's virtuous and manifest destiny to conquer and civilize the west. Perhaps not distantly removed from this meaning, in a foreshadowing moment during the film's opening monologue, Margo ponders, "Maybe what happened was bound to happen, like destiny."

Bonnie Jo Campbell is distinguished for her ability to effectively convey themes of "sexual violence and the internalization of warped cultural norms about female sexuality" while also bringing some dignity to poor, rural, working-class people of the Midwest in her writing (Fine 519). This chapter examines these themes in relation to further reprehensible stereotypes involving Indigenous women, which, as Deer has described, serve to justify sexual violence against them. Such violence is linked to another persistent myth that many Americans hold, which is that they have an "Indian Princess" ancestor, another stereotype that serves to attenuate Indigenous identity and diminish the legitimacy of Indigenous peoples' legal claims.[2]

Regarding this chapter's terminology, Indigenous peoples, Native Americans, and Tribe, as well as "Indian" and specific nomenclature like Potawatomi and Cherokee, encapsulate historical, essentialist, and creative processes, summed up as Indigeneity, which "functions as both a fluid and grounded form of identification with its basis in indigenous cosmologies and survival amid colonialism" (Teves et al. 116). General terms like Native Americans and Indigenous peoples are convenient for referring to people who share (1) belonging to independent, self-determined communities, with distinctive languages and cultures, on lands that predate European and other colonizing populations coming to these lands; (2) oppression, domination, and discrimination by and within nation-states formed through these processes; and (3) global solidarity in struggles to redress the wrongs emergent from these historical legacies and ongoing settler-colonial relations. However, as the United Nations Permanent Forum on Indigenous Issues notes, the term Indigenous is useful to identify but not define who people are. Broad terms problematically homogenize the vast diversity of the estimated 370 million Indigenous persons in over five thousand communities across seventy countries internationally and are ultimately classificatory terms imposed and "derived by the colonizers' worldview" (D'Errico).[3]

Certainly, as Vizenor explains, the term "Indian" is a misnomer, and it is "Eurocentric . . . because it suited centuries of European newcomers rather than respecting the nations' words for themselves" (Dunbar-Ortiz and Gilio-Whitaker 146). "Indian" caricatures, such as those used in sports mascots and rituals, normalize the exclusion of Indigenous peoples "from full participatory citizenship by treating them as signs rather than speakers . . . replays colonialist appropriation and reproduces the subordinate place of Native Americans within settler society" (Strong 160).[4] That said, the label remains in use in the legal terminology of the United States federal government bound by treaties made with nations it recognizes as "American Indian Tribes." Reappropriations by Indigenous peoples, such as in the terms "Indian Country" and the "American Indian Movement," remind the federal government of its obligations to those agreements between nations.[5] For all the reasons mentioned previously, and as Cheyenne/Muscogee writer and activist Susan Shown Harjo once told Oprah Winfrey, Indigenous peoples should always be referred to with their specific national names, and thus non-Indigenous peoples need to do the work to learn them (Dunbar-Ortiz and Gilio-Whitaker 145).

All of this context situates how Indigeneity is represented in *Once Upon a River*, even as both the book and the film do not overtly focus on "Native American issues." Regardless of intentions or the privileges of choices made by authors and film directors, Arvin cites Lyons to articulate how representational practices manifest in the "'actual existing diversity' inside and outside of the many given taxons our Indigenous lives are formed in" (Arvin 126). The differing lenses through which Campbell and Rose engage with these representational practices in their most Indigeneity-charged scenes and scenery illustrate this interpretive process from intention to effect.

"The Indian"

Contrasting depictions of the same encounter between *Once Upon a River*'s lead character, Margo Crane, and the man referred to only as "the Indian" in the novel (who is named Will in the film) encapsulate several dimensions of the representational politics outlined above. In the book,

Margo is immediately skeptical: "'You don't look like an Indian,' Margo said, although when she studied him more closely, she saw that he did resemble the guy in the Indian Hunter book" (206). In the film, however, she claims an ambiguous Indigeneity; when Will asks, "What Tribe?" about one-third of the way into the film, she replies, "I'm not sure. Somewhere out west." These versions of the same encounter include naming, ambiguities in personal tribal identity, and fictional and racialized reference points for "Indianness." The particularities of the intersectionality of Indigeneity, gender, and power are also highlighted in the continuum of tension and ease that occur in the interactions between the two characters and from the effect of the landscape, both of which are distinctively strong qualities in Campbell's writing overall.

In the book, "the Indian" appears mainly in chapter 15 and a few subsequent passages. Indigeneity also appears sparsely elsewhere, yet key tropes significantly situate Margo's personality, and her possibilities and limits. The novel begins with what Mihesuah describes as the powerful force of the family legend of Indigenous ancestry widely claimed among Americans. This legend is usually vague and undocumented, and involves a distant or dead, often female, forebear of indistinct tribal affiliation, who either "passed for white" or was phenotypically "full-blood," and was either ashamed of, or had lost and did not pass on, cultural knowledge (99).

Margo's father, Bernard Crane (played in the film by Tatanka Means), is "said by some" to be the bastard son of "part Indian" Dorothy Crane (*Once* 16–17). In both the novel and the film, this device sets up tension between Margo and her white Murray family relatives, which allows them to both claim and discard her. White masculinities shape the patriarchal power in the Murray household and the misogynistic gestures toward Margo and her mother, ranging from naming them "whores" to rape; these are interlaced with additional normalization of violence against Indigenous women. Bernard Crane is shot dead challenging this norm even as he tries not to directly confront Margo's rapist, her uncle and his half-brother Cal Murray.

These tropes will likely be less subtle to Indigenous audiences of the film. Joshua Cook, a reviewer of the novel, asks, "Margo's story seems wildly unbelievable—how can a single soul encounter so much awfulness in such a short time?" This question loses merit when Margo is read as an Indigenous female character, which she is more visibly portrayed as in the film than in the book. Indigenous women are sexually assaulted twice as much as the national average (*Maze*) and "bear the brunt of colonial violence, specifically sexual violence, both within families and by settler predators, and increasingly, sex traffickers" (Dunbar-Ortiz and Gilio-Whitaker 140). Colonial violence is both historical and ongoing in the multiple ways legal and other systems that govern Indigenous peoples' lives developed in the absence of the fulfillment of treaty obligations, in that they not only fail to protect Indigenous women but are deeply entrenched with the exploitation and destruction of Indigenous women's bodies.[6] According to Lucchesi and Echo-Hawk, this results today in a highly disproportionate rate of missing and murdered Indigenous women and girls, which is an extension of the mundane, everyday sexual violence that Margo experiences and is compounded for Indigenous girls.

When Margo meets "the Indian" he startles her while she is cleaning a rabbit she has just killed. Campbell writes him in with ironic dialogue that simultaneously pulls on and pushes against several stereotypical representations. In the book, "the Indian" is somewhat expected in his appearance, while he also doesn't act like an Indian or sound like an Indian, as Margo repeatedly admonishes him based on her cherished books *The Indian Hunter* and *Annie Oakley Little Sure Shot*, after which she also models herself. "The Indian" loves school, has finished college, teaches math, and organizes math conferences. He was adopted but seems to have some contact with one possibly Indigenous cousin who has told him some stories about his people's relationships to the local landscape, plants, and animals. He is here looking to see and experience these. He hates guns and pollution, is married, and has a bit of a problem controlling how much he drinks.

While he and Margo share interests in Indigenous practices and feel connections to the land and water, they talk past each other. His quest is for self-understanding and recovery of a collective cultural identity—what Allen refers to as blood memory. Hers is for knowledge that confirms what she read and can use to build and sustain her individual independence. Margo does not mention to him, or anyone else in the book, the family "Indian lore" about her grandmother, who got pregnant during an affair with Margo's Grandpa Murray. This has the representational effect of affirming her whiteness by bolstering how her methods of knowledge acquisition and abilities to survive in this landscape are of her own making. An attempt to reverse this trope in the film version only partially succeeds, as described below.

In other ways, the through lines of Margo's and "the Indian's" stories dance together, for example with their understandings of the relationalities between human/nonhuman animals, plant life, and the river itself. Margo starts to enjoy teaching "the Indian" what she knows, and even listening to his stories (as Sitting Bull told stories to Annie Oakley). She begins to wish he might stick around. They have sex, and unlike with other men, Margo is fully engaged as she is unable to imagine a reason "not to trust her body" (*Once* 240). She wants to know his name, but he is unable to tell her. Is he referencing what might have been his lost real "Indian name," his adoption, or just thinking he doesn't want her to track him down later? "The Indian" leaves the next day, never to return. A few weeks later Margo realizes she is pregnant. Like her grandmother, she is left by a married man, pregnant with an Indigenous child, except where Grandpa Murray remained present, "The Indian" vanishes.

Most of this complexity is abandoned in the film. Although "the Indian" gets a name, Will, he has no ancestral connection to the place that "the Indian" said he had. Will identifies himself as Cherokee from Oklahoma and is vaguely "studying" the routes of Indigenous people as they came down from Canada. This is a choice made for the film that is bewildering, as is the addition that Margo suggests her ancestors may be from "out west." Another odd change relates to the use of controlled substances, which facilitates their dalliance. Where "the Indian" seems to get, and need, a high from his whiskey, he is suspicious of the foraged mushrooms Margo has cooked for him because he worries they are hallucinogenic. Will doesn't drink and is the one who entices Margo to partake from his baggie of "magic" mushrooms. This reversal changes the power dynamics of the sexual encounter between the two characters to position Will as another, albeit different, male exploiter in the chain of Margo's users.

In these forty-five or so pages of the novel, Indigenous gender identities are implicated in several ways with the representational practices Barker explains as a "movingly malleable narrative of Indigenous womanhood/femininity and manhood/masculinity that reenacts Indigenous people's lack of knowledge and power over their own culture and identity in an inherently imperialist and colonialist world" (2). While "the Indian" is unexpected in some ways, Campbell weaves in dimensions to this character that are recognizable devices of the narrative strategies Barker describes. He ascribes the authority of his knowledge about the landscape and the Potawatomi people to anthropologists, librarians, his own study, and to a cousin whom it is unclear if the reader should identify as Potawatomi like "the Indian" himself. The lack of knowledge that drives his travels and study through the area, and which is at the center of his interactions with Margo, ties him to the trope that no "real" Indigenous people exist who know anything about the lands they supposedly want to claim back, and aligns him with the Indian caricatures described earlier that are used in sports mascots.

Importantly, however, Campbell attributes "the Indian's" unfamiliarity to the circumstances of his ancestors being removed from their lands in what is now southwest Michigan to Kansas, and to his own adoption. Do these mentions only affirm and bolster the settler-colonial trope of the "vanished Indian"? Or can they prompt readers to ask about how the settler-colonial processes of United States policies shape their own present attachments to their beloved Michigan landscapes, or how Indigenous people are recovering from these actions today? These include the nineteenth-century United States Indian Removal Act, which mandated the Potawatomi Trail of Death, and the subsequent assimilation policies of the twentieth century that broke up Indigenous families, including through adoption of children by white families.[7] Similarly, that "the Indian" struggles with alcohol represents one of the most insidious, intractable, and damaging tropes in U.S. social narratives, which—according to Dunbar-Ortiz and Gilio-Whitaker, as well as Innes and Anderson— is often understood through the false stereotype that Indigenous people, particularly men, have a tendency or predisposition to drink. Instead, "the Indian's" drinking might better be understood in terms of what Mihesuah has described as "the degree of suffering which Indians as a population endure [which] often encourages recourse to alcohol" (98). As Dunbar-Ortiz and Gilio-Whitaker, and Duran and Duran have shown, this suffering is directly relative to the effects of the implementation of United States policies, which Campbell has signaled are in "the Indian's" experience.

Other gendered figurative characters who appear in the narrative of "the Indian" (but not in Will's) include his wife, whose blood-quantum-measured "quarter-Sioux" identity authorizes the Indigeneity of the meanings of love, loss, and attachment to land in a "heartbroken Indian maiden" story he tells Margo. Frustrated with Margo's disruptive questions about the story, the essentialist feminine constructs of the wife and the maiden push Margo outside Indigenous womanhood. However, this scene, like his searching and drinking, may also operate to diminish the "Indian's" authenticity. The Indian maiden is another recurring stereotype that "reiterates particular structures of power and racial hierarchies in the articulation of Americanness or national identity based on a white, heterosexual, male norm" (Marubbio 5). These kinds of "Indian maiden" stories are usually told by white people. This complexity, and the disservice of this tale-telling scene may have been recognized by Rose, as well as being a convenient lengthy segment to drop from the film. Moreover, in the film, Will does not talk about a wife, but rather a sister he brings up as an Indigenous woman Margo should not emulate; she quit school like Margo, and "all she can do now is clean houses."

In both the book and film, Margo's Indigeneity is significantly muted, even regressed, yet her identity is aligned in some respects with what Rayna Green termed the "Pocahontas Perplex," most notably in that she is a precocious wild child of nature who, according to Strong, "stalks Smith [men] like a wildcat and then rolls with him in the grass, a 'free spirit' who embodies the joys of belonging to an uncommodified world" (149). Margo's wildness is signaled throughout *Once Upon a River*, where others label her a nymph, sprite, and a wolf child. In the book she pushes back against this when "the Indian" also labels her a "river spirit." "I'm not a river spirit. Why do guys always want to make a girl into something other than she is? Margo asked . . . even her Grandpa's naming her Sprite and River Nymph seemed odd now, as though he wanted her not to be a person, exactly" (*Once* 240). Despite Margo's refusal, reviewers of the novel frequently describe her as a wild animal. Several film reviewers also link her survival in the wilderness to innate Indigenous qualities. Delgadillo frames the "close ties to nature" depicted in the film as "obvious respect and attention put towards the beliefs and values of the Native American people," and Nerber writes that "Margo is uniquely equipped for life in the wild—her father, who is Native American, taught her to hunt and fish." That this latter information is elicited from Margo directly by Will raises questions about the essentialism suggested when there is otherwise nothing in Margo's hunting and fishing techniques that suggest they derive from her father's Native Americanness.

The perplex is a very old representational practice Green traces to the sixteenth century. As a new world princess or queen, "draped in leaves, feathers and animal skins . . . she appeared aggressive, militant, and armed . . . often she stood with her foot on the slain body of an animal or human enemy" (702). This imagery is transferred to the Annie Oakley Margo so much adores, fulfilling the way wild femininity stands in for America, but is also subsumed in American "blood memory" as an entity to be conquered and tamed along with her lands. Sexually, however, Green writes, the princess's "darker twin the Sq**w must serve this side of the image, and again, relationships with males determine what that image will be" (711).

Campbell effectively shifts this dynamic by bringing Margo some relief in the form of "the Indian" lover, from the treatment she has received from most of the males she has known so far, which ranges from being quietly but confusingly raped by her uncle to the overt hatred of his son. This cousin of Margo's recurringly acts to exclude her from her Murray family inheritance, both because he is jealous of his father's attentions to her and because he can be seen as the white male lineal descendant, whereas she is the brown female daughter of a "bastard" son. Although the portrayal of Margo in the film skews toward her searching, youthful innocence, and in the book she is more profoundly resourceful, in both cases there is an instinctual survival drive that shapes how she moves through the world, and a grayness or fog that masks the complexity of her sexuality. Other men are enraged supposedly on her behalf about her rapes, but they also circulate freely with men who rape and use the trope of the slut to justify their violence and control. In both the novel and the film, this imagery is complex and unpleasant, but as Miltho argues, serve some productive functions to be "mobilized to different aims . . . and [can be] adept at reappropriating these images for generative ends, including critiques of white culture" (154).

Potawatomi Lands and Landscapes

Once Upon a River takes place along the fictitious Stark River, a tributary of the real Kalamazoo River within the real Indigenous lands of the Potawatomi in southwest Michigan. Margo's encounter with "the Indian" follows logically as the prequel to Campbell's first novel *Q Road* (2002), in which Margo's daughter, Rachel, is the lead character and grapples with her own "Indianness" and themes of Indigeneity on the landscape. Campbell read extensively from the Michigan Pioneer and Historical Society journals to give *Q Road* an awareness of the Potawatomi and white settlers who left their marks on Rachel's landscape ("Midwestern" 4). In *Once Upon a River*, some features include "a stone wall and tower that her grandpa had said were built by Indians" (*Once* 72), and the "Pokagon mound, a hillock maybe six feet high, twenty feet in diameter, that was full of Indian bones, if the stories about it were true" (199). The mound has been turned into a nature park, and Margo stays here for some time following on what is, at this point in the novel, her third exile-escape from violence on white properties, and this is where she meets "the Indian."

The landscape is devoid of living Indigenous people. They are either dead or long gone, with the specific people mentioned scattered to Florida, California, and Nebraska. This trope is possibly deepened in the film even if the actors are Indigenous. In reality, the area is home to three Potawatomi communities, descendants of people who resisted removal or came back. At the time *Once Upon a River* is set in the late 1970s, the federal government maintained its refusal to acknowledge them as an extension of the intended erasure of its past policies. Erasing people on paper goes a long way but does not actually obliterate them. The federal government reaffirmed its recognition of the Pokagon Band of Potawatomi in 1994 (*Pokégnek*), the Nottawaseppi Huron Band of the Potawatomi Tribe in 1995, and the Match-E-Be-Nash-She-Wish Band of Pottawatomi Indians in 1999.

"The Indian" sounds self-assured in his accounts of Potawatomi land history, telling Margo how he is retracing their "migration route" from the Upper Peninsula specifically to Kalamazoo (*Once* 207). Is he referring to those who fled removal to the Upper Peninsula and beyond to Canada, and since returned? Nichols, for example, shows that many of them stayed in Canada, in the Upper Peninsula, and with their relatives in Potawatomi and other Indigenous communities in Wisconsin who did not remove or returned. The Hannahville Indian Community is a fourth federally recognized Potawatomi Tribe in Michigan (*Keepers*) located in the Upper Peninsula. On the other hand, the Potawatomi are, as a nation, part of the broader "Three Fires Confederacy" along with the Ojibway and Odawa collectively known as Anishinaabe (Neshnabe in the Potawatomi language), which covers a huge area surrounding most of the Great Lakes. A central theme in their origin story, described in the published works of Clifton, Noodin, and others, is a great migration from the east and distribution of the Anishinaabe along the way. Is the "Indian" referring to this migration story? As noted earlier, a third possibility is his own journey of self-discovery and family history as it is marked by generations of repeated displacement and relocation including to urban areas, which

Low has demonstrated in the relationship between the Pokagon Band and the city of Chicago.

These complex tropes have centered in a lot of Indigenous film and literature to grapple with Indigenous loss of heritage, high rates of alcoholism, and violence alluded to in both the novel and film version of *Once Upon a River*. In the film, this is further confused when Will explains that he is in this place "studying the routes from Canada on down." He does not portend any personal connection to the Potawatomi or their landscape. Along with Margo's "out west" identity and her disinterest in his lectures, they are both disconnected from the Indigenous story of the place in which they find themselves. This depreciates the Potawatomi in ways that perhaps the novel does not. Will has one line that seems intended to explicitly message a key issue: "The people who came to this country and took over, they never intended for us to survive." He draws this issue together with the pollution of the water, which helps to include Margo in a sense of belonging to a larger community—the shared dimensions of Indigeneity—but her disinterest and the incongruity of their identities with place deflate this message.

A significant but very brief and perhaps too subtle suggestion of representational politics of Indigeneity is also made by "the Indian" in the book. One of the first things he asks Margo is if she is poaching as he tries to make a joke about asking her for her hunting license (*Once* 205). It is an especially ironic joke in the way it marks Margo's poverty and the threat to people who generally survive on hunted food taken illegally on state land or private property. Additionally, as both Doherty and Nesper have shown, threats of being discovered or reported, as well as excessive fining, have been used aggressively as a tool against Indigenous people to specifically target the exercise of their treaty-based hunting and fishing rights in the Great Lakes region.

Coloniality is perpetuated through fantastical, historical, and voiceless representations of Indigeneity on the landscape. Timmerman demonstrates this tendency through Indian mounds, while similarly, Beck examines how the masculinized appropriation of place-naming is so complete that even Kalamazoo, a Potawatomi word, and thousands of other Indigenous-language place names in the United States are not known as present, living Indigenous places. When "the Indian" tells Margo that the place they are in "used to be called the River of Three Herons," she flatly rejects this, telling him it is the Stark River after the "explorer Frederick

Stark" (*Once* 207). For the film, Haroula Rose visited the St. Joseph River in Michigan with Campbell because it is supposed to be the fictitious Stark (Golus). St. Joseph is named after the French fort established there in in the seventeenth century and is the site of numerous battles for Indigenous lands and resources. Renaming the landscape is a totalizing act of colonization, but as Goeman explained in "Land as Life," it only works in tandem with other ongoing acts of settler-colonial erasure.

The Possibilities of Generative Counternarratives from
Once Upon a River

Representational practices like those described in this chapter illustrate what Barker sums up as processes in which "Real Indigeneity is *ever presently* made over as irrelevant, as are Indigenous legal claims and rights to governance, territories, and cultures" (3). *Once Upon a River*, the novel and the film, recasts the Potawatomi territory and story as a past, exotic, now empty Indigenous land open for current settler-colonial narratives. Although they do this in different ways, neither is just a story about a girl in which some people happen to be Indigenous. However, this story can, as Miltho argues, also mobilize a counternarrative to subvert stereotypical distortions. Counternarratives highlight the "inability to bind land to settler societies or expunge Indigenous sense of place [and are] . . . the anxiety producing thorn in the side of nation-states" and therefore attenuate acts of elimination and erasure (Goeman, "Land" 76).

This means anyone who reads *Once Upon a River* or sees the film can change the operative narratives that contextualize how the story is read and have consequences in real human lives. What might happen, for example, with a counternarrative that is allied to Potawatomi ways of knowing and telling, which Low and Pokagon show are operationalized through generative reintegrations of human relationships? As Mihesuah describes in the appendix to her book "Do's and Don'ts for Teachers and Parents," simple actions such as using appropriate terminology, and valuing diversity and more complete and accurate histories, should also be grounded in learning about why these are important for everyone (119–22). In another river story, Lynda Gray describes a place in Canada where a clear river and a murky river meet: "Despite their effect on each other, they are stronger together" (263). Gray uses this analogy to suggest a way forward for Indigenous and non-Indigenous people to choose to come "together to strengthen all of our lives" (263), by not letting opportunities to do so be swept away.

Notes

1. For an in-depth discussion of the health impacts, see Greenwood, de Leeuw, and Lindsay. Allard provides a Michigan-specific discussion of suicide among Indigenous youth.

2. See Dunbar-Ortiz and Gilio-Whitaker (137–44) and Miltho for a complete discussion of the implications of the "Indian Princess" stereotype.

3. Dunbar-Ortiz and Gilio-Whitaker cover the complexities of naming in more detail (145–49); and see Timperley for a comprehensive discussion of Indigeneity. *Do All Indians Live in Tipis?* from the Smithsonian Institution is a very good resource for younger audiences.

4. See also Howe, Markowitz, and Cummings; and Little and Little.

5. Deloria Jr. and Lytle provide an authoritative overview of the history of treaties between American Indian Tribes in the United States and the implications of these in the present. See Lebeau for a Michigan-specific discussion.

6. Deer and Goeman provide complete discussions of these intersections between colonial violence, contemporary law, and the disproportionate violence experienced by Indigenous women in the United States.

7. For a full discussion of Potawatomi cultural revitalization, see Wetzel. See Jacobs for a comprehensive discussion of policies focused on the disproportionate removal of children from Indigenous families into foster care and adoption out of their communities.

Works Cited

Allard, Seth. *Guided by the Spirits: The Meanings of Life, Death, and Youth Suicide in an Ojibwa Community.* Routledge, 2018.

Allen, Chadwick. "Blood (and) Memory." *American Literature,* vol. 71, no. 1, 1999, pp. 93–116.

Arvin, Maile. "Analytics of Indigeneity." *Native Studies Keywords,* edited by Stephanie Nohelani Teves, Andrea Smith, and Michelle H. Raheja. U of Arizona P, 2015, pp. 119–29.

Barker, Joanne, editor. *Critically Sovereign*. Duke UP, 2017.

Beck, Lauren. "Euro-Settler Place Naming Practices for North America through a Gendered and Racialized Lens." *Terrae Incognitae*, vol. 53, no. 1, 2021, pp. 5–25.

Campbell, Bonnie Jo. "Midwestern Writers Need Midwestern Historians." *Studies in Midwestern History*, vol. 4, no. 3, 2018, pp. 1–6.

———. *Once Upon a River*. Norton, 2011.

———. *Q Road*. Scribner's, 2002.

Clifton, James A. *People of the Three Fires: The Ottawa, Potawatomi, and Ojibway of Michigan* [*Workbook and Teacher's Guide*]. Michigan Indian Press, 1986.

Cook, Joshua. "Bonnie Jo Campbell's *Once Upon a River*." *Iowa Review*, 12 Feb. 2012.

Deer, Sarah. *The Beginning and End of Rape: Confronting Sexual Violence in Native America*. U of Minnesota P, 2015.

Delgadillo, Nicholas. "'Once Upon a River' Review—A Personal Odyssey That Loses Itself." *Discussing Film*, 29 Sept. 2020.

Deloria, Vine, Jr., and Clifford M. Lytle. *The Nations Within: The Past and Future of American Indian Sovereignty*. U of Texas P, 1984.

D'Errico, Peter. "Native American Indian Studies: A Note on Names." Peter D'Errico's Law Page, 2005, people.umass.edu/derrico/name.html.

Diamond, Neil, director. *Reel Injun: On the Trail of the Hollywood Indian*. Rezolution Pictures and the National Film Board of Canada, 2010.

Do All Indians Live in Tipis? Questions and Answers from the National Museum of the American Indian. Smithsonian, 2007.

Doherty, Robert. *Disputed Waters: Native Americans and the Great Lakes Fishery*. UP of Kentucky, 2009.

Dunbar-Ortiz, Roxanne, and Dina Gilio-Whitaker. *"All the Real Indians Died Off" and 20 Other Myths about Native Americans*. Beacon, 2016.

Duran, Eduardo, and Bonnie Duran. *Native American Postcolonial Psychology*. SUNY P, 1995.

Fine, Laura. "Sexual Violence and Cultural Crime in the Country Noir Fiction of Bonnie Jo Campbell." *Critique: Studies in Contemporary Fiction*, vol. 60, no. 5, 2019, pp. 515–26.

Goeman, Mishuana R. "Land as Life: Unsettling the Logics of Containment." *Native Studies Keywords*, edited by Stephanie Nohelani Teves et al. U of Arizona P, 2015, pp. 71–89.

———. "Ongoing Storms and Struggles: Gendered Violence and Resource Exploitation." *Critically Sovereign*, edited by Joanne Barker. Duke UP, 2017, pp. 99–126.

Golus, Carrie. "The Making and Remaking of *Once Upon a River.*" *University of Chicago Magazine*, Winter 2020.

Gray, Lynda. *First Nations 101: Tons of Stuff You Need to Know about First Nations People*. Adaawx, 2011.

Green, Rayna. "The Pocahontas Perplex: The Image of Indian Women in American Culture." *Massachusetts Review*, vol. 16, no. 4, 1975, pp. 698–714.

Greenwood, Margo, et al., editors. *Determinants of Indigenous Peoples' Health: Beyond the Social*, 2nd ed. Canadian Scholars, 2018.

Hearne, Joanne. *Smoke Signals: Native Cinema Rising*. U of Nebraska P, 2012.

Howe, Leanne, et al., editors. *Seeing Red—Hollywood's Pixeled Skins: American Indians and Film*. Michigan State UP, 2013.

Indigenous Peoples, Indigenous Voices: Who Are Indigenous Peoples? United Nations Permanent Forum on Indigenous Issues, www.un.org/esa /socdev/unpfii/documents/5session_factsheet1.pdf.

Innes, Robert Alexander, and Kim Anderson, editors. *Indigenous Men and Masculinities: Legacies, Identities, Regeneration*. U of Manitoba P, 2015.

Jacobs, Margaret D. *A Generation Removed: The Fostering and Adoption of Indigenous Children in the Postwar World*. U of Nebraska P, 2014.

Keepers of the Fire. Hannahville Indian Community, 2013, www.hannah ville.net.

Knopf, Kerstin. *Decolonizing the Lens of Power: Indigenous Films in North America*. Brill, 2008.

Lebeau, Patrick R. *Rethinking Michigan Indian History*. Michigan State UP, 2005.

Little, John, and Kenn Little, directors. *More Than a Word: A Film about Native American–Based Sports Mascots and the Washington R*dskins*. Media Education Foundation, 2017.

Low, John N. *Imprints: The Pokagon Band of Potawatomi Indians and the City of Chicago*. Michigan State UP, 2016.

Lucchesi, Anita, and Abigail Echo-Hawk. *Missing and Murdered Indigenous Women and Girls: A Snapshot of Data from 71 Urban Cities in the United States*. Urban Indian Health Institute, 2018.

Lyons, Scott Richard. *X-Marks: Native Signatures of Assent*. U of Minnesota P, 2010.

Marubbio, M. Elise. *Killing the Indian Maiden: Images of Native American Women in Film*. UP of Kentucky, 2006.

Match-E-Be-Nash-She-Wish Band of Pottawatomi Indians. Gun Lake Tribe, 2017, gunlaketribe-nsn.gov.

Maze of Injustice: The Failure to Protect Indigenous Women from Sexual Violence in the USA. Amnesty International USA, 2007.

Mihesuah, Devon A. *American Indians: Stereotypes and Realities*. Clarity, 1996.

Miltho, Nancy Marie. *"Our Indian Princess": Subverting the Stereotype*. School for Advanced Research, 2008.

Miroux, Frank. "Richard Wagamese's Indian Horse: Stolen Memories and Recovered Histories." *ACTIO NOVA: Revista de Teoría de la Literatura y Literatura Comparada*, no. 3, 2019, pp. 193–230.

Nerber, Matthew. "Review: Despite Some Clunky Moments, *Once Upon a River* Delivers a Beautifully Filmed Coming-of-Age Drama." *Third Coast Review*, 3 Oct. 2020, thirdcoastreview.com.

Nesper, Larry. *The Walleye War: The Struggle for Ojibwe Spearfishing and Treaty Rights*. U of Nebraska P, 2002.

Nichols, Roger L. "American Indians and US-Canada Transborder Migration." *Permeable Borders: History, Theory, Policy, and Practice in the United States*, edited by Paul Otto and Susanne Berthier-Foglar. Berghan, 2020, pp. 19–36.

Noodin, Margaret. "*Wanitoon ani Mikan Odenang*: Anishinaabe Urban Loss and Reclamation." *Urban History Review*, vol. 48, no. 2, 2021, pp. 16–31.

Nottawaseppi Huron Band of the Potawatomi. Nottawaseppi Huron Band of the Potawatomi, 2020, nhbp-nsn.gov.

Pokagon, Simon. *Ogimawkwe Mitigwaki (Queen of the Woods)*. Michigan State UP, 2011.

Pokégnek Bodéwadmik. Pokagon Band of Potawatomi, 2021, www.pokagon band-nsn.gov.

Robinson, Gary. *Native Actors and Filmmakers: Visual Storytellers*. 7th Generation Native Voices, 2021.

Rose, Haroula, director. *Once Upon a River*. Thirty Tigers, Chicago Media Angels, Neon Heart Productions, Glass Bead Films, 2019.

Stewart, Alison. "Once Upon a River." *All of It*, WYNC, 9 Oct. 2020, www .wnycstudios.org/podcasts/all-of-it/segments/once-upon-river.

Strong, Pauline Turner. *American Indians and the American Imaginary: Cultural Representation across the Centuries*. Paradigm, 2013.

Teves, Stephanie Nohelani, et al., editors. *Native Studies Keywords*. U of Arizona P, 2015.

Timmerman, Nicholas A. "Contested Indigenous Landscapes: Indian Mounds and the Political Creation of the Mythical "Mound Builder" Race." *Ethnohistory*, vol. 67, no. 1, 2020, pp. 75–95.

Timperley, Claire. "Constellations of Indigeneity: The Power of Definition." *Contemporary Political Theory*, vol. 19, no. 1, 2020, pp. 38–60.

Todorov, Tzvetan. *The Conquest of America: The Question of the Other*. U of Oklahoma P, 1999.

Vizenor, Gerald. *Manifest Manners: Narratives on Postindian Survivance*. U of Nebraska P, 1999.

Wetzel, Christopher. *Gathering the Potawatomi Nation: Revitalization and Identity*. U of Oklahoma P, 2015.

The Radical Class Politics of *American Salvage*

CHARLES CUNNINGHAM

The title of Bonnie Jo Campbell's *American Salvage*, a collection of short stories, implies an aftermath, what can be salvaged after a disaster. On many levels, that disaster is the end of the so-called Fordist period in the United States, which we associate with high-paying union manufacturing jobs and the advance of the industrial workers into the middle class, an era of unprecedented economic prosperity. Post-Fordism, our current period, is characterized by the loss of manufacturing and its high wages, the attack on labor unions, and the radical economic instability familiar to workers. Most of the stories in *American Salvage* concern people the mainstream culture industry would represent as down-and-out failures of our times; many are poor, underemployed, geographically and emotionally isolated, or substance-addicted. Yet, I would argue that in *American Salvage*, Campbell does not passively observe the destructive aftermath; rather, she implicitly condemns the capitalist social order, implying that it produces mental and physical misery that can be assuaged to some extent but cannot be overcome in existing conditions.

This condemnation of the status quo emerges, however, by negation; the necessity for a more just and humane society is made manifest to the reader by its absence. Socioeconomic analysis is not thematized explicitly or foregrounded in the stories; there are no moments of "discourse" where an omniscient narrator or knowing character comments on social conditions.[1] In fact, the characters do not seem to reflect on the fact that their lives are conditioned by the grand socioeconomic shifts of the post-Fordist era, much less by the class structure of capitalism. They feel their suffering, but they typically lack any means to step back and analyze its overarching causes. They do not belong to unions, political groups, or even churches. For them, the only antidote to complete alienation is the possibility of small-scale solidarity—often in families, makeshift groups, or even couples.

Yet, to work politically by negation, *American Salvage* must transcend two aesthetic tendencies that threaten to reduce it to a text offering a sympathetic portrayal of poverty and alienation while stopping short of condemning the social order that produces them. First, such beautifully written and emotionally powerful stories could effectively aestheticize suffering, making the characters human ruin porn, the objects of a fascinated but distant gaze from above. The young Tillie Olsen was well aware of this threat in her unfinished proletarian novel, *Yonnondio*. In one scene, families watch for miners to emerge from a coal mine after an explosion. In a discursive departure from the narrative, a voice that seems authorial comments:

> And could you not make a cameo of this and pin it to your aesthetic hearts? So sharp, so clear, so classic. The shattered dusk, the mountain of culm, the tipple; clean lines, bare beauty—and carved against them, dwarfed by the vastness of night and the towering tipple, these black figures with bowed heads, waiting, waiting. . . . Surely it is original enough—these grotesques, this thing with the foot missing, this gargoyle with half the face gone and the arm. (Olsen 20)

Besides an apparent swipe at those who hold that art is apolitical, Olsen seems to condemn the gazers, the "you" who would transform human life and the social relations of capital into things, what Marx called "reification" ("the conversion of social relations into things" [qtd. in Foley 73]). Yet she could be warning herself—another writer known both for her working-class affinity and for her emotionally powerful prose style—against objectifying by aestheticizing. Like Olsen, Campbell resists that possibility by depicting her characters as having rich, complex emotional lives and as being subject to conditions they have little control over; in effect, she salvages them from aesthetic reification.

In *The Political Unconscious*, Fredric Jameson identifies another political aesthetic tendency that Campbell's stories avoid. For Jameson, some literary works can be understood to "invent . . . imaginary or formal 'solutions' to unresolvable social contradictions" (79). Furthermore, "the social contradiction addressed and 'resolved' by the . . . narrative must . . . remain as an absent cause, which cannot be directly or immediately conceptualized by the text" (82). This formulation might seem to apply to *American Salvage*: the social contradiction many of its stories address is the alienating, exploitative character of capitalism that works to disrupt human connection and well-being. The stories "salvage" or resolve those disruptions narratively, in poignant renderings of interpersonal communion that often occur in endings. What "cannot be . . . conceptualized" in this case would be the broader scope of communion or solidarity—presumably mass organizing—necessary to change the social order. Yet, Campbell has acknowledged that she sees her work as political, which is readily apparent in her choice of subject matter.[2] Moreover, the stories' aesthetically powerful narrative resolutions clearly do not resolve the social problems they describe.

To make this argument, I will focus on four stories. "The Inventor, 1972" depicts an obvious victim of industrial capitalism, while "Family Reunion" suggests more subtle impositions of post-Fordist historical realities on an extended family. "Falling," which is less directly about work relations, shows the effects of inadequate social welfare on poor people in the United States, and "The Yard Man" describes how humans and nature have been continuously disrupted by the grand shifts of capital accumulation. Together, these stories demonstrate the broad scope of Campbell's radical political critique and how it emerges by negation.

"The Inventor, 1972" begins with a thirteen-year-old girl being struck by a car. The driver is a man in his thirties who has been profoundly disfigured in an industrial accident. The focus of the third-person narration shifts between the girl and the man. As she lies on the snowy road seriously bleeding from a compound leg fracture, she quickly discards her adolescent illusions of an idyllic future: "There are no songs about one-legged girls, and at school, everybody avoids the two girls in wheelchairs. Nonetheless, she realizes, one-legged would be better than dead. She has long imagined her future spreading out before her, gloriously full of love and discovery; she had been waiting for the future to arrive . . . like the biggest birthday cake with the brightest candles, baked and lit by people who love her" (*American Salvage* 41). Thus, grim as her situation is, it becomes life-affirming for her. She chooses to live, not to be shielded in an illusion presumably shaped by popular-culture representations of fulfillment. Nor will she be subject to the tyranny of wholeness, implicitly a commodification of the body in which a lost limb would make her damaged goods. In effect, she refuses to see herself as a thing—refuses self-reification.[3]

Yet, "the hunter," as the narrator calls the man, endures a much bleaker possibility for living—one dominated by unfulfilled longing. Moreover, the damage to his body is more profound than hers, even if she were to lose her leg. His face and hand have been horribly burned and his lungs seared by an explosion at the foundry where he used to work. His looks now frighten people; his face is "a scary mask" (42) scarred "chin to temple, edged in white, a swath of flesh so raw-looking it seems as though it might melt and drip" (39). Some teeth are missing, and others are infected and rotting (46). These injuries make his speech hoarse and difficult to understand. The hunter's reveries are about hopes he once had that are now—to him, at least—tragically unrealizable: "He thinks his body was once a vessel filled with hope for the future, ideas for invention—as a teenager, he ordered the inventor's guide out of the back of a comic book—but he long ago became a sack of broken glass. Now he has broken this girl, too, and she will never be her whole young self again" (46–47). Unlike her, he sees himself not just as maimed but as worthless—which is likely how society treats him. While the girl's image of the future is sobering but still hopeful, the hunter is bereft of human connection or contact, both because of his injury and because of the legacy of his upbringing. Most painful is the fact that "He has no women or girls in his life, no daughter, no little sister. He has had a few girlfriends over the years, none lately, not since burning his face. After his parents' divorce, his mother moved to Indiana, where his older sister lives" (45–46).

Intensifying this absence is his father's remoteness and austere sense of masculinity. When the hunter's car first strikes the girl, he hopes he has hit a deer so he can bring venison home to his disapproving father, who "thinks his son should have more to show for his life" (48), to be worth more. The rabbits the hunter has trapped will be a paltry offering by comparison. His mind wanders to a time in high school when he borrowed his father's gun to shoot a deer. But when he saw a buck with a group of does, he could not shoot:

> They stepped across the ice, lifting their hooves high, setting each hoof down again delicately; five deer clicking like one machine whose parts were too complicated to synchronize. This would have been his first kill, and he always felt shame at his inability to shoot the buck, but that's not what has haunted him all these years. It is more the complication of overlapping bodies, the mystery of the herd. Their legs seemed impossibly thin on the ice, and their delicate

bodies combined to become one powerful creature; they reminded him of the gangs of girls who passed him in the school hallways. (50)

What is suggested here, and in other parts of the story, is that a notion of masculinity culminating with life-taking vies with the hunter's longing to be part of a group or herd, to feel the solidarity that for him is complexly tied both to the feminine and to creativity—the idea of invention signaled by the story's title. His father has apparently advocated a more alienating, reified sense of masculinity that has left his son with no herd—no solidarity with others—a condition now presumably permanent for him. As he waits with the girl for an ambulance, he fantasizes poignantly about an alternate life he might have led had he killed the deer. He imagines "that buck already hanging in the garage when his dad got home. His dad would have spent the day in the garage with him and gone to work that night bragging about his son, and maybe that would have changed everything" (51). This is, of course, magical thinking, an attempt to assuage the hunter's overwhelming sense of isolation.

Yet he also entertains a more rational, and arguably valid, complaint about his predicament. The foundry has now closed, and he wonders, "If the foundry . . . has become obsolete, then shouldn't the world outside the foundry be noticeably more advanced? He had intended to work at the foundry forever (his burns were a pact the foundry made with him), but they disassembled and dissected the equipment with torches and sold it as scrap iron in a world unprepared to reshape those materials into advanced medical machinery" (47). Note the parallels between the torches and his burns and the use of the word dissected, which implies once-living bodies like his being cut into. Like the foundry, the hunter has become obsolete, but he has been discarded rather than scrapped. He has been maimed by a superseded modern industry, but he cannot even afford the ointment he needs to treat his wound. As the police arrive, he hopes he will be sent to jail so he can be fed, and then to prison where he can get his teeth pulled. Arguably then, the more harmful magical thinking is the American ideology, the narrative in which "economic" change, however destructive, is rationalized as progress.[4] The hunter's life is now primarily suffering, and only the reader can see his value as a human being. Even if he does not fully realize it as such, his yearning is for solidarity, both at an intimate, interpersonal level and at the mass level—the latter suggested by his dream of a just social order premised on advanced technology.

If, as we will see, other stories in the collection depict some examples of precarious, small-scale solidarity, this one offers no such solace. The hunter's clash with the contradictions of capitalism will not be resolved, and it is doubtful if rendering them as art will do so symbolically. The story ends with him fondly remembering playful, but intimate, contact with a friend, another "inventor," who drowned as a youth. (Though neither she nor the hunter know it, the friend was the girl's uncle, whom she never met.) One could argue that this is a "formal" resolution where nostalgia assuages the contradictions—or even where pathos becomes purely aesthetic, and thus also a kind of resolving movement. Yet, these operations would require an extraordinarily naive reader for the twenty-first century. Post 2009 (the year of the book's publication), readers are likely to notice, for example, that the lack of adequate healthcare in the United States unnecessarily dooms people like the hunter to misery, and that deindustrialization has produced widespread working-class income loss. The social problems described in the story would hardly seem "resolved," despite the fact that they are not articulated narratively.

"Family Reunion" depicts a different aspect of these social structural failures. The story, which became the seed of Campbell's novel *Once Upon a River*, is about the aftermath of fourteen-year-old Marylou's rape by her uncle. She and her father, Strong, live across the river from her mother's brother Cal Murray, his wife Anna, and their sons. After Marylou's mother "ran off to Florida with a truckdriver," Anna became a surrogate for her— her guide to a traditionally feminine experience—while her uncle and his sons taught her how to shoot and to fight for herself. As her grandfather would maintain before he died, "family was all you had, and . . . a strong family like the Murrays would protect a person" (80). Yet belying this sanguine assessment of paternalism, Cal has raped Marylou at the annual Thanksgiving "reunion party" (73). Now, a year later, the Murrays signal that they want her back in the fold by inviting her to the event, which infuriates Strong. In the intervening year, Marylou has responded to the trauma of the rape not only by refusing to speak but also by hunting and killing several deer. That all have been bucks suggests that the killing is a displaced response to the rape, which is actually avenged when she shoots off the tip of Cal's penis at the end of the story. Thus, "Family Reunion" is about the power relations of patriarchy, wherein Cal can get away with raping his niece, effectively force his wife and children to accept it, and then expect his victim to return to the fold.

Perhaps less obviously, the story concerns the precarious experience of working-class people under capitalism, specifically in post-Fordist America. Strong assaults Cal after the rape and loses his job as a result. Cal is not only "the head of the Murray family," he is also "the president of Murray Metal Fabricators, the only shop in town paying a decent wage" (73). Thus, to be cast out of the family is to be cast into the low-wage workforce. As the story proceeds, the reader begins to discern that Strong's current job—which is unspecified but possibly could be in retail—is both a profound demotion and degrading. It "pays only about half of what he made at Murray Metal Fabricators" (80). He can no longer sport a beard and he must wear a "blue work smock" (83), which suggests a degrading, forced conformity, a corporate aversion to employees distinguishing themselves as individuals. Also, he must now work on Saturdays, and significantly for the end of the story, on holidays, too. When he comes home during a break on Thanksgiving Day, he sees that Marylou has taken a boat to the Murrays' side of the river to watch the party. Before Strong can confront Cal—which Marylou thinks will result in her father's death or imprisonment for murder—she shoots off her uncle's penis. In doing so, she has attacked both the symbol of Cal's power and the literal instrument of her rape. However, the ending should not be seen as a Jamesonian resolution of social contradictions; shooting off the tip of his penis will not solve her immediate problems—or end patriarchy.[5]

In fact, Cal's patriarchal control of the family is inextricable from economic conditions and labor practices. Strong does not challenge his firing because he likely has no union to defend him.[6] In effect, he must choose between the "protection" of the Murray patriarchy—which requires acquiescing to his daughter's rape—and the vulnerability and apparent indignity of low-wage work. Marylou has to make a similar choice: on the one hand is the maternal love and guidance from her aunt and the belonging that comes with being part of the clan—but with rape a traumatic memory and a future threat; on the other is safe distance from her uncle, but also loneliness. The story strongly implies that no one should have to make such choices. The social structure itself has failed Marylou—not simply a bad actor like Cal; he can get away with abuses of other human beings because the society effectively tolerates it. Terrible choices are forced on anyone vulnerable, which, to some extent, is the majority of the population. Thus, the title, "Family Reunion," emerges as ironic, of course. The "family" as a unit of social welfare is inadequate to the challenge produced by a rapacious global capitalism, which is profoundly unsentimental. As collective units, families do not guarantee nurturing experiences for their members; in fact, the Murray clan reproduces violent authoritarianism. The idea that the family is adequate protection from socioeconomic forces is naive at best and dangerous at worst.

The story "Falling" is about a more nurturing collective, a small group of unrelated people who rely on one another as a bulwark against precariousness. Its unnamed narrator, who is in her early sixties, has been contemplating the sadness of her life since the farmhouse she lived and grew up in burned down. Now residing in a camper on the property (she had no insurance), she regularly imagines suicide, apparently less out of a death wish than as a means to cope with the loss of both the house and a more promising future. In sardonic, yet poetic passages like the following one, she weighs prospective methods: "I have a plan. A .22 bullet penetrates the skull, but can't get out. . . . Maybe there'd be pain when the bullet hits the skin, but after that, it would just be lights flicking out, one after another, making one sad fact after another disappear forever" (110). With her daughter "two thousand miles away," she has no family close by, but Robert, implicitly a former lover and now a disabled, "broken-up man I'm stuck with," lives in her garage (109): "He's got emphysema, he's been crippled by heart surgery, and he's coming off a long treatment for one of those bad staph infections" (109). Compounding his problems is that he has not received social-security disability benefits two years after applying.

Yet, rather than being a burden on the narrator, as she initially implies, he motivates her to keep living: "Some mornings I think there's no reason to get out of bed, but then I see Robert's light come on in the garage" (111). In the past, she also let "a neighbor girl stay upstairs, because her dad kept beating the hell out of her" (109). She also took in Jonas, who is twenty years younger and a former occasional lover. His father is a "useless piece of shit, and a mean drunk besides" (111). As the story opens, Jonas comes to visit the narrator when he is released from the hospital after a failed suicide attempt. We learn that he and "a few of the local kids" had burned down the house "cooking their drugs" (109). Although she is furious with him about the house, and is biting in her exchange with him, she grudgingly acknowledges to herself that she still cares for his welfare. Near the end of the story, when she learns that he has already been solicited by drug dealers in the "room downtown" a social worker has recently arranged for him, she invites him to live in a tent on her place (112). Also important to her is that Jonas "might be the closest thing Robert has to a son" (109). In effect, by caring for abused young people, the addicted, the sick, and the elderly, the narrator provides a safety net absent in post-Fordist America.

To one kind of reader, this story could be an exposé of the bad decisions of down-and-out people: the narrator should have had insurance; should not have taken in a disabled person she cannot afford to help; and should not accommodate drug users, who in turn should not use drugs. The title "Falling" would then refer to those falling in the social order. But in Campbell's hands, this material becomes a story about a powerful affection between people who do not fit the standards of bourgeois propriety. "Falling" refers more to the danger of their precarious circumstances than failures in decision-making, as the last image of the story implies. Robert has emerged from the garage and is trying to walk down the driveway. In his apparent excitement at seeing Jonas, he is literally close to falling: "He lifts his hand off his cane and gestures to us with two bent fingers, but I wish he hadn't. His hips waver, his legs seem unable to support him, his cane slips a little in the dirt. Jonas is watching, too, his trembling jaw setting up, his big body clenching beside mine, until Robert regains his balance. We wave back . . . and when Jonas lets his hand fall, I catch it and hold it steady in both of mine" (113). Their affection for one another prevents them from falling metaphorically; Robert stays on his feet, and presumably, so do they all. In a sense then, the story resolves the social contradiction of precariousness aesthetically. Yet, their lives do not end when the story does, and the reader knows this: tomorrow, the same problems will remain; it is unlikely that Robert will live much longer, which will be an emotional blow for the narrator. Even if he does, he will need increasingly more care, and they have little money. Jonas has escaped the drug dealers and his addiction for now, but for how long? The social support for him is highly limited. He cannot live in a tent through the winter, and neither can Robert in the garage. Thus, the narrative resolution does not adequately solve the problems described. The end may serve as a diegetic and aesthetic culmination, but the story implies a more radical politics by way of negation: small-group salvation cannot fix the failures of the social order.

The politics of "The Yard Man" also emerge by negation, but the story is less obviously about the need and longing for solidarity with others and more about the embrace of a non-reified relation to living. Jerry, the title character, is the caretaker of a former industrial site that is being slowly reclaimed by nature. He lives in a small house on the grounds with his wife Natalie and her two children from a previous marriage. With subtle humor that is nonetheless tinged with sadness, the narrative focuses on the conflict between Jerry's love for the returning wild animals and Natalie's fear of them. While he is steadily integrating with the natural world, she needs the boundaries of houses, fences, and orderly yards that strictly separate human from animal. The conflict escalates when wild animals begin to breach these domestic boundaries. The first instance opens the story: a huge, fantastically colored snake thought to be extinct begins to appear in the garden. When Natalie sees it, she wants Jerry to kill it, but he makes only a pretense of trying to strike it with a shovel. He imagines (and later dreams) that killing it would be like killing a human. Next, a honeybee colony is trapped in a wall of the house, ironically because Jerry has inadvertently sealed their outlet by closing gaps in the siding through which a bat had come. Natalie wants to "call the exterminator," but Jerry has a beekeeper rescue them instead (15). Finally, when an ermine gets into the house, leaving a "rich and musky smell," Natalie decides to move out (29). What for her is abhorrent only fascinates him; he realizes that though he loves her, she is "somebody that didn't belong here" (31).

Superficially, the story seems to establish a binary opposition in which Jerry's human/nature integration is privileged over Natalie's clinging to an inorganic modernity. In that formulation, the return to nature would be an uncomplicated mythologizing. But the simplicity of this opposition is first complicated by Jerry's view of Natalie as a wondrous creature. He stares at her in fascination and appreciation just as he would the snake or ermine. Even after she leaves, "Jerry couldn't think anything bad about his wife. He didn't know why he'd started loving her in high school, why he kept on loving her, loved every move she made, every expression that showed up on her face—he just did. With her soft skin and long hair, she was a beautiful mystery, and even her fear of all the other beautiful creatures was something special about her" (30). I would argue that he does not objectify her in the conventional patriarchal sense; rather, he appreciates all living things non-hierarchically. His love and wonder do not demand that she change, nor does he reduce her to an impediment on the road to a New Age–tinged enlightenment. She does not simply represent a postlapsarian foil in Jerry's paradise; like the snake (who only appears in the story when she is present), Natalie is part of Eden, which suggests a rejection of the opposition between fallen and unfallen nature. There is no premodern refuge to escape to. For him, the site is Garden-like, but it does not exist outside of time or history. It evolves as an ecosystem, and, critically, it is subject to sociohistorical forces, as are the humans who share it.

In fact, their circumstances are far from Edenic. Although he receives a small stipend for maintaining the site, his primary job is as a school custodian, and he has been relegated to part-time, resulting in a "devastating" pay cut (7). Natalie's hours as a bookkeeper at the school have been drastically reduced, and by the end of the story, she has been laid off altogether (22). Together, they experience the post-Fordist shift of public resources to private capital. Moreover, the industrial site is changing. As the old buildings or "sheds" on the property deteriorate, Jerry must demolish them; when they are gone, his job will be, too. Most ominously, the woman who owns the property is getting old, and Jerry fears that when she dies, her son will sell it to developers who will turn it into a subdivision. He wishes that all would remain as it is "forever" (26), but he is well aware of both his mortality and that of his paradise. The previous yard man, Holroyd, whom Jerry sees as a father figure, is old and in ill health, and *his* predecessor, Hammermill, has recently died. Thus, merging with nature does not provide him an escape from precariousness—it is not a live-off-the-land fantasy. At the end of the story, as he and Holroyd sadly contemplate that Jerry may be the last of the yard men, he thinks, "Anything seemed possible now that Jerry's wife was gone, any kind of sadness" (31). On the one hand, this implies loneliness, but on the other, Natalie represents modernity's attitude toward nature, including, perhaps, the false belief that natural processes such as death and decay can be thwarted. Giving up that illusion opens Jerry both to the peace of acceptance and the sadness of loss. In the story's last image, he pictures the snake, an archetypal symbol of renewal: "In spring, he'd poke his head up, stick out his tongue, sniff, and know he was where he belonged. Then he could get to the business of shedding and eating and seeking warmth" (32). Jerry, too, is where he belongs, but it is precarious and perhaps lonely. Though the last image is powerful, and shades towards optimism, it offers no resolution.

In this story, as with many of the stories in *American Salvage*, there is a complex dialectic at work: "The Yard Man" is at once about the impermanence of all things—and about renewal. Yet, it takes place in modernity—in history—where capital is restless, always exercising its own kind of destructive renewal, perhaps best captured by Marx and Engels's famous observation that under capitalism, "All that is solid melts into air"

(476). "The Yard Man" encompasses both the lives of individual people and the grand sweep of an always unfinished history. By presenting the depth of their suffering, their heroic efforts to endure, and their occasional successes, Campbell will not allow her characters to be reified; she resists the trap of aestheticizing their plights. And though these stories are beautifully rendered, their political thrust is not subsumed by narrative resolution. Working by negation, *American Salvage* indicts the social order—and insists that there must be an alternative.

Notes

1. For the story/discourse distinction, see Chatman.
2. After her keynote reading at the Society for the Study of Midwestern Literature Conference on May 17, 2019, Campbell was asked if she saw her writing as political, and she replied in the affirmative. At a panel earlier in the day, she noted that her characters do not belong to unions or political organizations because the people that she bases them on do not.
3. My thinking is influenced here by Marx's notion of reification, but also by Horkheimer and Adorno's *Dialectic of Enlightenment*, where they discuss the pervasive nature of commodity logic in thought itself. They note the tendency of Enlightenment and capitalist thought to reduce all phenomena into units that can be exchanged. Thus, a "damaged" body would be anathema to a culture of abstract equivalencies.
4. I am thinking of Schumpeter's notion that capitalism is characterized by "creative destruction," an apology for inflicting suffering that would appeal only to the comfortable.
5. In *Once Upon a River*, the Marylou character, called Margo, must endure the murder of her father, being raped again, and, of course, banishment from the family. She is not defeated by her suffering, but the novel is no simple paean to endurance. Like so much of Campbell's writing, it is about women navigating an often threatening and violent world.
6. The vast majority of workers in the United States are employed "at will," meaning they can be fired without cause. Union contracts often require just cause for termination.

Works Cited

Campbell, Bonnie Jo. *American Salvage.* Wayne State UP, 2009.

——. *Once Upon a River.* Norton, 2011.

Chatman, Seymour. *Story and Discourse: Narrative Structure in Fiction and Film.* Cornell UP, 1978.

Foley, Barbara. *Marxist Literary Criticism Today.* Pluto, 2019.

Horkheimer, Max, and Theodor Adorno. *Dialectic of Enlightenment: Philosophical Fragments.* Translated by Edmund Jephcott. Stanford UP, 2002.

Jameson, Fredric. *The Political Unconscious: Narrative as Socially Symbolic Act.* Cornell UP, 1981.

Marx, Karl, and Friedrich Engels. *Manifesto of the Communist Party.* 1848. *The Marx-Engels Reader,* edited by Robert C. Tucker. Norton, 1978, pp. 469–500.

Olsen, Tillie. *Yonnondio: From the Thirties.* 1974. Delta/Seymour Lawrence, 1989.

Schumpeter, Joseph A. *Capitalism, Socialism, and Democracy.* Harper, 1976.

The Cultural Critique of American Patriarchal Capitalism in *American Salvage*

Regional literature must strike a balance between depicting the everyday life of a location while being accessible to the wider social concerns of readers within other areas of the United States. Midwestern author Bonnie Jo Campbell does just that by capturing the lived experience of those residing in southwest Michigan through the lens of rural noir fiction (also known as country noir) in order to critically examine the structural effects of American patriarchal capitalism. Court Merrigan writes that rural noir "carves out a space for the small, the local, the defiant, and the defeated" and addresses the "hubris of the American dream" by looking "to the broken-down farmhouse, abandoned in a pasture, with its dreams long gone and broken." There is a sense of isolation within rural noir fiction. Communities feel abandoned by both cities and society at large, and therefore focus inward on their own social circumstances. Campbell has commented on her interest in capturing this feeling in an interview with the *Kenyon Review* when she explained that her collection of short stories *American Salvage* makes "the case that not all Americans are on the same page heading into the twenty-first century. It's as though there was some kind of apocalypse and nobody noticed, and now a large number of folks are living off the debris that's left behind" ("Conversation").

The characters of Bonnie Jo Campbell's oeuvre are those who have been hit the hardest by life's misfortunes, both economic and otherwise, and they find themselves disenfranchised within the structures of American life. These individuals are often perceived as damaged, distraught, misfits, or outcasts who struggle to survive day-to-day. This collection of fourteen short stories features women abused by society, parents, children, and significant others. It also offers a look at the difficulties men may endure when they cannot live up to the masculine middle-class expectations (including a successful profession, a beautiful home, and a loving, doting family). The characters experience poverty, post-traumatic stress disorder (PTSD), anxiety, depression, drug addiction, unemployment, or abusive bosses (if they are fortunate enough to have a job). Yet while Campbell's characters have narratives that may be gut-wrenching to read, they are vivid representations of the lived experience individuals may face under the weight of patriarchal capitalism.

Torben Iversen and Frances Rosenbluth argue that patriarchal male dominance can be seen in social, economic, and political organization as far back as agrarian societies because "men have a bargaining advantage that derives from their ability to leave the household more easily" (18). Over time, it has become so ingrained within society that patriarchal practices are nearly invisible. Market economies prioritize male labor because it is presumed that there is often a chance that women could leave the workforce for childbearing and other family work, which often leads employers to select men over women when hiring. Still, Sylvia Walby notes that any definition of patriarchy should engage with the way it affects a system of social structures in order to reject "the notion that every individual man is in a dominant position and every individual woman in a subordinate one" (214). With this in mind, we can more clearly address the ways the system favors most men while also establishing a structure that may be difficult for all men to aspire to. The patriarchal structure thus leads to a system dependent on kin groups defined by men. Competition between kin-based groups not only legitimizes patriarchal control but also encourages capitalist authority over workers. This authority can become further oppressive during times of crises. *American Salvage* was published in 2009 and thus reflects on both the 2001 and 2008 recessions. These economic crises deeply affected the working class, especially in southwest Michigan where *American Salvage* is set. The crises and their effects shifted our understanding of American cultural values and forced some to directly address how the patriarchal structures that frame capitalism may negatively affect all working individuals.

Campbell's stories also contain a common narrative thread of meth addiction. There is a connection between capitalism and the production of meth in the rural Midwest, as Jason Pine shows, because an intersection has developed between work and everyday consumption. This sense of consumption goes beyond drugs, as Midwestern workers participate in a form of embodied capitalism that extends to their work in the farming, motor, and retail industries. Pine argues that "in embodied capitalism, bodies, and not just those of meth users, are at once fuel and machine, resource and product, point of departure and the obstacle. They register the exertion of immaterial labor and the symptoms of precarity" ("Embodied" 179). As meth serves as a haunting presence in all of the stories in this collection, Campbell displays not only how addiction is a pervasive problem, but also how it becomes embedded in effects of capitalism and gendered violence.

By tracing Campbell's examination of patriarchal capitalism within *American Salvage* it is possible to address the way these systems create a divide between social classes in order to permit certain individuals to stay at the top of the proverbial ladder. Campbell's depiction of Midwestern automotive and agricultural workers struggling to survive day-to-day in the wake of the economic recessions highlights what Sharon Harrigan refers to as "honest violence" (170) within Campbell's stories. Harrigan labels the violence as "honest," because of the way these narratives "admit that those who transgress have often been transgressed against" (171). Addressing violence against both women and men demonstrates how a deteriorating American culture of patriarchal capitalism generates a disordered environment where individuals must challenge their morals and go to great lengths to survive. Ultimately, this chapter shows how Campbell uses the rural noir genre to examine the complexity of everyday life as individuals endure the consequences of perpetuating American capitalist culture.

Remnants of Patriarchal Capitalism

It is poignant that Campbell named this collection *American Salvage*. Although the title is a gesture to one of its stories, the word "salvage" is also an apt description for the collection as a whole. The word suggests an act of retrieving or preserving something from potential loss or destruction. The loss referenced here could point to the myth of the American Dream that has become inherent within American culture. It is drilled into Americans' heads at a young age that if they just work hard enough, they can make a prosperous, honest living for themselves. However, the characters in *American Salvage* are examples of those who pursued the American Dream and were unable to obtain the promised results. Rather, they are struggling to make ends meet. As Marcia Noe, Mollee Shannon, and Laura Duncan note, Campbell's work (and *American Salvage* in particular) draws attention to the question that if a country such as the United States is "so rich in resources," then it should be able to address its "problems of homelessness, corporate greed, addiction, poverty, un- and under-employment, juvenile delinquency, rampant consumerism, and the patriarchal oppression of women" (34–35). These characters strive to retain what they believe to be true American culture. However, they often struggle or fail and, in turn, find themselves scrapped on the salvage heap of American culture. Even when some of the characters try to work within the system of patriarchal capitalism, they find themselves suffering further because of it.

The process of salvaging is directly tied to the short story that inspires the collection's title: "King Cole's American Salvage." The titular King Cole is the owner of a scrap junkyard and purchases used cars to salvage for parts. Johnny (King Cole's nephew) lets slip to his friend, Slocum, that his uncle does not like banks and instead keeps "thousands of dollars in hidden pockets in his jackets" (*American Salvage* 115). With this information, Slocum goes to King Cole's home under the pretense of needing a jump for his car (that he stole). He instead beats the old man with a metal pipe and steals his money. Slocum justifies his actions by stating that King Cole is a "cheap bastard" (115) who stiffed him on the price of an old Mitsubishi Montero, and also by suggesting that he and his girlfriend, Wanda, need the money more than King Cole does. King Cole survives but has significant brain damage, leading to Johnny caring for both him and his scrap junkyard. As the story progresses, we watch Slocum's trail unfold and learn more about the man as those around him (including Wanda and Johnny) provide testimonies. Campbell describes him as feeling "like a bull for slaughter" (127) when he is presented to the judge, highlighting the way he understands his role in this story. Johnny's ability to carry on his uncle's work after the attack suggests that Slocum's sacrifice is necessary so men like King Cole and Johnny can continue to maintain their livelihoods.

King Cole serves as a representation of one who is still trying to make a living within the automotive industry. Drawing on the nursery rhyme, Campbell's rural King Cole is heavy and hides behind a synthetic appearance of control. He is described as a "small man with one hand on his potbelly. His long beard and shoulder-length hair were black . . . the old man dyed it because he thought it made him *attractive to the ladies*" (115). Like the Old King Cole of the nursery rhyme, Campbell's King Cole's girth shows the reader the character's ease of accessing food and resources. He is living off of what was left behind by the automotive industry crisis of 2008, which led two of the "Big Three" automakers to receive emergency loans to address impending cash shortages and their imminent bankruptcy.

Jobs were significantly scaled back in car plants during this period. The U.S. Bureau of Labor Statistics notes that there was a 35 percent decline in manufacturing in the car industry, leading to employment being cut by about one-third (Barker 30). Because of this, men like Slocum cannot make ends meet, while men like King Cole find ways to profit off what remains. Consequently, Slocum is not beating King Cole the person. Rather, Slocum is seeking to punish the men of the auto industry for the way they took advantage of the Michigan working class. Noe, Shannon, and Duncan observe that "all that's left of a country that used to make things are the junkyard remnants of an erstwhile manufacturing economy that used to provide a decent life for many Americans" (35). While capitalism focuses on the profit margin, workers like Slocum suffer significantly. Slocum's act of assault and robbery is his desperate attempt to reclaim what he believes to be his from a system that used and discarded him. This becomes clearer as Slocum explains during the trial that he never intended to cause so much harm to King Cole: "If he just would've stayed down when I told him to I would have stopped hitting him" (*American Salvage* 128). However, Slocum does not defeat one of the men involved in perpetuating the established system. In the end, King Cole manages to continue his work with the assistance of his nephew, proving that subsequent generations will inevitably work toward preserving the system if it means they too can survive another day.

Although the theme of salvage is clearest in the short story that contains the word in its title, the closing story of the collection further addresses this theme from the perspective of the Midwestern farmer. In "Boar Taint," Campbell tells the story of Jill, a woman who was only meant to stay in southwest Michigan for as long as it took to complete her postgraduate studies. Her family tries to dissuade her from staying full-time to become a farmer, arguing that "just because she'd studied agriculture for six years didn't mean she knew a damned thing about farming. All she'd ever wanted, from the time she was a kid, was to work with land and animals, to work beside a good man, but there was so much more to it" (161). Yet Jill is determined to make a living with the farm she is building with her husband, Ernie. Jill's new idea to help their farm is to raise pigs for pig roasts (152). To bring this dream to life, Jill answers an advertisement to purchase a poorly treated boar hog from the Jentzen family farm for $25. Through her innovative ideas, Jill is seeking to salvage what she can of the farm's future.

Although the primary narrative of "Boar Taint" is centered on the struggles of Jill and Ernie, the Jentzen family proves to be the clearest image of the struggling Midwestern farmer on the brink of collapse in the twenty-first century. When she arrives at their family farm, Jill finds a home that stands as a shell of what once might have been a thriving space:

> Jill stepped inside the hot, dark kitchen, felt her work boots press grit into the plank floor. . . . Although a fire burned in the stove, not even a candle was lit to defend against the oncoming darkness. . . . As her eyes adjusted to the dim light, three more silent men materialized at the table, and a boy. . . . The men all had a forward curve to their shoulders, with their forearms resting on the table as though they were defending bowls of food, only there were no bowls. (155)

The grit on the floor, the lack of food, and the hunched men create an image of starvation and a life without livable means. These men may still have the farm to work on, but they cannot construct the patriarchal capitalist expectation of a controlled household. The Jentzen boy that is tasked with showing Jill the boar can only inherit the hollowed-out home and swampy pigpens. Through this, Jill recognizes that the men are not selling the boar as an act of everyday business but rather as an act of survival. At this point, she has yet to see the boar, but the reader is given hints that the Jentzen men believe the animal is not even worth eating. In an interview with the *Kenyon Review*—where the short story was first published— Campbell commented, "The Jentzen men are the failing farmers, ghosts of the men they once were, so far gone they don't even bother to communicate anymore" ("Conversations"). The invocation of "ghosts" here is reminiscent of the implied remnants in "King Cole's American Salvage." The word "ghosts" can imply that while the men are no longer self-sustaining farmers, the lingering nature of ghosts prove that the men refuse to fade from existence, just as the remnants that are meant to be discarded instead accumulate and demand recognition. The Jentzen men remain long past their use within the capitalist structure. When Jill finally sees the boar, she notices that "its visible eye looked as dull as the eyes of those men in the kitchen" (*American Salvage* 157), and thus places the Jentzen men and the male boar as parallel figures struggling to survive.

Despite the ghost-like Jentzen men, Campbell's "Boar Taint" offers an image of hope for the Michigan farmer. This hope is not found through the survival of the Jentzen men but rather through Jill's innovation. Andy Oler comments that Jill's risk-taking endeavor is a direct result of being "part of a system that compels risk" (177). Yet, more importantly, Jill's ability to remain optimistic through this new direction for the farm, Oler argues, is rooted in Campbell's interest in "rethink[ing] rural decline through this combination of uncertainty and opportunity, which is linked to her construction of gendered behavior" (177). The transfer of the boar between the farmers results in a transfer of the responsibility of the boar's survival onto Jill—and, by extension, the transfer of watching over the survival of the farming profession. In her efforts to devise new ways for the Midwestern farmer to survive, Jill becomes an extension of the family. Her plans for the boar are reflective of her desires to reimagine the material production of her farm. When Jill takes the boar home, it manages to pull itself up on its legs, proving to her that it is "a creature even bullets could not stop" (*American Salvage* 167). The closing image of the boar's determination to continue living reflects Jill's own determination to survive despite the looming weight of the capitalist expectation of constant material production. Her efforts to rethink the structure of farming as a profession despite this system offers a note of possibility at the close of the short story collection that seeks to address the ways patriarchal capitalism as a system has broken down industries that are crucial to Michigan's economic survival.

Navigating Gendered Violence

Throughout the collection, Campbell carefully weaves in an examination of how patriarchal capitalism can generate gendered violence. Two notable stories that address this topic as it affects both men and women are

"The Trespasser" and "The Solutions to Brian's Problem." Because human behavior is shaped by gender and class interests, the term "patriarchal capitalism" leads to an understanding of the innate problem of inequality created by class arrangements that are defined and controlled by men. Anna Pollert notes that "the only explanation for men's alleged control over women's labour power lies in their acts of exclusion and control" (642). As a system, capitalism has an internal self-perpetuation, as production cannot exist without clear profit. Although there is no intrinsic dynamic of the same kind within the system of patriarchy, learned behaviors of personal value are passed on through generations, encouraging the favoring of male labor over female labor.

Furthermore, as these values are passed on, as both stories suggest, a person is only worth something to society if they can contribute as is expected of their gender. Yet while there is an encouraged difference between men and women, there is also an established difference between classes and races of women. As Nancy Folbre explains, "More extreme class inequality seemed to mute gender inequality, because it intensifies differences among women" (208). This can most prominently be seen in the way affluent women manage their care responsibilities for children and the elderly by hiring women at low wages (who are often women of color) to do the work for them. Therefore, Folbre notes, "Poor women suffer both from low wages and a low level of public support for care provision" (207). Ultimately, there are consequences for all genders because the expectations of patriarchal capitalism perpetuate the economic development of specific individuals. While it is important to note that race and ethnicity can further affect individual oppression, because it is not explicit whether or not Campbell is addressing individuals of color in *American Salvage*, this chapter focuses on general gendered oppression and violence within my examination of her short stories.

While meth is always on the margins of her stories, it is most clearly displayed in the narratives that engage most with gendered violence. Meth becomes connected to capitalism, as it brings together the acts of production and leisure. Pine's interviews of meth addicts show how the drug increases the feeling of productivity, thus further fueling the anxiety individuals feel when struggling to keep up with the expectations of surviving in a capitalist society. Furthermore, he highlights how meth "oversexes the body" ("Economy" 364). The user's focus on productivity and promiscuity leads them to go for prolonged periods of time "without nourishing or giving their bodies rest, or protecting it from disease," leading to the body's needs being abandoned "in the pursuit of pure speed" (365). Yet the heightened feelings of invincibility and sex generates further violence upon both the body of the user and the bodies the user encounters. Campbell takes up both concerns in *American Salvage*.

In the opening story, "The Trespasser," a family enters their summer cottage to find the place in disarray. Three men and a sixteen-year-old girl had at one point invaded the cottage and turned it into a space for sex and drugs. Noe, Shannon, and Duncan extend their discussion of this story to engage with all three intruders to argue that the story emphasizes "the toll [capitalism] takes on its youth, in many cases doomed before adulthood through no fault of their own to a life of poverty and drugs" (36). Yet the lasting image of the titular trespasser, a young blonde girl escaping out the back door to the river, haunts the short story by demonstrating the effects of patriarchal violence. The trespasser becomes a parallel to the family's wholesome daughter. The two live separate lives, but both become scarred by the hardships of society. The thirteen-year-old daughter becomes forever changed by the image of her invaded bedroom and her newfound awareness of the threat of violence, whereas the sixteen-year-old trespasser, already very familiar with violence, continues to struggle to survive.

In the *Kenyon Review*, Campbell noted how she intended for *American Salvage* to examine the ways men devoured women. She explains that in "Boar Taint" the male farmers sitting around the table seemed as if they had devoured the woman in their kitchen. Similarly, Jill is seeking to find a reason to stay in the farming business and not get devoured by her partner, Ernie. Yet where Jill may still be able to find a way to survive on her own, not all women in Campbell's collection are as successful in their efforts. The teenage girl in "The Trespasser" offers a look at how the process of devouring women within this patriarchal capitalist system can start from a young age. The trespasser's body is consumed by the men in exchange for hits of meth to satisfy her drug addiction. Here the reader can see that violence only begets violence. Specifically, male violence begets violence upon women.

Although the sixteen-year-old girl is named for her crime of trespassing, Campbell makes the character sympathetic by showing how the girl was robbed of innocence. After the men left, the trespasser actively "pretended to be visiting her own family's cottage, pretended that the bones in the faces in the photographs were her inherited bones and that she inhabited this place as naturally as the furniture and relics" (*American Salvage* 2). She cares for the home by vacuuming the living room and polishing the objects in the hallway. The trespasser falls back on characteristically domestic chores, attempting to create a sense of what she believes to be normalcy—albeit superficial normalcy as constructed by a patriarchal society that defines women's roles through housekeeping. While the family is distraught to find the kitchen was used to make meth, the most horrifying image is of the daughter's closet, "where the trespasser slept five nights in a nest created from all the pillows in the house. She curled there with two stuffed ponies and a unicorn, the pink flannel pajamas that say Daddy's Girl, and the secret purple spiral notebook that is identical to the one the daughter keeps in the city" (3). The trespasser had read the notebook repeatedly and pretended to be the girl in the diary entries. The clear attraction the trespasser has to the soft, girlish items demonstrates that despite the crimes described at the start of the short story, the trespasser, at the end of the day, is still just a girl. Laura Fine notes that Campbell's version of country noir shifts from a question of who performed a crime to the question of what makes a crime. She argues that, in Campbell's interest in the effects of violence, "sexual violence and the internalization of warped cultural norms about female sexuality are conceived . . . as cultural crimes" (519). By the end of the story, it is clear that the crime suggested at the start—the trespassing and cooking of meth—is not the focus, but rather the violence against the girl's body and overall well-being.

Campbell's honest violence may primarily focus on violence against women, but "The Solutions to Brian's Problem" highlights how the patriarchal capitalist system can enact violence on men. The short story breaks traditional narrative form to instead feature a list of seven possible solutions to Brian's problem of caring for a baby with his abusive, meth-addicted partner, Connie. Campbell has noted that the collection is "about troubled men" ("Interview"). Fine takes this further to argue that *American Salvage*'s male-dominated stories show that men "make compromised moral choices in a dark world they accept but do not understand" (516). While this analysis is true for most of the stories in the collection, Brian fully understands the world he resides in, and at times he appears to accept it. For example, solution #3 begins, "Put the baby boy to bed in his crib and sit on the living room couch until Connie comes home" (*American*

Salvage 52). Other solutions range from abandoning his partner to helping his partner curb her addiction, committing suicide, or changing nothing about the situation. Each solution offers a snapshot of Brian's life, conveying to the reader how he not only endures physical violence from Connie but also places pressure on himself to continue performing as the male provider of their home.

Although the structure of the short story purposefully places the solution that Brian will accept at the close of the narrative, his navigation through each no-win solution shows Brian struggling to retain his sense of self through expectations society has placed upon him. He struggles with finding a balance between the social expectations (of providing for his family, building a comfortable home, and retaining status in a profession) and the violence enacted by his partner. In almost all of his solutions, Brian actively engages with his sense of responsibility. He only contemplates full abandonment in two of the seven solutions. This focus on responsibility shows his awareness of the care his son requires as well as the expectations placed upon him by the patriarchal capitalist society to remain both faithful and committed to the family structure. Many solutions prioritize his son's care: along with solution #3's emphasis on bedtime, solution #1 starts with "Put the baby boy in the car seat, and drive away" (52). Solution #6 shows him seeking outside help through counseling. Yet, even in this solution, he recognizes the uneven power dynamics between himself and Connie: "Try to be patient when the counselor seems awkward in her responses, when she inadvertently expresses surprise at the nature of your distress, especially when you admit that Connie's only five foot three" (54). Here, the expectation of female victimhood makes it easier for the counselor to accept a woman's cries for help, rather than a man's. Campbell's acknowledgment of the existence of gendered violence against men in this story allows for a consideration of how men can become trapped within a system that is seemingly made to favor them.

American Salvage is a series of windows into the lives of individuals struggling to persevere despite the odds against them. Stories like "King Cole's American Salvage" and "Boar Taint" address the different methods individuals employ to survive. While some manage to hang onto the hope of possibilities, others become overwhelmed by the pressures of the system. The violence that becomes a product of patriarchal capitalism is shown in "The Trespasser" and "The Solutions to Brian's Problem."

When men and women cannot fit within the established parameters of gender roles expected, they are left to fend for themselves. Through the genre of rural noir, Campbell's short story collection presents an image of Michigan that is deeply affected by the patriarchal capitalist culture of the United States as a whole. Since the start of the twenty-first century, unanticipated consequences have been piling up, further exacerbating the instability that made capitalism dependent on patriarchal familial structures. As working-class Americans fall further into the collapse of this culture, we can see how individuals, such as those represented in Campbell's rural noir fiction, have become remnants of American ideals.

Works Cited

Barker, Megan M. "Manufacturing Employment Hard Hit during the 2007–09 Recession." *Monthly Labor Review*, Apr. 2011, pp. 28–33.

Campbell, Bonnie Jo. *American Salvage*. Wayne State UP, 2009.

———. "A Conversation with Bonnie Jo Campbell." *Kenyon Review*, kenyonreview.org/conversation/bonnie-jo-campbell/.

———. "An Interview with Bonnie Jo Campbell." *Nashville Review*, 1 Apr. 2012, as.vanderbilt.edu/nashvillereview/archives/5124.

Fine, Laura. "Sexual Violence and Cultural Crime in the Country Noir Fiction of Bonnie Jo Campbell." *Critique*, vol. 60, no. 5, 2019, pp. 515–26.

Folbre, Nancy. "Varieties of Patriarchal Capitalism." *Social Politics*, vol. 16, no. 2, 2009, pp. 204–9.

Harrigan, Sharon. "Honest Violence and Women." *Pleiades*, vol. 36, no. 1, 2016, pp. 170–71.

Iversen, Torben, and Frances Rosenbluth. *Women, Work, and Politics: The Political Economy of Gender Inequality*. Yale UP, 2010.

Merrigan, Court. "New Genres: Country Noir." *Electric Literature*, 27 May 2014, electricliterature.com/new-genres-country-noir/.

Noe, Marcia, Mollee Shannon, and Laura Duncan. "The Dark Fairy Tale in the Fiction of Bonnie Jo Campbell." *Midwestern Miscellany*, 2014, pp. 33–44.

Oler, Andy. *Old-Fashioned Modernism: Rural Masculinity and Midwestern Literature*. Louisiana State UP, 2019.

Pine, Jason. "Economy of Speed: The New Narco-Capitalism." *Public Culture*, vol. 19, no. 2, 2006, pp. 357–66.

———."Embodied Capitalism and the Meth Economy." *The Body Reader: Essential Social and Cultural Readings*, edited by Lisa Jean Moore and Mary Kosut. New York UP, pp. 164–79.

Pollert, Anna. "Gender and Class Revisited; Or, the Poverty of 'Patriarchy.'" *Sociology*, vol. 30, no. 4, 1996, pp. 639–59.

Walby, Sylvia. "Theorising Patriarchy." *Sociology*, vol. 23, no. 2, 1989, pp. 213–34.

Power Tool Mishaps

Women and Alcohol in "Playhouse"

ELLEN LANSKY

One of the most effective performance artists of the nineteenth century, Carry Nation gained fame in Kansas as a fierce opponent of the saloon. Indeed, she was infuriated by the saloon culture that produced, enabled, and promoted a male homosocial environment of public drinking. Her fury sprang from the deleterious effects of alcohol on heterosexual families—women, children, and the drinking men themselves—in her own domestic life, in her own home. She responded to this unhappy situation through protests that often included violence and destruction of property.

Carry Nation's protests against saloon culture began when she developed rudimentary but powerful tools. At first, propelled by righteous indignation, she would enter a saloon with a tool she called a "smasher"—a big brick that she used literally to smash the place to bits: breaking mirrors and windows, demolishing bottles, and threatening the saloon keepers and their clientele. Her performances became even more powerful when she took up a more complex and threatening tool: a hatchet. In a performance piece she dubbed the "hatchetation," she would enter a saloon, raise high her hatchet, and bust the place ("Nation"). The fact that she was six feet tall and strong gave her performances even more fortitude. Her hatchetations became known far beyond the dusty, hot borders of Kansas, and she went on tour, selling hatchet pins as part of her act. The hatchetation and, eventually, just the hatchet pin, became her brand.

Carry Nation's hatchet serves as an emblem for the national fixation on alcohol and saloon culture. While Nation's temperance hatchet has now been transposed into popular bars where people go to throw hatchets for fun, early to mid-twentieth-century American writers understood that women who drink in public are more vulnerable to violence and sexual assault, not to mention scorn, derision, and castigation. In the short story "Playhouse," Bonnie Jo Campbell extends this tradition into the twenty-first century, rendering an unfortunately all-too-familiar situation involving Janie, a bottle of tequila, sexual assault, and an accident. In the story, Janie's brother Steve's cordless drill is the most obvious power tool that causes the "mishap" to which this essay's title refers. However, as the story develops, Campbell shows that the power tool that does the most damage to Janie, and portends even more damage to Pinky, is not the cordless drill but the remnants of saloon culture. In "Playhouse," Campbell reexamines a familiar figure in the canon of American modernist fiction writers: a woman under the influence of alcohol.

Drinking Women

The history of alcohol as it pertains to women in general and, as in Campbell's story, to white, working-class, heterosexual women, is complex and fraught. To begin, Michel Foucault's method in *History of Sexuality, Vol. 1* provides a useful theoretical implementation. Foucault posits sexuality as a "discursive production"—not a cause or originary moment but rather an effect of a particular kind of exercise of power (10–13). One might apply his tracing of the history of sexuality to the history of alcohol and drug addiction in nineteenth-century American culture. For example, in *Dark Paradise*, David T. Courtwright traces the origins of the drug addict to the nineteenth-century physician and his female patients. With the advent of hypodermics in the 1860s and 1870s, morphine, an opium product, became a wonder remedy. Courtwright explains that "[a] syringe of morphine was, in a very real sense, a magic wand. Though it could cure little, it could relieve anything; doctors and patients alike were tempted to overuse" (47). This overuse, combined with the addictive properties of opium and morphine, produced drug addicts.

Throughout most of the nineteenth century, drug addiction, like sexuality, was confined to the house. Significantly, most nineteenth-century opium or morphine addicts were women. According to Courtwright, "doctors liberally dispensed opium and morphine to their patients, many of whom were female and many of whom subsequently became addicted"

(2). Doctors administered opium and morphine for a range of "female complaints"—from "nerves" to menstrual pain; in fact, Courtwright reports that "as late as 1908 the State Hospital at Independence, Iowa, reported that most of the female addicts became addicted through palliation of dysmenorrhea" (48). Opium's euphoric effects quelled "female complaints," but unfortunately, many of these quelled females became addicts—dependent not only on a substance but also upon the man who administered it. Thus, doctors who prescribed and administered opium and morphine to their female patients used this substance as a strategy of subordination and disempowerment, intentionally or not.

Paradoxically, the same people who helped create drug addicts later helped create the negative image of addicts. The addict underwent a paradigm shift from complaining white bourgeois female to furtive underclass male junkie. Courtwright explains that "as the nonmedical addict emerged as the dominant type, an increasing number of physicians and public health officials came to view addiction as a manifestation of psychopathy or some other serious personality disorder, to support mandatory institutionalization of addicts, and to refuse to supply addicts (especially the nonmedical type) with drugs" (123). The enthusiastic creation of the drug addict recalls Mary Shelley's *Frankenstein*, in which an enthusiastic doctor/scientist cobbles together a creature and then repudiates it.

A similar effect can be found in the history of alcohol. During what William Rorabaugh calls the "national binge" (ix) of the late eighteenth and early nineteenth centuries, drinking seemed to cross gender and class boundaries. Rorabaugh notes that women mostly drank at home (13). Furthermore, Mary Jane Lupton reminds readers "[not to] forget the countless American women, many from the middle class, who periodically and even habitually comforted their aches with Lydia Pinkham's Vegetable Compound, a medicine containing herbs, vegetables, and a solvent of 21 percent alcohol" (577). For much of the nineteenth century, respectable white ladies had consumed alcohol only in private, often for medicinal reasons or alongside their husbands. In *A Shoppers' Paradise*, Emily Remus notes that in Chicago and elsewhere, "public drinking was a male privilege and a vital component of masculine camaraderie; a woman who so imbibed was thought to be a 'public woman,' her body available for sale" (117). As drinking disrupted white bourgeois homes and posed a threat to Victorian domestic order, proponents of Victorian domesticity took action. Perhaps as a result, the scene of solo binge drinking moved out of the house and into the saloon.

Saloon culture, especially as it affected white heterosexual domestic life and the lives of white women and children, hastened the rise of Carry Nation, and her physical presence in saloons constituted a direct challenge to white male privilege and power. For example, in dry states like Kansas, white men gave themselves permission to operate saloons while simultaneously prohibiting them by law. When Carry Nation entered her first saloon in Kiowa, Kansas, and then proceeded to smash the joint, she was busting up a site of patriarchal privilege and power. Indeed, her presence in a saloon exposed the duplicity inherent in the state's prohibition laws. She hatcheted the hypocritical rhetoric of white male Kansas lawmakers.

By 1919, eight years after Carry Nation's death, the Volstead Act brought writing and talking about alcohol into the fabric of the Constitution. Prohibition, a result of the Volstead Act and, one might argue, of Carry Nation's hatchetations, became the moniker of a complicated era in which alcohol was deemed illegal and meant to become a scarce commodity. Instead, it proliferated. During Prohibition, creative writers added to the multiplicity of discourses by writing stories and novels and poems and plays and memoirs that were specifically "about" drinking and alcohol, and many of these texts featured women at their centers. Rather than drying out, the culture became literally (and discursively) saturated with alcohol. Twentieth-century writers contributed to a discourse that both normalized and complicated the culture of alcohol. Indeed, a woman drinking alcohol became a central figure in modern American literature.

Rather than raising smashers and hatchets, women now participated in public drinking practices and in writing about drinking. Dorothy Parker, for example, was a "regular" at several New York speakeasies, and so is Hazel Morse in Parker's story "Big Blonde." Zelda Fitzgerald also spent much time in speakeasies and wrote about it in *Save Me the Waltz*, and Djuna Barnes wrote about Prohibition-era drinking women in her novel *Nightwood* (published in 1937 but set in the 1920s). At the same time, men were writing about drinking women as well. For example, at the center of Ernest Hemingway's *The Sun Also Rises* is the hard-drinking Brett Ashley. On the stage, Tennessee Williams's women characters were often affected, including Maggie in *Cat on a Hot Tin Roof*, as well as Blanche DuBois in *A Streetcar Named Desire*, who spends most of her summertime visit with her sister, Stella, and brother-in-law, Stanley, taking baths and drinking Stan's liquor.

Despite the presence and central role of alcohol, the critical tradition has mostly declined to analyze the presence of alcohol and alcoholism in American fiction. For example, the influential critic—and participant in the expatriate Paris drinking scene—Malcolm Cowley documents the coming of age of those who "fled to Europe and then came back again": the cocktail-drinking modernists (296). Cowley's contention is that American writers went to Paris in the 1920s as a gesture of escape, a way to find home, following "a larger pattern of exile . . . and return from exile" (292). Then they returned to the United States and became active participants in American culture and everyday life. While Cowley recognizes that "there seemed to be more drinking than before in literary and business circles" at the time of the expatriates' return to the United States (305), his narrative largely mutes the alcoholism that many of these writers experienced, as well as the simple fact that many young writers and other people flocked to Europe in the 1920s because it was cheap, and liquor was legal.

The ordering, serving, and drinking of alcohol is a primary activity in many modern American novels and stories, and the cocktail is an iconic presence. Alcohol and drinking are so pervasive in American modernism that to ignore it or to dismiss it is a major critical shortcoming. Another exclusion is the refusal to examine the presence of women in the culture of alcohol in modern American fiction. In her short story "Playhouse," Bonnie Jo Campbell centralizes a figure whom the classic criticism of modern American fiction has often overlooked: a woman under the influence of alcohol who must negotiate conflicting gender and power positions in her relationships and everyday life.

The Drinking Woman in "Playhouse"

Bonnie Jo Campbell's "Playhouse," published nearly a century after the passage of the Volstead Act, reiterates those dangers in her characterization of Janie, the narrator who was raped in a blackout after drinking at her brother's party, and also Pinky, Janie's three-year-old niece. "Playhouse" opens with Janie returning to a crime scene, though the fact that a crime was committed and she was its victim is not immediately evident to her or to Steve, her brother. She pays a visit to Steve, whom she hasn't seen in three weeks, since his Summer Solstice party, and finds herself in the difficult spot of trying to remember a "blackout."

The story's opening invites further investigation into two key features: Steve's Summer Solstice party and Janie's bottle of tequila, which situate drinking and the culture of alcohol as part of a larger enterprise of cultural appropriation, disempowerment, and violence against women masquerading as fun. Both features bear the traces of what Mikhail Bakhtin calls, in *Rabelais and His World*, "folk carnival culture." Mary Russo observes that the carnival has a "complicitous place in dominant culture" that poses, she suggests, "especial dangers for women and other marginalized groups within the carnival" (217). While drugs and alcohol may fuel the carnival spirit, an intoxicated woman in a carnival scene is not in a position of power. In fact, she is in danger. The crime scene in Steve's twenty-first-century Michigan backyard bears traces of dangerous, degraded forms of carnival revelry that quickly devolve into drinking too much, vomiting, passing out, and laughter that is scornful and ironic. At first glance, the Summer Solstice seems like a fun and amusing theme for a backyard party. One might recall that Shakespeare uses the Solstice as the situation and setting for *A Midsummer Night's Dream*. In his article "What Is the Summer Solstice? An Astronomer Explains," Stephen Schneider notes that "people around the world observe the change of seasons with bonfires and festivals and Fete de la Musique celebrations." However, in Campbell's story, Steve's staging of a Summer Solstice party suggests not a celebration of the seasons or any kind of expression of the "folk culture" in Kalamazoo, Michigan, but instead an enactment of cultural appropriation that serves as a backdrop or just a simple reason for a group of people to get together and get drunk.

Moreover, the scene at Steve's party bears none of the marks of an authentic Summer Solstice event. There is no celebration or even a mention of the change of seasons; there is no bonfire, no music, no joy or fun. There is some horseplay and general rowdiness, and it degrades into a sexual assault on Janie. The event does not take place in the woods outside of a city, as in Shakespeare's version, or at a fairgrounds or marketplace, as Rabelais would have it. Instead, the Summer Solstice party takes place at Steve's modest one-story house with a privacy fence and "a big back yard where he grills out in the summer" (Campbell 17). Steve "lays floors for a living" (17), which suggests a kinship to Shakespeare's "rude mechanicals" in the midsummer night woods (190) or to Bakhtin's marketplace carnival revelers, but his domestic situation suggests a transience and a disconnection from the rituals of family life and a wider, authentic culture. For example, Steve is not a carpetmaker or a weaver or a craftsman; he sells his labor for wages. Steve lives in his modest house with his three-year old daughter, Pinky. It's not clear if he is or was married to Pinky's mother, but their relationship is perhaps best illustrated by the fact that he calls her "the Bitch," and she "lost her custody rights when she was convicted of cooking meth" (Campbell 18). In his kitchen, Janie notes "the lingering smell of what must have been brats for dinner . . . [and] greasy paper plates in the garbage" (17); the structures of family life that might make the small house feel like a happy home instead feel tenuous, disposable, smelly. Steve and Janie exchange small talk and some banter on a range of topics: Steve's horrible ex, Janie's bad hair-dye job, her boyfriend who is a dud, her dead-end job at Smart Mart. They watch the news on TV and laugh about a report on a "fair tax," but their laughter, unlike the Bakhtinian carnival laughter that is regenerative and liberating, is harsh, scornful, and ironic. Steve may have had the idea of the spirit of carnival from the "olden times" in mind when he planned his Summer Solstice party in his big backyard, but the event that results is a monstrosity that is neither amusing nor fun.

Another marker of cultural appropriation that contributes to the scene of violence at the Summer Solstice party is the bottle of tequila. Tequila is a modern and contemporary "party drink," and it has an older history as a signifier of conquest and violence ("Tequila"). The bottle of tequila at a Summer Solstice party in the backyard of a small, not-very-domestic house in Kalamazoo, Michigan, is a long way—geographically and culturally—from its Mexican roots, as the Summer Solstice party is a long way from its roots on, say, the Salisbury Plain or a wild Rabelaisian carnival scene or even the woods outside the court of Athens. Also, Janie sells her labor for wages at Smart Mart so that she can buy tequila—a marker of subjugation and violence in Mexico. According to Teret and Michaelis, and other scholars of the history of alcohol, alcohol was similarly used as a tool for theft, domination, and disempowerment of Native Americans in Michigan and throughout North America. Teret and Michaelis historicize the use of alcohol as an agent of colonial domination and note that "the effects of excessive alcohol consumption by Native Americans was recognized by both the European settlers and the Indians themselves" (248). Steve's party bears traces of this history of violence, as it takes place on land that was originally the home of the Council of the Three Fires— the Ojibwe, the Odawa, and the Potawatomi ("Land"). In other words, a bottle of tequila is a power tool.

In "Playhouse," Janie drinks to feel relief or to get completely, utterly, dangerously drunk. Janie relies on tequila for "the relief [she feels] when she takes that first sip . . . after work" (Campbell 33). When she goes to visit Steve, she throws up in the bushes before she goes in, and then she drinks two glasses of wine and swallows a Vicodin she finds in Steve's medicine cabinet, thus thoroughly vanquishing any pain she might feel. At Steve's Summer Solstice party, she clutches a bottle of tequila as if it is her companion and friend. Beyond a few celebratory shots at a party, she drinks so much tequila that she does not remember the details of what happened to her "among the peonies" at the Solstice party. After the party, she recalls only that somebody dropped her off at her house and her boyfriend found her "passed out alone, with puke on [her] shirt" (25).

In addition to making her black out and vomit, the bottle of tequila also makes Janie vulnerable to actions often associated with conquest: sexual violence, especially when alcohol is involved. For example, an important story in the twentieth-century short fiction canon that features the combination of alcohol and sexual assault is Ernest Hemingway's "Up in Michigan." Hemingway's story is a textured study of a young woman's heterosexual desire and its vicissitudes. It also marks the ways that the influence of alcohol can easily blur the lines between desire and fear, consent and assault—even when the young woman in the situation is not drinking, and especially when the man is.

In Hemingway's story, Liz Coates's sexual desire for Jim Gilmore is mercurial. Liz, "the neatest girl [her employer] has ever seen," is attracted to a blacksmith named Jim Gilmore: "short and dark with big mustaches and big hands" (Hemingway, "Up" 59). She is willing to go with him on a "walk," which sounds like a sexual euphemism, after he's had several "big shots" from a jug of whiskey (61). When Jim begins touching her, Liz becomes "frightened" and then "very frightened": "She was frightened but she wanted it. She had to have it but it frightened her" (61). Several times, she says to Jim, "Don't" or "You mustn't" or "No" or "You can't," but he persists. After he finishes, he passes out on the dock. Liz feels uncomfortable and hurt and even more confused. Jim's wanted and then unwanted assault "had hurt her," and Liz runs through a range of actions and emotions (62). At the end of the story, Liz is alone with her emotional turmoil and physical pain in the "cold mist" that rises as she leaves Jim in his whiskey-sodden torpor and walks "across the dock and up the steep sandy road to go to bed" (62). She may have "wanted it" and "had to have it," but not like that.

Traces of "Up in Michigan" appear in Campbell's "Playhouse" in terms of the differences between desire and consent and sex and rape. A key difference between Hemingway's Michigan story and Campbell's is that in "Playhouse," Janie is drunk. At Steve's party, she has drunk too much tequila. When Roger and Mickey approach her in Steve's backyard, it's not clear if Janie says or is even able to say "no" or "you mustn't" or "you can't." She was drunk at the time, and afterward, she does not remember what did or did not happen. As is the case with Liz Coates up north, it does not matter if Janie says "No" because the men who "want it" are not listening. Jim Gilmore on the dock and Roger and Mickey in Steve's backyard take things that they want, rather like the conquistadors in Mexico and the European "settlers" in North America, regardless of social contracts such as consent in sexual relations. In this respect, their actions repeat the attitude of "I got to. I'm going to" that Jim espouses in "Up in Michigan," which are the same actions and attitudes that the Europeans brought to the Great Lakes Indigenous people, the same actions and attitudes that the conquistadors brought from Spain to Indigenous people of Tequila.

As Campbell's story progresses, the conversation between Steve and Janie reveals to both Janie and the reader that, according to Steve, Janie was "screwing" two guys at Steve's party. Janie does not remember the details, so Steve provides them: "you were humping your bottle of tequila down by the peonies, and they [Steve's friends Roger and Mickey] were out of booze, so I told them to go down and harass you" (Campbell 26). Without even realizing his complicity in the ensuing action, Steve tells Janie, almost cruelly, that Roger and Mickey took off Janie's clothes, assaulted her, and took cellphone photos. Steve continues, "After I erased the pictures, I went down and put your damned clothes back on you. . . . At first I felt bad for you, but then I was just pissed" (28).

In the course of the conversation, Steve, the big brother who orchestrated the scene, takes the position of prosecutor, judge, and jury. His jurisprudence follows the contradictory and self-serving logic of the Kansas legislators in Carry Nation's time, trying simultaneously to outlaw and protect saloons. Janie is agog. She remembers scraps and pieces of the crime, but other details seem impossible to conjure. She says to Steve, "It had to be somebody else," but Steve shuts her down: "Oh, it was definitely you. The first picture was Roger licking the Tasmanian Devil tattoo on your boob. No mistaking that" (27). She tries again. "Was it really sex, like sex . . . with both of them?" (31). Steve shrugs, and Janie shifts her questions to a statement: "Damn, Steve. You should have stopped them," to which Steve replies, predictably, "'Don't put it on me, sister. . . . You should have told them no if you didn't want it'" (31). In a familiar judgment that is a particularly fallacious kind of power move, Steve places the blame squarely on Janie for her own inability to say no because she was drunk.

Steve also passes judgment on Janie's contention that the two guys at the party raped her. When Janie tells him he should have protected her, and when she says, "'I think maybe they raped me, Steve,'" Steve issues a familiar denial: "Roger? Get real. . . . He's a decent guy. Maybe not the brightest bulb on the planet, but he's not a rapist, Janie" (31). His tone is admonishing, as if he were speaking to Pinky. Janie backpedals: "Or something like rape" (31). Steve gets the last word: "That's not how it looked to me, that's all I'm saying" (32). Then, as if to toss her the tiniest bone of cold comfort, he adds, "I guess you're the one who should know, though" (32). He goes off to bed; the conversation is over, and the case is closed. If there was a crime, it was that Janie got too drunk to handle herself, and she ended up naked in the peonies. Wittingly or not, Steve has destroyed the evidence when he erased the cellphone photos, and while he does concede that Janie would know if she had been raped, he makes it clear that she'll have a difficult time proving her point in any court of law, including the one in his living room. Thus, he uses his power as a big brother and a white heterosexual man to pass judgment on a crime he helped facilitate and then cover up, exonerating himself and his two rapist friends, and laying the burden on the victim, his little sister who had drunk too much tequila.

Steve's judgment is one of the many mishaps that befall Janie when she finds herself under the influence of alcohol: she was "screwing" those two guys, and now she is "screwed." Then, as the story continues, Steve "screws" her in a different way. Three weeks after the Summer Solstice party, while trying to stabilize the plastic structure, Steve wields a cordless drill and drives a screw through the roof of Pinky's playhouse into Janie's arm.

Pinky's playhouse sits in the middle of Steve's living room, in the middle of the story. It sits like an anomaly, a rupture that at first "looks bright and safe" (17). However, the playhouse takes on sinister qualities. Janie thinks to herself, "I hate the way the playhouse makes the room feel crowded," and she asks Steve, "Aren't you going to put that thing outside?"—as if it were an untrained house pet, a monster (17–18). Steve explains why the playhouse is in the middle of the living room, crowding the house: "It was a hundred degrees today. My crazy kid'll sit in there and cook herself" (18). Now Steve's words suggest that the playhouse is an oven, a furnace, a crematorium. Then Pinky offers another way to think about the playhouse. "It's my fun-fun-funhouse" (18), she says, which puts the playhouse into yet another category—first a toy then a hateful obstacle, then a death-oven, and now a funhouse—a carnival attraction designed, with its tilted floors and peculiar mirrors, to disorient people who walk through it.

The funhouse makes yet another transformation, one that raises the specter of Carry Nation and brings the saloon from the dusty plains of Kansas into the house in Michigan. Janie notes that Pinky "runs to the playhouse and opens the saloon-style doors" (18). In the hateful, dangerous, pretty house-within-a-house saloon, the proprietor is a three-year-old whose idea of fun-fun-fun is running around at Steve's Summer Solstice party and "drinking out of glasses people left on the table" (19). Janie wonders "whether [Pinky] really would let herself cook in the name of having fun," but the answer is already clear. Now, the fun-fun-funhouse is Pinky's tiny saloon, operating in the middle of the living room—as if it were Main Street in Kiowa, Kansas.

By the end of the story, it is clear that Pinky's funhouse saloon is exactly the kind of structure on which Carry Nation would have made a hatchetation. Steve literally screws Janie's arm in his effort to "keep the roof from falling on [Pinky's] head" (19). His effort to stabilize an already dangerous structure is a procedure that causes more harm to Janie, who has already suffered greatly from the effects of drinking tequila in a saloon culture that has been transposed to the backyard of a one-story ranch house up in Michigan (19). As she sits in the emergency room, the story's pathos arises from Janie's thoughts that conflate herself and her fun-loving, drink-sipping niece: "I don't know how anyone can stop a girl from drinking so much she doesn't know what she's doing, what's happening to her. All the precautions in the world might not be enough for a girl who loves fun" (35–36).

Janie's musings extend a tradition of alcohol-related final scenes in modern American literature. To name a few, Hemingway's *The Sun Also Rises*, in which Brett Ashley yearns for the "good time" she and Jake Barnes could have had together (263); the more desperate end of Parker's "Big Blonde," in which the unhappy Hazel Morse stares into a glass of whiskey and "prayed without addressing a God, without knowing a God. Oh, please, please let her be able to get drunk, please keep her always drunk" (210); and a dazed Blanche DuBois's ironic dependence on "the kindness of strangers" as she takes her sorrowful journey to an asylum at the end of Williams's *A Streetcar Named Desire* (178). Campbell's Janie and her story "Playhouse" evince this simultaneously historical and contemporaneous message: For a girl in a saloon who loves drinks and fun fun fun, the roof is going to fall in no matter what. In short, she is screwed.

Works Cited

Bakhtin, Mikhail. *Rabelais and His World*. Indiana UP, 1984.

Barnes, Djuna. *Nightwood*. 1937. New Directions, 2006.

Campbell, Bonnie Jo. "Playhouse." *Mothers, Tell Your Daughters*. Norton, 2015, pp. 15–36.

Courtwright, David T. *Dark Paradise: A History of Opiate Addiction in America*. Harvard UP, 2001.

Cowley, Malcolm. *Exile's Return*. 1964. Penguin, 1994.

Fitzgerald, Zelda. *Save Me the Waltz*. 1932. Albatross, 2020.

Foucault, Michel. *History of Sexuality, Vol. 1: An Introduction*. Translated by Robert Hurley. Vintage, 1980.

Hemingway, Ernest. *The Sun Also Rises*, 1926. Edited by Séan Hemingway. Scribner's, 2014.

———. "Up in Michigan." *The Complete Short Stories of Ernest Hemingway*. Scribner's, 1987, pp. 59–62.

"Land Acknowledgment." Kalamazoo College, 2 Aug. 2019, land.kzoo.edu/.

Lupton, Mary Jane. "Ladies' Entrance: Women and Bars." *Feminist Studies*, vol. 5, no. 3, 1979, pp. 571–88.

"Nation, Carry (1846–1911)." *The Penguin Biographical Dictionary of Women*. Penguin, 1998.

Parker, Dorothy. "Big Blonde." *The Portable Dorothy Parker*, edited by Marion Meade. Penguin Classics, 2006, pp. 187–210.

Remus, Emily. *A Shoppers' Paradise: How the Ladies of Chicago Claimed Power and Pleasure in the New Downtown*. Harvard UP, 2019.

Rorabaugh, William. *The Alcoholic Republic: An American Tradition*. Oxford UP, 1979.

Russo, Mary. "Female Grotesques: Carnival and Theory." *Feminist Studies: Critical Studies*, edited by Teresa de Lauretis. Indiana UP, 1986, pp. 213–29.

Schneider, Stephen. "What Is the Summer Solstice? An Astronomer Explains." *The Conversation: An Independent Source of Analysis from Academic Researchers*, 2018. https://theconversation.com/what-is-the-summer-solstice-an-astronomer-explains-98270.

Shakespeare, William. *A Midsummer Night's Dream*. Oxford UP, 2008.

"Tequila." *The Hutchinson Unabridged Encyclopedia with Atlas and Weather Guide*. Helicon, 2018.

Teret, Stephen P., and Annie P. Michaelis. "Litigating for Native American Health: The Liability of Alcoholic Beverage Makers and Distributors." *Journal of Public Health Policy*, vol. 26, no. 2, 2005, pp. 246–59.

Williams, Tennessee. *A Streetcar Named Desire*, 1947. New Directions, 2004.

———. *Cat on a Hot Tin Roof*. 1955. New Directions, 2004.

Bonnie Jo Campbell's Millennium and the Infrastructure of Failure

Garth Sabo

The tepid response the undergraduates in my Midwestern literature class at Michigan State University in early 2021 had to "World of Gas" and "Fuel for the Millennium," the duo of stories in *American Salvage* that Bonnie Jo Campbell sets in the final days of 1999, at the height of millennium-glitch panic, is encapsulated in one student's insistence that these Y2K stories seemed irrelevant to the life she was living. Now, to expect undergraduates to care about something that *didn't* happen three years before most of them were born would be a failure of my responsibility to see the world through my students' eyes before training them elsewhere, and my students are far from alone in questioning the legitimacy and relevance of an event that is best remembered as a failure. In 2009, in her reader review of *American Salvage*, the short-story writer Ursula Villarreal-Moura singled out "World" and "Fuel," writing that "some of the subject matter wasn't for me." And as early as December 1999, the *Baltimore Sun* columnist Maria Blackburn was ready to dismiss the burgeoning subgenre of books about the then-impending millennial disaster as "a total waste of time" (11E), well before nothing happened.

Nevertheless, to see Y2K only as a punchline fulfills Michael Rubenstein, Bruce Robbins, and Sophia Beal's warning about the challenge of representing the role of infrastructure in maintaining modern life, which is that "infrastructure tends to go unnoticed when it's in fine working order" (576). Rubenstein, Robbins, and Beal detail a critical approach they dub infrastructuralism, which highlights the ways in which literary fiction can be used, in their words, "to defamiliarize our daily dependency on infrastructures and to resensitize us to a host of urgent questions about access and ownership, rights and responsibilities" (585). The millennium glitch need not be devastating to be valuable as a lens for looking at the Midwestern present in terms of what was imagined but never realized, and the need for such a perspective becomes increasingly urgent in a political and media landscape where the dystopian threat of infrastructure collapse seems less funny and more chilling the further we wade into the twenty-first century. Fortunately, between *American Salvage*'s "World of Gas" and "Fuel for the Millennium," and again with "Blood Work, 1999" in *Mothers, Tell Your Daughters* (2015), Campbell has thrice recognized the visible fragility that the material systems of modernity had in the waning moments of the twentieth century—and ought to have today.

To imagine the failure of power grids, gas lines, and financial networks is to draw their existence out of the shadows and recognize the dull, if precarious, comfort we derive from their presence. By focusing on Campbell's millennial stories, I hope to show the value of such an endeavor, even if said failure remains imaginary. These stories are more often treated as the seeds of interests that blossom elsewhere in her work, as when interviewer Matt Carmichael invokes Campbell's fascination with "the whole Y2K phenomenon and the people who bought into it" as a precursor to "the whole notion of survivalism that [she] often write[s] about" ("Bonnie Jo Campbell: Interview"). The traits they share, however, are distinctive enough to demand consideration as a thematic unit unto themselves. Each, for instance, begins with a beleaguered protagonist's reactions to others' preparations for the new year, and each ends in hopeful speculation that, despite the promise of disaster, the new millennium will bring more good than bad. Thus, as "Fuel for the Millennium" draws to a close, refrigerator repairman and doomsday prepper Hal Little imagines stepping out of his pole-barn bunker after the Rapture, knowing "he'd hear the sweet voices of birds and angels. He hoped he would smell flowers. He hoped there would be babies" (150). Marika of "Blood Work, 1999" enters the new year from the burn ward of the hospital where she works, convinced that "as the sun rose on the new millennium, there would no longer be rich or poor, weak or strong" (195). And though Susan, the put-upon office manager for the Pur-Gas propane company, is less sure of the transformative potential of the new year, "World of Gas" ends in contemplation of "some advantages to a real millennium breakdown" as well (38). "Life," Susan hopes, "would be quieter without power," and, ideally, "Men of all ages everywhere—men talking about football, auto engines, politics, hydraulic pumps, and the mechanics of love—would finally just shut up" (38).

Hal, Marika, and Susan join together in imagining what "would" happen rather than what "might" or "could" emerge from the wreckage of the preceding millennium, and in doing so they imbue these stories with a sense of material precarity that is no less meaningful for being misguided. None of these characters manages to abandon thoughts of ruin entirely. Even Susan, who spends most of "World of Gas" "so busy scoffing at the alarmists that she [doesn't] let herself really think about the year 2000," concedes that the "principle involved with the zero-zero date . . . could cause problems with computer systems controlling traffic lights and ATM machines" (American Salvage 37). The litany of possibilities that follows embodies the mixture of anxiety and assurance that attracts Campbell to the turning point between centuries. Susan ponders: "Maybe she'd allow extra time to get to work on Monday, January 3. Maybe she ought to have a couple hundred dollars on hand in case her first paycheck was screwed up. She could easily fill her bathtub with water, but probably she wouldn't bother" (37). Susan's decision to "probably" ignore the survival instructions she read in her brother-in-law's militia-style pamphlet makes her faith in the status quo remarkably tenuous. The rumors of Y2K and a cold, dark future in Michigan are persuasive enough that even those who are sure disaster will be averted plan for its effects nonetheless.

To be fair, Bonnie Jo Campbell did not invent the end-of-the-century brand of confident uncertainty found in her millennial stories, but she deserves credit for giving voice to the infectious quality the Y2K disaster acquired in the months leading up to the year 2000, when every reassurance that everything would be okay could be tinged with the possibility that many things might not. For instance, on September 17, 1999, Arthur Levitt, the chairperson of the Securities and Exchange Commission, opened his remarks to the President's Council on Year 2000 Conversion with the prediction that "the first day of trading after the New Year will be business as usual," but closed with the promise that "the Commission is also developing a coordinated plan to respond to any problems that arise." Like Campbell's "would," Levitt's invocation of "problems that arise" comes close to promising their occurrence, even while insisting that "the disasters that some originally predicted will not get even an honorable mention in the history books."

Campbell complicates Levitt's insistence that nothing could go wrong, and that the government would be prepared when something did anyway, with the attention she pays to the material forms of power throughout her millennial stories. "Fuel for the Millennium" begins with Hal Little's knowledge "beyond the shadow of a doubt" that "everything would fail—the stock markets, of course, but also the government and then the power company, the water and sewer, law and order, and most importantly, the gas stations" (*American Salvage* 144). Marika in "Blood Work" is closer to Susan in "World of Gas" than Hal in terms of her belief that disaster is imminent, and yet she also "knew that at the stroke of midnight, as the fireworks display lit up the sky over Kalamazoo, a hurricane or tornado could hit this hospital just as easily as any other place" (*Mothers* 194). Framing Hal's and Marika's convictions as forms of knowledge pushes us to see their actions as the rational recognition of patterns of interconnection, even if said patterns emerge as a practice of religious zealotry or flights of fancy.

An infrastructuralist perspective knows that "it would be folly to imagine knowing ourselves without also knowing our embeddedness in a network of large and sophisticated technological artifacts" (Rubenstein et al. 585), and so this type of network recognition is a vital component of Y2K fiction in general, and Campbell's Y2K stories in particular. Taken together, "World of Gas," "Fuel for the Millennium," and "Blood Work, 1999" show that embeddedness is a matter of kind as well as degree. That is, Campbell's millennial fiction reveals not only how much we rely upon technology but also how many technologies we rely upon. Thus, the silence that depends upon the world in Susan's vision of the first moments of the new millennium is instructive. Campbell describes the temporality of this closing passage as "Susan's millennium moment" (*American Salvage* 38), and she balances the language she uses to fill it between gradual and immediate experiences of newly silent time. For instance, Susan anticipates that "the headlights of the delivery trucks would dim and die as wheels stopped turning," "cars would grind to a halt," and "Men revving motorcycles, chain saws, and lawn tractors in garages would wind down, too, their machines becoming dead" (38), while she also acknowledges that the ensuing silence would last "if only for a moment" (38).

Campbell's attention to machines dimming, grinding, and "becoming dead" emphasizes the physicality of the infrastructural network and the vapid noisiness of the activities that rely upon it. This haptic sense of ruin, aware of the profound physicality over those soon-to-be-defunct structures that circumscribe life in Campbell's Michigan, permeates all three stories. "Blood Work, 1999" follows "World of Gas" in a similar vein, imagining the collapse of civilization with a marked tactility. Marika pictures buildings crumbling in much the same way Susan imagines men and their engines grinding to a halt, "envision[ing] the bricks falling away from the walls of the hospital, bricks and blocks falling off all the buildings downtown and becoming rubble" (*Mothers* 194). Likewise, the sudden decay of financial institutions in Marika's sunny view of the year 2000 emphasizes physical structures, like the "bars guarding the vault at the heart of the bank [that] would slide open" and "Bill Gates's private vault, too, [which] could crack open like a giant egg hatching" (194–95). Certainly, much of the drama of Marika's precarious financial situation, to which I will return shortly, comes from the reader's keen awareness of the difference between the physicality of the financial industry's settings and the long, invisible tendrils of their control, but there is no doubt that "Blood Work, 1999" works hard to bring networks of power into view, even if only in their (imagined) dissolution.

In much the same way, "Fuel for the Millennium" could be aptly summarized as the narrative attempt to render visible the physical and emotional exhaustion Hal Little experiences in his efforts to replace the systems he expects to fail with self-sufficient alternatives. Accordingly, Campbell details the capacity of every structure and supply in Hal's compound, whether that be the "half dozen fifty-five-gallon blue plastic drums of gas stored behind his pole barn" (*American Salvage* 144), the "fifty-pound bags of rice and beans" he anticipates purchasing but dreads eating (148), or the "reinforced steel-and-aluminum, solid-core front door" he imagines opening onto God's "New Holy Universe" once he survives the Rapture (150). The materials that compose Hal's world, far from receding into the background, are immediately present, visceral reminders of the lost comforts he aims to replace. Nowhere is this more evident than when he reflects on the naiveté of the unprepared, "thinking that nothing bad could happen, thinking that their parents couldn't be killed in a car crash so bloody that blood would stain the asphalt at that intersection for months" (145). Though the description of his efforts borders on the absurd throughout "Fuel," an undeniable effect of his attention to detail is to illuminate the degree of reliance we have on the equivalent structures that would go unnoticed or willfully ignored otherwise.

It is worth noting, however briefly, that Arthur Levitt's comments to the President's Council on Year 2000 Conversion in September 1999 accomplish something very similar, which should reiterate that the exhaustion Campbell renders in fiction was made manifest in countless official pronouncements about the end of the century. Levitt describes "the efforts of the industry" to prepare for the Year 2000 problem as "nothing less than Herculean," a phrasing that emphasizes the amount of toil needed to render this glitch inconsequential. He quantifies the effort again shortly thereafter, this time not as a measure of sweat and tears but rather as a function of the "over $1 billion" that had been spent "on Y2K remediation" by the "top eight broker-dealer companies alone" in the months preceding his address. My intention here is simply to make clear that Y2K is unique for the opportunity it affords to see the material effort and fiscal investment required to keep an apparatus as complex as America's digital infrastructure running seamlessly in the background. Anticipating the possible crises of the Year 2000 means making systems that would otherwise remain spectral and determinative into something concrete and, for what may be the last time, vulnerable.

One of the great subtleties of Campbell's work comes in the deft way she differentiates these vulnerabilities between the men and women who populate these stories. "World of Gas" memorably condemns the masculine self-image of "a hot-headed Bruce Willis character, fighting against the evil foreign enemy while despising the domestic bureaucracy. Men wanted to focus on just one big thing, leaving the thousands of smaller messes for the women around them to clean up" (*American Salvage* 34–35). Campbell's approach serves admirably as an excavation of these thousands of smaller messes. Hal Little's doomsday preparation in "Fuel for the Millennium" brings this distinction between disaster preparation and domestic maintenance to the fore, as his actions throughout the story are predicated on viewing doomsday as better suited to his efforts than the "keeping up the status quo of the house" he inherits from his father and mother, whose recent traumatic death seems to drive the sense of urgency in Hal's actions. More compellingly, Susan's millennial dream of silence is inseparable from her fantasies of relief from the inane badgering of the men in her life, who would "finally just shut up" (38) if mechanically divorced from the "one big thing" of whatever sports media, engine overhauls, or political soapbox they turn to instead of assisting Susan with the dishes she washes as the clock strikes midnight.

Given that Marika's situation in "Blood Work, 1999" unfolds due to the constant sexual badgering of her patient Tiny, it is evident that Campbell's interest in the gendering of this disaster continues from *American*

Salvage to *Mothers, Tell Your Daughters*. The climax of the story becomes increasingly sexual as midnight nears, and indicators of Marika's sexualized satisfaction in conjuring the transformed world she imagines stroking into existence, as her own breathing starts to ring louder in her ears than Tiny's and "her own body shudder[s]" (*Mothers* 194), come to the fore in the story's final paragraph. The sudden flash of light and Marika's surprise gives way to an orgasmic feeling of "bursting open like flowers in sunlight, overflowing into the new millennium" (195). Part of the promise the new millennium holds for the beleaguered phlebotomist seems to come from the opportunity to disrupt the sexual hierarchies that govern the world alongside the financial, political, and infrastructural ones the story names more directly.

The seamless and insistently physical way that Campbell shows these various systemic ordering principles integrating and guiding her characters' lives represents an important feature of her imagined doomsday, and one that separates Y2K narratives from other tales of the end of the world. In *The Sense of an Ending*, Frank Kermode labors to discredit the significance of numerological signs of doom, by which the round numbers of the year 2000 could be taken to signify the coming of the biblical apocalypse. With the calm of a man whose career was made decades earlier, he insists that "there is no *intrinsic* connection between apocalypse and millennium" (183); elsewhere he calls the millennium "a calendrical fiction that makes available new attitudes to time and its passage" (189). James Berger, clearly influenced by Kermode's seminal text on this topic, strikes a similar note in his introductory essay on the apocalyptic in the twenty-first century with his opening description of the "arbitrary chronometric click of the millennium" (387). They are both surely right to point out that the zero-zero date carries no ontological capacity for destruction, but so too do they both overlook the degree to which the ubiquity of systems that were both essential to life and perceived as vulnerable to the computer glitch at the turn of the century. As Kavita Philip and Terry Harpold note, "Y2K panic was most forceful and general in the United States" due to this country's "deeply embedded ... fantasy-structures of crisis and redemption" related to computer networks. Not only were computer systems technically vulnerable to the Y2K bug, but the dominant storytelling apparatuses of the time made it difficult to see such a glitch as anything other than a material threat.

In other words, though Kermode and Berger are spirited in their critique of Y2K as nothing more than a software problem, Campbell incentivizes her reader to see how the computer glitch, though far from written into the fabric of the universe, is nonetheless inscribed upon the very heart of her characters' way of life. Her depiction of Hal Little, in particular, stands out for its nuance in this regard. The conservative orthodoxy he spouts throughout "Fuel for the Millennium" would seem to pigeonhole him as the type of apocalyptic Christian that feared the millennium for numerological reasons, whom Kermode would insist was mistaken and Berger would condescend to as quaint. Yet Campbell weaves together biblical and infrastructural fears in her bespectacled repairman, who urges his customers to accept "both Jesus and the millennium problem" as a way to avoid "the impending Y2K disaster" (*American Salvage* 145). The simile he uses to understand the millennium problem as being "like religion" further indicates that the two are entangled but distinguishable (145), and also suggests an ability to limn the borders of faith-based thinking in anticipation of doomsday in a way that other equations of Y2K and the apocalypse struggle to replicate. Campbell's millennial fiction, in other words, does not shy away from portraying the religious anxieties dredged up by the replacement of nines with zeroes, but she also pairs these depictions with real, materialist concerns that can be traced back to the data infrastructure of modern life. She remains ever attentive to the material precarity that her characters experienced and that scholars of the apocalypse presumably did not as the twenty-first century was born. Hal Little's fears of the darkness of January are complex and rooted as much in a pragmatic assessment of his risk exposure as they are in his Faith Channel convictions of a vengeful God.

Fitting Y2K under the umbrella of the apocalyptic, as Kermode does, would thus seem to sap it of any unique temporal quality or critical interest, but Campbell's triple investigation of the transition between millennia insists on some specificity in this liminal moment. To write about the millennium as she does is to eulogize a disaster that didn't happen. Y2K was a future that unfolded, or unraveled, in the past; for her characters, it became disastrous precisely in its failure to be a disaster, which is surely why her millennial fiction dwells on the moments preceding the New Year. "World of Gas" and "Fuel for the Millennium" are both set an indeterminate amount of time before December 31, though close enough for the date to loom over both stories. Hal remembers starting to hoard gasoline "a few months ago, in the heat of summer" (144), whereas Susan reflects on her problems in "a stream of cold night air" and "imagine[s] the hands of her kitchen clock spinning faster and faster, racing toward New Year's Eve, and then stopping" (37–38). The image of a clock stopping at midnight is fairly representative of Campbell's approach to the millennium in all three stories, as it serves equally well as a material reminder of the real fears of infrastructure failure as well as a symbol of her temporal fascination with the liminal moment between centuries.

The clock stops at midnight for Campbell because it is precisely at that moment where the mixture of anxiety and optimism for the future reaches its critical mass. "Blood Work, 1999" gets us closest to that pinpoint in time, ending just as one year gives way to the next. Marika, who has snuck back into the hospital where she works in order to fulfill the burn victim Tiny's request for her intimate touch, "hear[s] the popping of the fireworks," signaling the arrival of January 1, and along with it "the beep of [the] heart rate monitor" as well as a sudden surprise "when the overhead light came on" (*Mothers* 195), presumably as the night nurse enters the room to check on the patient and discovers Marika masturbating him. The rapid pace of Campbell's prose here encourages a reading of these various events all unfolding simultaneously at precisely the moment of transformation from 1999 to 2000. In particular, the sensory shock of the overhead lights flipping on, which causes Marika to "blink and [feel] herself bursting open like flowers in sunlight, overflowing into the new millennium" (195), obscures the physical setting of this moment and highlights instead the temporality. This moment is frozen in time, where the physical setting fades into the background in order to highlight the temporal experience of limitless promise in the face of an uncertain future, which is precisely how Campbell invites us to reflect on the millennium.

It is crucial to recognize the collectivity that drives these dreams of the year 2000. In all three instances, the promise of the future is inseparable from the hope for greater contact with a sense of community. Loneliness emerges as the core condition of the world that, with any luck, would dissolve at midnight. In pointed opposition to the cliché of Y2K preparation as an act of withdrawal and isolation, then, Campbell sees the millennium as a potential source of togetherness. Though most of Hal Little's actions ostensibly create distance between his farm and other survivors of the anticipated apocalypse, Campbell weaves his deep-seated need for closeness throughout "Fuel for the Millennium." Hal's repeated references to the bloody car accident that killed his parents frame his actions as a response to the trauma of loss. His preparations offer a palliative against the need to "fend for himself" (*American Salvage* 145), and thus his final reflection centers on his closeness to others in the Kingdom of Heaven after Jesus nestles his pole barn into the Heavenly Woods (149–50). Hal hopes to be "not right next to the other houses, but not far away, either" and follows this with a short list of possible neighbors he would be "pleasantly surprised" to gain: a Faith Channel minister; his parents; his skeptical customers from the beginning of the story (150). The implication here is that Hal's desire for community and his faith in the millennial apocalypse will restore the closeness that had been torn asunder by loss.

Likewise, Marika's decision to spend the last moments of 1999 pleasuring Tiny comes shortly after admitting that "lately [she] had been feeling sorry for herself for not having had a boyfriend in six years" (*Mothers* 184). As with Hal, Campbell couches Marika's endless desire to serve as a means to distract from her relational deficits: "Being alone wasn't nearly as bad as being a refugee or a victim of a famine or of debilitating burns" (184). Opportunities for contact multiply in the vision she receives after being touched by the regular patient she knows as the Lightning Man, such that Marika's millennium may be defined as the tearing down of boundaries between stranger and friend. After the sun rises on the new millennium, she foresees that "strangers would embrace and heal one another with touch" and feels "more than ready to ladle out [this] nourishment herself" (195). The Y2K glitch is thus valorized as a social leveler, and it is in "Blood Work, 1999" that Campbell pursues the implications of the openness that would result.

Even Susan, whose exasperation with the millennial hullabaloo and the "pain-in-the-ass alarmists in town these days" manifests as a desire for solitude by the end of "World of Gas" (*American Salvage* 34), shares Marika's optimism that a slower, quieter world will restore balance to her interactions with the men in her life. While she ruminates over the tryst she interrupts between her teenage son and his girlfriend, recalling how the room where the two lay was "lit only by the bluish glow of the television" (36), Susan's unspoken rejoinder to her son's insistence that she "wouldn't understand" focuses on this disruptive technological mediation: "If this girl means so much to you, then why don't you turn off the damned TV when you're in bed with her?" (37). The bright shine of starlight she invokes in the story's closing moment of millennial fantasy must then be seen as a corrective to the uncanny glow of the television.

Of course, any reading of these stories will inevitably be textured by the historical fact that civilization did not crumble at 12:01 on January 1, 2000. The poignant tragedy with which Campbell imbues these stories is the knowledge that these hopes for new communities lit only by starlight will be roundly dashed in the moments immediately following the last words on the page. Marika's case is the clearest example of this, due to the shorter interval between the end of her story and the beginning of the new millennium, as well as the extreme final action she took in 1999 and the equally extreme reaction it is likely to receive when the overhead lights dim in the first seconds of 2000. And indeed, Marika's brief return later in the closing story of *Mothers, Tell Your Daughters* reiterates that the new world she imagined the sun rising over on January 1 failed to materialize. "The Fruit of the Pawpaw Tree" finds Marika some years later, still entangled in her family's hardscrabble life in the semirural areas outlying Kalamazoo, and still part of the world that she thought would have changed at the turn of the century (*Mothers* 239–62).

Campbell makes it clear that the trajectory of Marika's life was not unduly altered by her midnight decision to soothe Tiny. She is still easily swayed by emotional appeals for aid and now serves on the board of directors for the local Humane Society, a position for which she is eminently well-suited. But this continuation in spite of the promise of change is precisely what Campbell's millennial fiction asks us to consider. Susan and Hal fare no better. The imagined reprieve the millennium would grant Susan from the relentless jabbering of the men in her life, including her newly and naively sexually active son Josh, never comes, and Hal Little's doomsday prepping leaves him without "anything left in the bank" (*American Salvage* 147) and ill-prepared for the self-sufficient farm life he has mortgaged his future on. The likelihood of financial ruin rears its head at several points throughout these stories, in fact, underscoring the inescapable capitalist gravity that holds the various systems that ought to have failed in orbit around each other. The Pur-Gas fuel company arranges to profit coming and going from Y2K preparations; Susan informs her brother-in-law that he will "have to pay double rent on the [propane] tank" if he doesn't "use a hundred dollars a month worth of this gas" (36), all but ensuring that the money spent to procure the propane tank will be followed with punitive charges. Campbell leaves these hardships implied but inevitable so that they enter the memory ephemerally, equal in substance to the imagined lives each character would have led had the millennium gone wrong in the right way.

Doing so allows Susan, Hal, and Marika to maintain a form of devastating optimism throughout their respective stories that Frank Kermode presents as characteristic of the apocalyptic genre. Kermode contends that, "even in its less lurid modern forms," the apocalypse "still carries with it the notions of a decadence and possible renovation, still represents a mood finally inseparable from the condition of life, the contemplation of its necessary ending, the ineradicable desire to make some sense of it" (187). It is worth noting that this detail comes from Kermode's 1999 epilogue to *The Sense of an Ending*, where he waxes philosophical on the then-current millennium fever. The apocalyptic, for Kermode, must be future-oriented. It promises to make sense of life by rendering the future knowable, even if that knowledge is of destruction assured. From his vantage point at the end of the twentieth century, Kermode looks ahead to the twenty-first and insists that the apocalyptic fears associated with the coming epoch are merely the latest rendition of a long cultural narrative of pending collapse.

Y2K gives Bonnie Jo Campbell an opportunity to reverse the temporality of Kermode's eschatology. Focusing on the moments before but never after the stroke of midnight means that Y2K always fails extradiegetically for Campbell, so the narrative leaves her characters' hope intact, even if history would prove them wrong. She plays the future orientation of her stories against the retrospective actions needed to read them from the twenty-first century in order to juxtapose the radical challenges that had been imagined against the mundane struggles that unfolded instead. Campbell looks back on the disaster with the optimism of what might have happened, aching for a time when the material systems that dictate modern fates were anything less than impregnable. Thus, the denunciation of such fears as "wild," as Marissa Michaels labels them in "The Rural Struggle for Survival," need not be seen as antagonistic to the work Campbell does there or in "Blood Work, 1999." Rather, these stories exert their greatest gravitational pull when the reader laughs at the very idea of the power going out or the gas running dry, and then realizes the layers of embeddedness required for such a fear to be coded as a joke.

The infrastructuralist approach empowers such realizations. Under that aegis, we turn to literary fiction like Bonnie Jo Campbell's millennial stories as a privileged plane for laying bare what is designed to stay hidden, and for recognizing the organizing principles that allow vast structures and monolithic technologies to masquerade as states of nature. Campbell's longing for a time when different futures were even legible, let alone possible, differs meaningfully from the "pleasant nostalgia [of] knowing that there were still a few people looking forward to the end of the world" (387) that James Berger invokes when he looks back on the Y2K phenomenon from one year later. "Most of us," he concludes without any apparent concern for the easy we/they distinction he falls back upon, "ultimately were convinced by government and business assurances that the problem had been addressed" (387), and he dismisses those who were not as quaint anachronisms dwelling on the physical and temporal fringes of society.

Bonnie Jo Campbell, by contrast, suggests that the best efforts of government and commerce could not prevent a world from ending at the stroke of midnight, and in fact may have contributed to a sense of disaster unseen. When she describes her work in *American Salvage* in an interview with Geeta Kothari for *Kenyon Review*, Campbell insists she is "making the case that not all Americans are on the same page heading into the twenty-first century. It's as though there was some kind of apocalypse and nobody noticed, and now a large number of folks are living off the debris that's left behind" ("A Conversation"). Her insistence that "not all Americans are on the same page" rings especially true alongside Berger's claim that "most of us" saw through the problem of Y2K, and his dismissal of those who didn't as "anachronistic." Campbell's willingness to contest the portrayal of millennial anxiety as correlated with a lack of intelligence or cultural savvy is consistent with her broader interest in the overlooked humanity of Michigan's rural and semi-rural areas. She evinces a type of nostalgia for Y2K anxiety that is very different from Berger's, if only for the experience of subtle hope that came with it and was subsequently crashed by the continuation of the status quo. Thus, by looking back on the millennium instead of forward to it, Campbell activates a desire for renewal that lives in retrospect rather than anticipation.

Campbell's retrospective futurity is well-suited to representations of the Midwest because it is grounded in the material and economic vulnerabilities that make the continuation of the status quo perilous. Y2K anxiety is not a uniquely Midwestern experience, but following the examples set in these three stories allows us to delve deeper into the implications of a regional temporality. Looking to the past to find hope for the future speaks to a condition of uncertainty and betweenness that is at home in the cities and towns along the Rust Belt. Campbell's nostalgia is for the opportunity, now lost but still remembered, to grow something new from the ruins of a futureless present. That is, though the new millennium is portrayed as a pending catastrophe in all three stories, Campbell opens up the possibility that the real disaster is that Y2K failed to ruin us in the way we hoped it might.

Works Cited

Berger, James. "Twentieth-Century Apocalypse: Forecasts and Aftermaths." *Twentieth Century Literature*, vol. 46, no. 5, 2000, pp. 387–95.

Blackburn, Maria. "Y2K's Worst Disaster: Gazillions of Rotten Books." *Baltimore Sun*, 26 Dec. 1999, p. 11E.

Campbell, Bonnie Jo. *American Salvage*. Wayne State UP, 2009.

———. *Mothers, Tell Your Daughters*. Norton, 2015.

———. "A Conversation with Bonnie Jo Campbell." Interview by Geeta Kothari. *Kenyon Review*, July 2008, www.kenyonreview.org /conversation/bonnie-jo-campbell/.

———. "Bonnie Jo Campbell: Interview." Interview by Matt Carmichael. *TriQuarterly*, 30 July 2012, www.triquarterly.org/interviews /bonnie-jo-campbell-interview.

Kermode, Frank. *The Sense of an Ending: Studies in the Theory of Fiction with a New Epilogue*. Oxford UP, 2000.

Levitt, Arthur. "Remarks to the President's Council on Year 2000 Conversion." Financial Sector Group Year 2000 Summit, 17 Sept. 1999, Washington, DC.

Michaels, Marissa. "The Rural Struggle for Survival: A Review of *American Salvage*." *Midstory*, 3 Nov. 2020, www.midstory.org/the-rural -struggle-for-survival-a-review-of-american-salvage/.

Philip, Kavita, and Terry Harpold. "'Party Over, Oops, Out of Time': Y2K, Technological 'Risk' and Informational Millenarianism." *NMEDIAC: Journal of New Media and Culture*, vol. 1, no. 1, 2002.

Rubenstein, Michael, et al. "Infrastructuralism: An Introduction." *MFS: Modern Fiction Studies*, vol. 61, no. 4, Winter 2015, pp. 575–86.

Villareal-Moura, Ursula. Review of *American Salvage*, by Bonnie Jo Campbell. *Goodreads*, 26 Dec. 2009, www.goodreads.com/review /show/82136593?book_show_action=true.

Mothers, Daughters, and Rape Culture in *Mothers, Tell Your Daughters*

LAURA FINE

Contemporary American writer Bonnie Jo Campbell, whose writing is sometimes categorized as "country noir," often focuses her stories and novels on rural Michigan working-class protagonists. Campbell's 2015 short story collection, *Mothers, Tell Your Daughters*, examines mother-daughter relationships in the context of rape culture. These stories pose a difficult question: how does a mother who internalizes the messages of rape culture, who is raised to believe girls and women should submit to unwanted male sexual advances, successfully parent her daughter? The title story of the volume depicts the voice of a mother on her deathbed who earlier in her life internalizes misogynist cultural values to the extent that she looks the other way when her boyfriend sexually abuses her pre-teen daughter. The mother's acceptance of these warped values damages her daughter, and of course, her relationship with her daughter. Another story, "Tell Yourself," depicts a mother who is filled with fear as she watches her thirteen-year-old daughter come to a sense of her budding sexuality at the exact same time she understands herself as a sexual object for men. This mother faces the dilemma of how both to keep her daughter safe and to maintain a relationship with her daughter. To ensure her daughter's safety, the mother must disrupt the patriarchal narrative through which her daughter is learning to express her sexuality. But a young woman trying to fit in with cultural standards unsurprisingly resists her mother's attempts to thwart the process.

This essay examines Campbell's remarkable portrayal of the difficulties mothers and daughters face in forging healthy relationships with one other in this current American cultural era. Campbell's stories suggest that if the mother accepts the detrimental cultural norms her daughter is in the process of internalizing, she in effect endangers her daughter, and in the long run, her relationship with her daughter. On the other hand, if she challenges the cultural norms her daughter is adopting, her daughter rejects and dismisses her, again potentially endangering herself. Rather than depicting a futuristic dystopian society, Campbell portrays in a realist style the current dystopia that is American culture, where so many girls and women so routinely face sexual assault, sexual abuse, sexual harassment, and/or unwanted sexual advances.

In "Persephone Rising: Struggles in Female Adolescent Development in the Aftermath of Rape," Wendy Winograd reviews evolving theories of conventional adolescent girl development and individuation. She starts with Freud's contention that penis envy is the catalyst for girls' oedipal crises and subsequent separation from their mothers, then moves on to Chodorow's theory in *The Reproduction of Mothering* that argues that mothers' strong identification with their daughters "complicates the process of separation, as [the daughter] will stay more connected, intrapsychically, to her mother" (qtd. in Winograd 287). Critic Marianne Hirsch makes the point about object-relations theorists like Chodorow and feminist psychoanalytical revisionists that their object of study is the daughter, not the mother: "The adult woman who is a mother . . . continues to exist only in relation to her child, never as a subject in her own right. And in her maternal function, she remains an object, always distanced, always idealized or denigrated, always mystified, always represented through the small child's point of view" (167). However, among other conceptions of female adolescent development that Winograd considers, she notes recent theorists' highlighting of the Persephone myth as a way of focusing on both mother and daughter. This myth serves as a metaphor for female separation from the mother and incorporation of sexual selves:

> The Persephone/Demeter myth describes the acute pain suffered by mothers and daughters alike in the process of separation as well as the conflicts girls experience as they begin to take ownership (or resist doing so) of their own sexuality. The myth's final compromise, by which Persephone gets to spend part of the year with her husband/lover Hades in the Underworld and part of the year reunited with her mother, demonstrates the conflict between the girl's and mother's need to separate and need to stay connected. (286)

It is significant that in many versions of this myth, Hades's rape of Persephone is the catalyst for her separation from her mother, Demeter. From one perspective, the girl's process of separating from the mother is so painful that it is conceived of in the myth as a violent abduction. The force that leads her to identify her sexual self, in other words, must be violent enough to tear her away from her beloved mother.

From another perspective, Hades's rape of Persephone at the very point that she becomes conscious of herself as a sexual being demonstrates that rape culture has informed girls' process of individuation from the start. Significantly, Persephone's mother, Demeter, was herself raped by Zeus. Indeed, countless rapes occur in classical Western mythology—Demeter, Persephone, Leda, Philomela, etc.—and female characters like Briseis in Homer's *Iliad* are used as objects of exchange. In the Bible, stories of rape abound, including the unnamed woman in Judges 19, the rape of Tamar, and many more examples. What is different now is that contemporary thinkers are calling this culture into question. While many theorists have studied the process by which girls separate from their mothers and come to understand their sexual identities in adolescence, we still need to give more attention to how rape culture affects this process.

Popular-culture and literary critic Roxane Gay defines rape culture as "a culture where we are inundated, in different ways, by the idea that male aggression and violence toward women is acceptable and often inevitable" (129). Buchwald, Fletcher, and Roth define it as "a complex of beliefs that encourages male aggression and supports violence against women. It is a society where violence is seen as sexy and sexuality as violent.... In a rape culture, both men and women assume that sexual violence is a fact of life, as inevitable as death or taxes" (xi). Jacob Beaudrow notes Holly Kearl's point that

> for women, the threat of rape is "part of the background" of their lives. Therefore, many women live with this subconscious awareness and take hundreds of daily precautions, such as not going out alone after dark, carrying mace, buying a dog for defense, not wearing headphones in public (so as to better hear if anyone is approaching), parking only in well-lit areas, and even having to guard their beverages to ensure they are not "spiked." (22)

Another critic argues that the predominance of rape, sexual assault, and sexual abuse in our culture derives in part from definitions of masculinity centering on "toughness, power, dominance, eagerness to fight, lack of empathy, and a callous attitude towards women" (Miedzian 161).

In her 2011 novel, *Once Upon a River*, Campbell explores the effects of rape culture on her adolescent protagonist, Margo Crane, who at fifteen years old is raped by her uncle and then later in the novel by an acquaintance. As a fifteen-year-old girl, Margo does not resist the sexual advances of her uncle. When Margo's dad, Bernard Crane, bursts into the barn as her Uncle Cal is buttoning his fly, and Joanna, Cal's wife, follows, Cal "whispered his defense to Joanna. . . . 'That little slut lured me in here, Jo, but I swear I never touched her'" (*Once* 24). Joanna, with whom Margo shares a close relationship, responds by looking at Margo and saying, "Damn you" (24). Cal both lies about his own role in the encounter and evokes the misogynist trope of the woman (girl) as male seducer. Having herself internalized the messages of rape culture, Cal's wife blames her fifteen-year-old niece for the sexual assault, even though Margo is under the legal age of consent.

As in the Persephone myth, Margo's sexual assault occurs in the absence of her mother, who shortly before the time of the rape has left Margo and her dad. Indeed, it seems her mother's abandonment enables the rape to occur as it leaves Margo unprotected. When her Uncle Cal rapes her, and her father physically assaults Cal as a result, she experiences a new season of separation from Cal and his wife and family, the Murrays, with whom she had been close. Similar to Persephone missing her mother during the fall and winter, Margo especially laments missing out on the family's annual Thanksgiving rituals. Worse, the rape results in the death of Margo's father when he shows up at the Murrays' looking for Margo, and his nephew kills him thinking he has come to kill Cal. In the end, as with Hades's rape of Persephone, this rape results in Margo's separation from her beloved family: "It had started with . . . the departure of her mother in July, and now the severing was complete between Margo and all the rest of them" (24).

Campbell illustrates the effects of rape culture later in the novel when Margo's boyfriend's brother brutally rapes her when her boyfriend, Brian, is away from the cabin where they are staying. When Paul pulls her down, Margo thinks, "In school she had wrenched away from boys who had grabbed her in the stairwell, but she had never fought a big man" (117). The fact that teenage boys feel it their prerogative to grab girls' bodies, that her uncle feels entitled to his niece's body, and that Paul brutally rapes her and then smiles pleasantly at her afterwards all bespeak the cultural acceptance of rape. Significantly, Margo does not tell the police who arrive after her father's death about her rape and does not consider calling them after Paul rapes her. Her conclusion is that "From now on she knew better. She would count on no one to help or protect her" (118).

The complicated intertwining of rape culture with girls' processes of separation from their mothers and integration of sexual identities also informs Campbell's stories. As I've written elsewhere,

> The opening flash fiction story, "Sleepover," provides a context through which to view many of the stories that follow in the volume, *Mothers, Tell Your Daughters*. Two apparently adolescent girls are being sexual with two brothers while the first person narrator's mother is not home. The narrator feels complimented when the brother she is kissing says, "We were wishing your head could be on Pammy's body," . . . "You two together would make the perfect girl" (13). Her feeling complimented suggests her internalization of the idea that she is a sexual object for men. (Fine 519)

It is the mother's arrival that stops the sexual objectification: "Ed's tongue was in my ear when Mom's car lights hit the picture window. Ed slid to the floor and whistled for his brother" ("Sleepover" 13). After the brothers escape and the mother enters, she makes a conventional maternal comment, "'You girls are going to ruin your eyes,'" and switches on the lamp for them (13). The mother's headlights in essence expose the brothers' objectification of the girls into body parts, and her turning on the light for the girls symbolically suggests her attempt to illuminate their objectification for them.

The cultural commodification of this objectification is emphasized by the girls' watching an old Frankenstein movie in which "the doctor . . . [cobbles] together body parts" (14). In the movie, a man creates a monster from body parts and, in the story's final line, "the men from the town band together to kill the monster" (14). The townsmen determine that a being made from body parts is not truly human, and so they destroy it. This equation metaphorically suggests the process by which men objectify women and girls and then denigrate the girls and women for being sexual objects. The final line of the story, which begins by noting that the narrator "stayed awake" to watch the men hunt the monster (14), implies that the girl in the story feels the menace involved in this process. It also highlights the shadow that rape culture will cast on mother-daughter relationships in several stories that follow.

The title story, "Mothers, Tell Your Daughters," is about a woman dying of lung cancer. She is on a morphine drip under hospice care and, as Emily Eakin writes, "She's raised six children, tamed wild horses, skinned a cow and been crushed against a barn wall by a Hereford bull. She's also been raped, beaten and abandoned by a string of men. Her life's a home-spun ode to an era of male prerogative and female submission that's not quite—and this is [Campbell's] point—bygone." Having recently suffered a stroke and no longer able to speak aloud, she imagines a conversation with her adult daughter who is beside her, a conversation in which she tries to make sense of their troubled relationship and to explain and jus-tify her allowing her daughter to be sexually abused, a decision for which she has paid with her daughter's unremitting anger for all the years since. This is a story about how the internalization of the damaging messages of our current dystopian rape culture ruins a mother-daughter relationship.

One theme that stands out throughout her narrative of her girlhood and womanhood is the unquestioned power that men hold. The dying woman remembers her own father as a man to be feared, especially since he ends up committing his wife, the narrator's mother, to a psychiatric institution: "I used to be afraid I'd end up in the nuthouse too, was afraid your grandfather would send me there if I didn't work hard. Later I was afraid your daddy would commit me, because I never knew the end of the powers a man had over his woman" ("Mothers" 89). The last clause is one that resonates throughout this story. The unnamed narrator mentions to her daughter, "Of course you were scared of your daddy—he was a fear-some man, and he scared me, too" (94). At another point to defend herself from her daughter's accusations, she says, "Your daddy gave you babies liquor, not me. He poured it, burning, into your tender mouths when you cried and kept him awake—men did what they did back then, and there was no stopping him. You complain about the way I raised you children, but I only wanted to survive another day" (90). These are matter-of-fact accounts of the power her father and husband held, and the narrative is filled with such examples of men's unquestioned authority.

One message about rape culture that the narrator internalizes is the acceptance of male superiority and concomitant admiration of all things male. This narrator repeatedly discusses her approval of men, their machines, their motorcycles, their power washers, and unsurprisingly prefers sons to daughters: "Some women might be happy with daughters, but there's a reason every place in the world the folks cry out for sons" (95). She defines herself by her ability or inability to hold a man and speaks matter-of-factly of a man who broke her nose as if it's all in a day's work of living with men. As she says, "a good-looking man can always find a place in somebody's stable, however bad his behavior" (92). Most significantly, she casually mentions her own rape as part of a litany of abusive behavior by men she has witnessed, including a man killing his wife. She recounts her own rape with "One night a stranger put a knife to my throat and cursed me while he took me from behind like a bitch" (88). She comes back to the rape several other times in the course of her narrative in a casual way that belies the effect it truly had on her. She explains it as an inevitable part of living as a woman: "Women get themselves hurt every day—men mess with girls in this life, they always have, always will—but there's no sense making hard luck and misery your life's work" (89). Given men's superiority and women's duty to give them what they want, it does not occur to this narrator to even consider whether she has been wronged or mistreated by a man.

For the narrator of "Mothers, Tell Your Daughters," the sexual abuse of girls and women is inevitable, a fact of life. Douglas Sheldon writes about sexual victimization in "Playhouse," another story in *Mothers, Tell Your Daughters*: "Through the story's dialogue, a discourse on notions of female promiscuity and victim blaming emerges which displays a male privilege of dismissing sexual violence" ("Conversational" 23). Here, though, in the title story, it is the female narrator who herself dismisses sexual violence, demonstrating that women internalize the values of rape culture as much as men do. In her imagined conversation with her daughter, she says of other men who would come around the house and casually abuse her daughter: "How was I supposed to know there was trouble with the way they pulled you onto their laps if you never told me you didn't like it? It seemed like you were having fun when they said how pretty you were" ("Mothers" 94). Indeed, since sexual abuse is so routine, she believes her daughter has made much too much of it: "You've got more than anybody else around here, but you still worry an old thing that got done to you worse than a dog worries a bone. A couple of nights of trouble makes your whole life bitter" (88). Interestingly, the only power she seems to grant women is in having the agency to decide not to question their own abuse, in refusing to let themselves feel mistreated.

The entire narrative in fact is meant as a justification for allowing her boyfriend, Bill Theroux, to sexually abuse her then eleven-year-old daughter. So indoctrinated is this mother in the warped values of her culture that she sacrifices her daughter in an attempt to keep this man. While she has pretended to her daughter that she wasn't aware of the sexual activity between the boyfriend (who also was married) and her daughter, the truth is that he did not hide it from her. In fact, she acknowledges the following conversation: "*I think I'll go teach your daughter to French kiss*, Bill Theroux said to me one time, the first time, I guess. *Is that okay?* he said" (100). She then contemplates why she allowed it: "Maybe it was the way he asked, so casual, like it was an ordinary thing, like, can I borrow your truck? . . . Maybe I thought it would've been selfish to say, *Hell, no, you can't kiss my eleven-year-old daughter*" (100). We see here her deeply embedded sense that it is her duty as a woman to provide for her man, even if the provision is her own daughter's body.

In a culture that elevates men over women and pits women against women to win the hand of a man, it is not surprising that the mother, instead of feeling protective of her daughter feels jealous anger: "You ought to know I was mad as hell about it. What did you, a kid, have to offer that man? I had a steak to cook for him. I could listen to his stories" (99–100). She actually feels competitive toward her eleven-year-old daughter for the affections of another woman's husband. In fact, in her desperation to keep this man's attention, she in effect offers her daughter as bait because she realizes after a point he is more interested in her daughter than in her. When her daughter runs away from home to get away from Bill Theroux, the mother hides her daughter's permanent absence from him, telling him she wasn't really gone, because she is afraid that without her daughter there to attract him, he will leave (101). When he determines the daughter is gone, he does in fact leave.

This culture is dystopian in the sense that a mother who herself has been raped and physically and emotionally abused by men feels that her most important object is to keep a married man she is seeing happy enough to continue seeing her, even though his happiness involves sexually abusing her eleven-year-old daughter. This unnamed narrator, like Demeter, has been raped, and also like Demeter negotiates a deal with the man who is abusing her daughter. Only instead of striving to hold onto her daughter at least part of the year as Demeter does with Persephone, this narrator is trying to hold onto the man abusing her daughter. Indeed, the songs the narrator mentions several times in the course of her narrative serve to enforce some of the same values that appear in these classic myths. She notes songs about "dying for love or waiting for a soldier to return from the war" (94) and songs about "women drowned by their lovers and snow white doves nesting on girls' graves" (100), this last reference made while she remembers looking the other way when her lover, Bill Theroux, sexually abused her daughter. These songs reiterate the messages the narrator has already internalized, that it is a given that men cheat; that men want sex from whatever woman or girl will allow it—or won't; that men rape; that men are violent; that men hold the power; and that women will do anything to keep a man.

The mother, though a tough, no-nonsense woman with no self-pity and little for anyone else either, seems to long for a different relationship with her daughter. She comments more than once on how nice it is in the present to be physically close to her daughter: "You sitting beside me, holding my hand and showing me old black-and-white photos of the farm, that's nice" (89). At the end of the story, she apologizes for all she has attempted to justify throughout the story: "Someday, I hope, you'll want to . . . gather me up in your arms, forgive me even if I can't say I'm sorry" (104). This woman has so thoroughly absorbed the cultural messages that help to destroy her relationship with her daughter that by the end of the story she has only a vague notion of her own responsibility for their estranged relationship.

In another story that examines how the threat of sexual violence affects mother-daughter relationships, "Tell Yourself" concerns a mother who, growing up in the rape culture of her generation, has suffered sexual abuse from more than one man and is now filled with fear as she watches her thirteen-year-old daughter's blooming sexuality and worries about what it means for her safety. The story is a remarkable evocation of many connecting issues: the mother's memory of her own sexual abuse as well as her adolescent sexuality, the mother's perception of her daughter's growing sexuality and concomitant potential for sexual abuse, the mother's desire to protect her daughter and remain close to her at the same time, and the mother's current fear of men's capacity for sexual abuse to the extent that she questions her boyfriend about whether he is abusing her daughter, which effectively ends their relationship.

The crux of the story is the mother's understanding that a girl's budding sexuality automatically spells danger in this culture. Her daughter,

Mary, is an adolescent girl whose girlish and womanish desires and behavior are in a constant mix. Her adolescence is captured in the following reflection from the mother's perspective: "Your daughter changes her shirt at your insistence, and as soon as her phone is charged, she heads out to Amber's house on foot, cracking her gum, shaking her head, rolling her eyes, and texting in a cloud of candy-flower perfume" ("Tell Yourself" 45). At the same time, Mary is newly aware of her changing body and of her sexuality, shown by the clothes she wants to wear that expose her midriff and emphasize her breasts. The mother narrates, "Under your gaze she tugs her jeans up and makes an effort to pull down her shirt, but the whole production leaves six inches of bare belly and hips" (37). Indeed, Mary has also recently engaged in behavior at school—"flashing boys in the stairwell"—that results in an in-school suspension (39).

The mother worries for her daughter because she remembers both her own budding sexuality and the danger that sexuality caused her. She thinks to herself, "You can't deny how thrilled you were at the way your body got attention when you were her age. You would have bared your breasts for cute boys on a dare, no doubt" (40). Yet she also remembers her own history of sexual abuse, how her mother's boyfriend would give her rides, compliment her, and eventually molest her: "At the time, it wasn't clear what happened in the back seat, but in retrospect it is painfully clear" (40). She also remembers her "pot-smoking neighbor whom you, as a fourteen-year-old, screwed while his wife was at work and while his young son napped in the adjacent bedroom" (38). She is filled with fear for her daughter when she remembers how it feels to be a thirteen-year-old girl who is coming to an understanding of her budding sexuality when she remembers the sexual abuse she suffered then, and when she understands the current rape culture her daughter lives in.

Most of "Tell Yourself" concerns the mother's attempts to reassure herself that her daughter is safe. When she hears that her daughter plans to go to her friend Amber's house to work on her science project with Amber's dad, the mother thinks, "Amber's father has never been convicted of diddling with minors or of any other sex crime (you've looked him up on the Internet)" (38). She tries to calm her sense of panic throughout the story. In one passage she thinks, "Calm yourself down, woman. Not all men will try to screw your daughter, however she dresses. There are men who will not even fantasize about touching her darling new breasts. Some men are distracted, for instance, or gay, while a few may actually prefer mature women" (38). She views every man as a potential predator, including her current boyfriend, whom she ends up confronting with the possibility: "He'd never shown any interest in Mary beyond joking around and asking her about homework and cheerleading, but you just wanted to be absolutely one hundred percent sure your daughter was safe with him" (42). She wishes to enlist her intellect to calm her feelings, but she has experience and knowledge that tell her that her fears could be all too real.

The mother tries to navigate protecting her daughter while maintaining a close relationship. While trying to calm her fears at one point she tells herself, "Mary is probably not going to confide in you if you seem out of your mind" (38). But finally, in probably the most powerful passage of the story, the mother lets out her true feelings to her daughter: "'God damn it!' you shout at last. 'Can't you see? I'm worried sick about you. I'm worried that all the motherfuckers in the world want to mess with you and get their lousy hands on your body. Yes, I'm out of my mind with worry about what you do with boys at school in the stairwell. And worse, I'm afraid some man is going to sweet-talk you and lure you into his car and molest you, Mary. And I'm worried that you might like it. Or you might go along with it even if you don't'" (44). Her daughter responds as only a thirteen-year-old girl could, with "God, Mom. That's just gross, . . . You know I don't like men that way. They're too hairy" (44).

This story is a poignant evocation of a mother who herself grew into her sexuality in a culture that condones the sexual exploitation and even abuse of young women and girls, a mother who wants to protect her daughter from what she herself has experienced. But this protection may have to come at the expense of closeness to her daughter because she must to some extent present herself as her daughter's antagonist in order to keep her safe. At the same time, this mother, because of her fear of men, because of her determination that she be 100 percent sure of her daughter's safety, sacrifices her relationship with her current boyfriend. Still, the end of the story concerns her longing for his comfort: "Sitting that way with his strong arms around you, with his belly pressing into the small of your back like a support cushion, made you forget about the day's appalling customers. . . . When you allowed your head to fall back against Stan's shoulder, the warmth and size of him made you feel small and pretty, like a girl again" (46).

———

Interestingly, when I discuss "Tell Yourself" with my students, who are all women, I ask them if they think the narrator's fears are legitimate or if she is simply paranoid, since, indeed, the story indicates her fears about her boyfriend are unfounded and unnecessarily cause her to lose a potentially good relationship. Based on their own experiences and their understanding of our current culture, my students always uniformly support the legitimacy of this narrator's fear. She may be wrong about her boyfriend, but she is not wrong about her culture.

The mothers in both "Mothers, Tell Your Daughters" and "Tell Yourself" were sexually abused, the first minimizing the effects the abuse seemingly had on her. The first mother's internalization of rape culture results in her overseeing the sexual abuse of her own daughter, while the second mother's challenging of rape culture makes her fear her daughter's budding sexuality and what it might mean in terms of potential sexual abuse, a fear that results in her sacrificing her own romantic relationship out of the concern that even her partner might prey on her daughter. Critics have read the Persephone myth as demonstrating the fraught process of daughters' separation from their mothers from both mothers' and daughters' perspectives, and the myth as advocating a compromise: "It suggests that it is possible for a girl to enter into adulthood without necessarily destroying her relationship with her mother and indeed that a girl can be a sexual adult and still remain strongly connected to her mother" (Winograd 286). But also of importance is the fact that Hades's rape is an integral part of the separation process. These stories, then, examine the normalized, often violent process by which a girl living in our current rape culture moves from the protection and comfort of her mother to sexual relationships with men. Bonnie Jo Campbell depicts through these stories not only the ways in which rape culture damages girls and women but also its potential to disrupt and even destroy the mother-daughter bond.

Works Cited

Beaudrow, Jacob. "The Culture of Rape: Examining Causes and Educating for a Rape-Free Society." Lakehead U, PhD dissertation, 2014.

Buchwald, Emilie, et al., editors. *Transforming a Rape Culture*, revised edition. Milkweed, 2005.

Campbell, Bonnie Jo. "Mothers, Tell Your Daughters." *Mothers, Tell Your Daughters.* Norton, 2015, pp. 85–104.

———. *Once Upon a River.* Norton, 2011.

———. "Sleepover." *Mothers, Tell Your Daughters.* Norton, 2015, pp. 13–15.

———. "Tell Yourself." *Mothers, Tell Your Daughters.* Norton, 2015, 37–46.

Eakin, Emily. "Bonnie Jo Campbell's 'Mothers, Tell Your Daughters.'" *New York Times*, 9 Oct. 2015.

Fine, Laura. "Sexual Violence and Cultural Crime in the Country Noir Fiction of Bonnie Jo Campbell." *Critique: Studies in Contemporary Fiction*, vol. 60, no. 5, 2019, pp. 515–26.

Gay, Roxane. "The Careless Language of Sexual Violence." *Bad Feminist.* HarperCollins, 2014, pp. 128–36.

Hirsch, Marianne. *The Mother/Daughter Plot: Narrative, Psychoanalysis, Feminism.* Indiana UP, 1989.

Miedzian, Myriam. "How Rape Is Encouraged in American Boys and What We Can Do to Stop It." *Transforming a Rape Culture*, edited by Emilie Buchwald et al., revised edition. Milkweed, 2005, pp. 159–72.

Sheldon, Douglas. "Conversational Dissonance: Assault and Dialogue in Bonnie Jo Campbell's 'Playhouse.'" *Midwestern Miscellany*, vol. 44, no. 1, 2017, pp. 22–29.

Winograd, Wendy. "Persephone Rising: Struggles in Female Adolescent Development in the Aftermath of Rape." *Clinical Social Work*, vol. 38, no. 3, 2010, pp. 286–97.

Up the Road, Down the River

The Novels of Bonnie Jo Campbell Side by Side

MONICA FRIEDMAN

Editors' Note

Friedman's comic analysis of Campbell's novels *Q Road* and *Once Upon a River* bridges the scholarly and teaching sections of this collection. As a scholarly essay, it demonstrates how Campbell develops key themes from one book to the next, as well as the way these novels engage the iconography of rural southwest Michigan. While most scholarship serves a pedagogical function on some level, this chapter's visual form makes it an accessible teaching object in itself. For an example of how Friedman's work might be used in the classroom, see Doug Sheldon's contribution to this volume.

In this chapter, Friedman extends a project that began with comic versions of all forty-six short stories in *Mothers, Tell Your Daughters, American Salvage*, and *Women & Other Animals*. In those comics, Friedman extracted and analyzed meaningful images and quotations from each story, re-creating them in a linear fashion. While this chapter continues to mine the relationship between imagery and comprehension, it does not simply retell the stories visually. Instead, Friedman reimagines them by grouping analogous images to compare the human and environmental influences on Campbell's development of gun-toting teenage protagonists Rachel and Margo.

Throughout the comic, where the page is divided, *Q Road* material appears on the left or top half of the page. *Once Upon a River* material appears on the right or bottom of the page. Similarly, on the splash pages, *Q Road* is on the left, while *Once Upon a River* remains on the right. Citations follow the comic in the notes section.

BONNIE JO CAMPBELL COMICS

volume 4

graphic
literary
criticism
by
monica
friedman

Up the Road, Down the River: The Novels of Bonnie Jo Campbell Side by Side

Q Road	Once Upon a River
(2002)	(2011)

Both novels: set in Michigan, around Kalamazoo • tough, laconic, independent, gun-toting teenage girls with trust issues • lush descriptions of land and animals • search for home and family • inappropriate sexualization of a minor • murder • mysteriously vanished mothers • destruction of meaningful historical artifacts

This pumpkin symbolizes cultivation and seasonality.

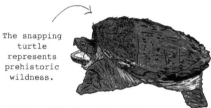

The snapping turtle represents prehistoric wildness.

- October 9, 1999
- day-in-the-life
- ensemble cast
- land in transition
- desire for rootedness
- gardening
- familiar faces

- Late '70s/early '80s
- road (river) novel
- limited point of view
- land is timeless
- urge to travel
- hunting
- new people

"At the eastern edge of Kalamazoo County, autumn woolly bear caterpillars hump across Queer Road to get to the fields and windbreaks of George Harland's rich river valley land."

From the novel's first page, we are taught the inherent value of George Harland's fertile farmland and given a hint as to the importance of the oldest barn in the county. In one sense, the caterpillars help set the narrative firmly in time and place, and also help establish the richness of the earth. In another sense, their migration sets them in opposition to Rachel, Margo's daughter, who thinks them stupid for feeling compelled to move, when she herself intends to stay put.

"The Stark River flowed around the oxbow at Murrayville the way blood flowed through Margo Crane's heart."

Setting, exposition, and backstory precede character and action in chapter one because the Stark River itself is a main character; the book's opening helps the river come alive for the reader as it's always been alive for Margo. The first page mentions eleven different types of animals Margo sees on the river, and three specific plants. It introduces Margo's famously laconic nature, her love of the river, and the importance of a small teak boat called The River Rose.

foul-mouthed

WILD

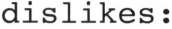

"The mystery of her face was that, while no individual aspect was freakish, the striking sum of her features demanded a person stop and stare, and then, after dragging his eyes away, look back for confirmation."

dislikes:
Todd
unnecessary killing
wasting food
explaining herself
animal haters
asphalt
concrete
ignorance
vulnerability

likes:
land
gardening
money
David
swearing
local history
Potawatomi legends
staying put
sex

"Whenever she was standing somewhere, you got the idea that she'd already been there a long time and it would take a lot to move her."

"David knew Rachel worked hard to put swear words into every sentence; she'd told him that plain talk, without swearing, was weak and invited argument."

"Her body in twilight was almost too much to look upon; her hipbone, her strange out-poking navel, her breast, the side of her throat were of some other world, and even in that world, where beauty was but the crudest version of whatever power Rachel possessed, there were no words for the fierce line of her jaw or the wing of her cheekbone."

strong

Rachel

strange

Secretly able to love

101

CHILD!

"Nobody ever expected her to say anything. ...Before she could answer a question ...she always had to figure out how a thing she was being asked connected to all the other things she knew. She might answer hours later, when she was alone...."

"Margo learned that when she was tempted to speak or cry out, she should, instead, be still and watch and listen."

dislikes:
rapists
Cousin Billy
Johnny
pollution
marijuana
alcohol
unsettled
scores
talking
feeling
helpless
confinement
bullies

likes:
parents
Grandfather
Cousin Junior
Aunt Joanna
cinnamon bread
the river
dogs
herons
Annie Oakley
trick shooting
Smoke
self-reliance

"You're so lovely," he whispered. "It's unholy."

beautiful

"I've never shot like that in my life. That's unholy."

lethal

Margo
Doesn't get mad; gets even

Roots

While many neighbors believed Rachel's mother to be dangerous and insane, Rachel found Margo an adequate parent who taught her to care for herself and connect to her home. Margo may have not have offered affection, but she vigilantly protected Rachel from the sexual assault that marred her own adolescence. When she vanishes, Rachel understands and doesn't miss her much. Her secret was the identity of Rachel's dad.

"Are you sure you're a daughter of mine?"

"If men could feel anything at all, they wouldn't want to own women."

"When you think about a woman like Margo, it reminds you that you're going to die someday."

"I thought I could raise a girl to be something on her own, but you act no better than a creature clawing its way up the riverbank to get caught in someone's trap."

The Murrays called Margo's mother free-spirited like it was a bad thing. She never loved the river or the land, and while Margo has fond memories of her, she was drunk and unhappy as a mother. When Luanne vanishes, Margo doesn't understand, and holds out hope that Luanne will nurture her again. Luanne would like to be a nurturer, but she doesn't have much to give. Her secret was her affair with Margo's uncle.

"I would have given anything to see you, but it wasn't the right time."

"I know I didn't take care of you when I should have, but I will now."

Rachel never knew her father; her mother only spoke of him once, had never even learned his name. All Rachel has of his is a single legend Margo passed down despite herself, the myth of Corn Girl, a Potawatomi maiden who enjoyed gardening the Three Sisters so much that she killed herself rather than marrying a man who would take her away from the land she loved.

Corn Maiden is another element linking the two novels, in a playful use of oral history. Margo tells Rachel the story with disdain, to demonstrate how ridiculous her father was. Rachel embraces the story and embellishes it, with the knowledge that she is writing her own history. She shares it with David, who revises and repeats it as a kind of truth. An earlier version appears in *Once Upon a River*; The Indian tells it to Margo. His cousin originally told it to him after hearing it from his great-uncle. To him it serves as both history and folklore.

Margo adores her father, especially in the wake of her mother's disappearance, and makes decisions she believes will keep him safe, although they backfire, so that Margo thinks herself complicit in his death. Bernard Crane was the result of an adulterous affair, and was a latecomer to his own family, but Margo's birth allowed for a degree of reconciliation.

"Don't you ever forget, Margo, you're the only reason I'm alive and sober in this world."

"You think before you shoot. You consider the consequences."

"You look like an angel, but you smell like a rutting buck."

George Harland's family has owned this farm for a hundred thirty years. With the land, George inherited family mythology: stories of the forced displacement of the Potawatomi people in 1840, which his ancestors silently witnessed; stories of the regretted discrediting of Mary O'Kearsy, a beautiful schoolteacher shamed out of Kalamazoo in 1934 after George's grandfather ratted her out for being sexually active, right before a tornado struck, as if in retribution.

"Like all the farmers, George's great-great-great-grandfather had thought he was glad to see the Indians go. For hours he heard the wailing and watched.... Two decades later...[he] told about those heartbroken people.... He described that sad despair.... He saw that barn...as...a memorial to the gone people."

The Murrays own Murrayville, and none of them have ever been anywhere else. Cal Murray will never fill his father's shoes as a businessman, He does enjoy adultery like the Old Man did, but prefers to keep it in the family, as if incest is a respectable value. Joanne Murray tolerates his philandering; she's the type who can't seem to stop nurturing. Their children are troubled; likely this will be the last generation of Murrays to rule Murrayville.

"I admired the old man, your grandpa, may he rest in peace, but I've got to tell you, girl, I'm not so fond of some of them other Murrays of Murrayville."

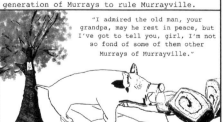

The Land

Rurality vs Suburbanism

Rachel's southwest Michigan, in the 1990s, has succumbed to modernity and largely embraced the inevitability of **change**. Rachel is able to visually track and categorize the so-called progress of suburbia creeping across her beloved farmland.

Spectrum of Attitudes toward Farming:

- Farms are gross; tract housing must sanitize the land
- Farms were nice in their time, but that time's passed
- Still mourning the inevitable loss of local farms
- We must save this beloved historic farm at all costs

Living on the Land

Rachel occupies the land, seeking to transform it according to her desires.

George Harland's great-great-great grandfather bought the land over 100 years ago, displacing those who came before, just as the suburbanites displace farmers now. George's father and brother felt farming was a trap. Rachel sees freedom in being bound to the earth, which offers nourishment in exchange for work.

Rachel imagines Jonathan apples and honeybees, raspberries, and ripe tomatoes.

Farming and gardening means choosing what you intend to cultivate.

"She rubbed her hip and belly with a handful of cool black dirt.

Rachel's almost erotic relationship with the land is a love palpable in her gardens and her willingness to trade part of her life and freedom for access to it. She trusts the land to overcome human failings.

Wilderness vs Civilization

Margo's southwest Michigan, in the 1970s, clings to a prehistoric, untamed nature that summons a sense of **timelessness**. Pockets of development are carved out of land that resists change, embracing its own ancient systems and cycles.

Spectrum of Attitudes toward Hunting:

- Hunting? Ew! You skin dead animals with your hands?
- Nice to know about, but not immediately necessary
- We cannot financially afford to run afoul of DNR
- Hunting is the only legitimate way to live freely

Living in the Land

Margo blends into the land, transforms herself for optimal survival there.

The Murrays rule Murrayville, but none of them ever go anywhere else. Margo's grandfather claimed he was "stuck on the Stark," but the smallness of the Murrays' world is a choice. Luanne felt trapped there; Margo cannot begin to formulate what freedom might look like until she escapes the confines of their realm.

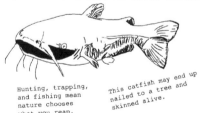

Hunting, trapping, and fishing mean nature chooses what you reap.

This catfish may end up nailed to a tree and skinned alive.

"I wish I didn't have to be on any person's land."

Margo's distrust of the land reflects her experience learning not to trust men. She'd rather be outside than in a house, and she'd rather be on the river than on land, which is only good for hunting and trapping.

Structure

Q Road depicts the pivotal events of a single day, but frequently jumps back in time to events from the past, some recent enough to be clearly remembered, some so distant as to function as myth. While it keeps three target protagonists — George, Rachel, and David — at the fore, it constantly shifts perspective to show every character's point of view.

Although Margo's journey is anything but straightforward, *Once Upon a River* unfurls in a generally linear fashion, occasionally focusing on the past, but only when Margo lacks forward momentum. The reader sees only Margo's experience, and can decode the other characters' actions and motivations only through the filter of her limited perception.

[This panel was meant to be a graphic illustrating the relationship between past and present, and the path of the narrative as it jumped between the two, twining the events of October 9, 1999 with preceding incidents. However, that graphic would have been as long as this entire comic. Instead, here is a short list of stories, history, and myth referenced throughout the text.]

[Similarly, this panel would have traced Margo's movement up and down and back and forth the Stark and the Kalamazoo, per the map that precedes Part I of the novel, and it would have been not just long, but probably also boring. Instead, ponder these drawings of important, guiding imagery Margo enjoys thinking about, which don't appear elsewhere in this comic.]

Long Ago

Corn Girl
Potawatomi expulsion
Expulsion of Mary O'Kearsy
Tornado
The old barn

Recent Past

Rachel and Margo
Rachel and Johnny
Rachel and George
Rachel and David

Stories for Now

Christianity
Marriage & monogamy
Parks's theories
Suburbia

For the Future

Aliens
David's strength
Rachel's gardens
George's new barn

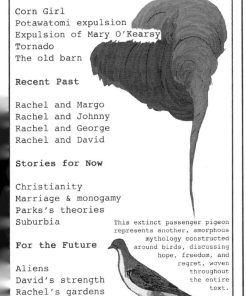

This extinct passenger pigeon represents another, amorphous mythology constructed around birds, discussing hope, freedom, and regret, woven throughout the entire text.

Annie Oakley has stood as an enduring hero to badass little girls for 145 years.

"For the Indian hunter, a wolverine ...meant he should return to his tribe. But this animal was not threatening to Margo."

"Did you ever hear about a deer eating a bird?"

Margo's travels up and down the Stark and the Kalamazoo have been compared to Huck Finn's backward journey down the Mississippi; an artful reader could also establish parallels between Rachel's and David's experiences and those of Tom Sawyer. I see even more comparisons to the work of Jack London. *Once Upon a River*, like *Call of the Wild*, depicts a journey from domesticity to wildness; while *Q Road*, like *White Fang*, illustrates the journey from wildness to domesticity.

More Characters

The Neighbors

Familiar faces: Rachel grew up isolated with her eccentric, emotionally distant mother, never trusting others, although many of her Q Road neighbors have known Rachel her entire life. When Margo disappears, Rachel learns to accept the benefit of community.

David Rettaker

Practically an orphan. Chronically malnourished but determined to be tough. Obsessed with George Harland, farming, the loss of a single knuckle, and the irrational belief that smoking pilfered cigarettes can cure asthma. Probably Rachel's only friend; Rachel is probably his only friend. Kid could have really used an ashtray.

Elaine Shore

Sad, plastic person, hates nature, farms, animals. The human equivalent of astroturf, if astroturf spied on grass and passed unfavorable judgement on it. Obsessed with aliens. Takes comfort in her own boobs and the paving over of natural resources.

Steve Hoekstra

Adulterous door-to-door salesman. Unaware of the ridiculousness of his life, lying just below his handsome facade. Takes the penetration of strange women's homes way too seriously. Pushy, in an unctuous way.

Nicole Hoekstra

Desperately, comically unhappy housewife, forgot to plan for life after her wedding. Mildly homicidal, but fun about it. Forgettably pretty. Needs SSRIs and a volunteer job.

Milton Taylor

Sold the family farm; turned his historic barn into a bar and grill in a complicated but ineffective plot to convert the neighbors to Christianity. Gentle and kind, but deluded by his own faith. Always encouraged Rachel's gardening, but that was probably also a complicated but ineffective attempt at proselytizing. Thinks the old way belongs in a museum.

Sally Retakker

Agreeable but pathetic barfly type; doesn't seem to remember she has a child. Wandering aimlessly in the general direction of her next drink/lay. Would be a joke if she were less pathetic.

Tom Parks

Sold the family farm and moved away, but couldn't stay away. Recently returned to Kalamazoo in his new incarnation as a small town police officer. Wishes he still owned a farm. President of the "I Can Never Admit How Much I Envy George Harland" Club.

Riverfolk

New folks: Margo, raised among extended family, no longer feels safe with the Murrays. On the river she meets new humans, different from the people she has always known. She learns to assess risk so she can figure out how and who to trust again.

Brian Ledoux

The kind of guy who says just what he's thinking but acts without thought. Not evil, per se (when he's sober) but not a saint either. Margo got in bed with him to protect herself, but if he wanted to protect her he would have said no. Has knowledge and assets Margo wants. Prone to violence when drunk. Not as good at hiding out as he thinks he is.

Paul Ledoux

Drug addicted rapist who sort of respects his brother as long as his brother is around to witness that respect. Lawless bully. Justice is served on his stupid face.

Michael Appel

Wants desperately to know that he's a decent guy. Totally civilized but wishing for a little wilderness in his life. Trying to be self reliant, trying to save Margo, trying to abide by the law.

The Indian

Native American professor searching for his roots who says things like, "by golly." Both cynical and easily impressed. Definitely never cheated on his wife before he met Margo. Acts like this is his first time outside.

Smoke

Suicidal print setter (retired), immediately trustworthy because he's too old, sick, and weak to hurt anyone. Almost takes the place of Margo's dead dad. Has a bunch of stuff he doesn't need or use, that Margo really wants. Bullied by his nieces, with love.

Fishbone

Loves the river at least as much as he loves the fifteen extended family members all living in his house with him, maybe more; has all the knowledge Margo needs to live the life she wants.

Characters Appearing in Both Novels:

George Harland

A decent guy, even if he did bribe an underage girl to marry him. Worries about the past. Worries about the future. Generous to women who aren't very nice to him. Missing part of one finger. Not selling his family farm.

Johnny Harland

Drunk pedophile, serial seducer of underage girls, will hump anything including the carcass of a dead deer, and everybody knows. Hates farming but resents others appreciating the farm. Apparently handsome? Dead.

April May Rathburn

Doing her best despite the things she's seen in her life. Loves children, birds, pumpkin carving, and local history. Survived a tornado-related injury. Understands that alternative justice is better than no justice.

Animals: Wild and Domesticated

Aside from the danger of being run over by humans, the woolly bears' lives have remained unchanged for millions of years. Their ancestors have always hibernated here; if George and Rachel hang onto the farm, their descendants will do the same.

George's neighbor still farms Duroc hogs, but the cattle that used to sometimes get loose and eat his crops have all been sold. George's animals all seem ornamental. When they get out, they just poop on the suburban lawns. The long haired llama was left behind by George's first wife, who was bored of farming. Presumably, someone could shear it and make wool, but George and Rachel don't have time for that. The pony and the donkey could theoretically work as well, but George has a tractor, so the pony and donkey are really relics of the past.

Margo passive-aggressively skins a skunk as she tells Rachel what little she knows about her dad. The stench lingers long after Margo is gone.

English sparrows, like George Harland's family: an invasive species that displaced natives so long ago they seem to belong.

April May enjoys bird watching because she finds birds less complicated than people.

Like Rachel, Margo, and Kipling's Cat who walks by himself, Gray Cat straddles the divide between wild and domesticated.

Martini the spotted pony

A long haired llama

This requisite donkey

Once Upon a River features countless animals, a diversity of organisms along the river. For Margo, they represent freedom: the freedom of their wild lives, and her freedom to live on the river as long as she can hunt and fish to feed herself.

Many of the creatures appear as features of the river, like visible aspects of character.

The herons function as guides for Margo throughout her journey:

- As an only child who craves a secure place in her boisterous extended family, Margo counts the herons in the heronry by the cemetery
- Cold, starving, and exhausted after rowing away from home, Margo begins to drift when she is startled back to her senses by a heron
- After drifting away from Michael and Cleo, Margo watches a heron stalk a .22 caliber long-rifle cartridge, which it drops on her hip like a sign.

Margo begins hunting deer to cope with her trauma. Later, she chooses to kill only what she needs.

Cleo, the fishing dog, loves the river just as Margo does, but she also serves as an enticement to return to domesticity. Margo later adopts another river-loving dog, Nightmare, as she figures out how she can live according to her own rules. Margo's parents didn't allow her to keep a dog, but the Murrays had a black lab, Moe, she liked. All dogs are good dogs.

"Good" Guys. Sex. Consent?

From a legal perspective, Margo and Rachel are both too young to consent to most of their sexual experiences; however Campbell writes them each as understanding whether or not they have consented to intercourse with older men.

Rachel has been raised with Margo's distrust of men, but her experience with Milton, her adolescent rebellion, and her natural physicality lead her to reject her mother's misandry and draw her own conclusions regarding experimentation with men and sex. None of her experiences lead her to reject the possibility of future sex.

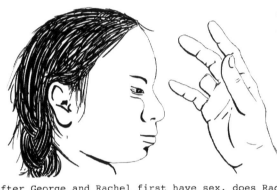

"He didn't want to think of what they just had together as sex. The phrase *making love* seemed like nothing.

"'Will you please marry me?' he said."

After George and Rachel first have sex, does Rachel say "damn you," because she feels violated, is angry he seduced her, just likes to swear, or is disappointed, "he couldn't stop himself from coming apart after only one minute"? How is George's initial sexual interaction with her different from Johnny's? Would Rachel have come back if George didn't own that land?

Until her uncle rapes her at the family reunion, Margo's childhood sexual experiences are developmentally appropriate: a few stolen kisses, and once, an egalitarian exploration of intercourse with a friend of her cousin's only slightly older than herself.

"...she had nowhere else to go, and she wondered if she could make herself welcome here."

"She did not know if Brian would force a girl, but he couldn't force her if she went to him on her own."

Margo invites herself into both Brian and Michael's beds out of survival instinct. She craves the safety and security she had when she knew her father would do anything to protect her, and she wants to be warm and fed. Michael, who thinks of himself as a decent Christian, puts up more of a fight than Brian, who lives by a much less stringent moral code. Ultimately, Michael's ethics drive Margo away, just as Brian's lack of principles end his relationship with Margo. Her single encounter with the Indian, and her disappointment in him, lead her to swear off sex forever.

"She was surprised at how much she wanted to keep kissing him, though he was practically a stranger."

SEXUAL ASSAULT

Rachel and Margo both have early sexual experiences thrust upon them by older men; although neither of them objects in the moment, they are not legally old enough to consent at the time. Margo's history leads her to want to protect Rachel from any sexual assault. Margo's experience of sexual violence is greater than Rachel's due to that fact that Margo's parents were not available to teach and protect her from men the way she chooses to teach and protect Rachel.

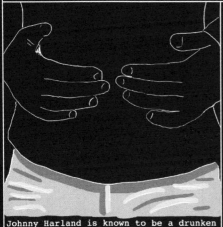

Johnny Harland is known to be a drunken serial deflowerer of pubescent girls.

Paul is an amoral drug addict; his worser nature was only held in check by his brother Brian's disapproval. Uncle Cal is also a disgusting failure of a human being in multiple categories.

Margo Shoots a Man and Runs

When Margo shoots Johnny Harland in his brother's barn, she runs away in the belief that she can protect Rachel by disappearing. Possibly, she also runs because she long ago vowed that she would never murder another person.

Margo doesn't run immediately after shooting Cal, and is chagrined that her actions lead to the death of her own father; then she runs away. After shooting Paul, she runs to protect both Michael and her own freedom.

Despite her love affair with the rifle, the only person Rachel has ever shot at is David, and it was an accident, and she stops shooting at coyotes afterward.

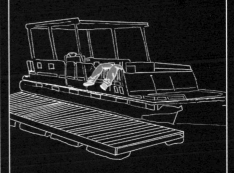

After Paul's death, Margo vows not to kill another person again. Perhaps she is not in her right mind when she shoots Johnny, but she never liked him.

Gardening vs Hunting

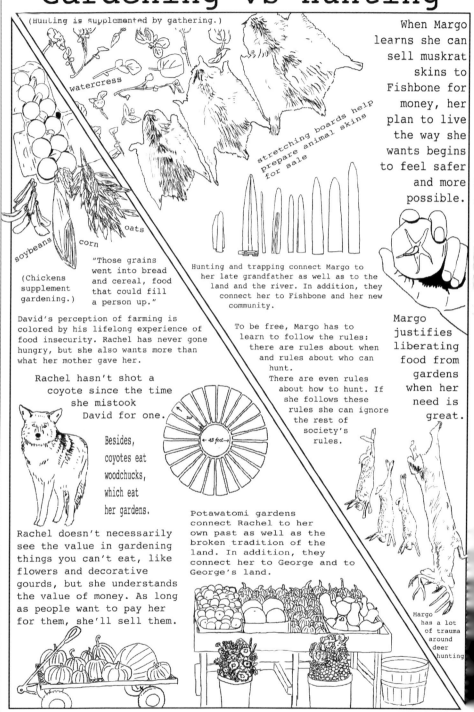

(Hunting is supplemented by gathering.)

watercress

oats

soybeans   corn

(Chickens supplement gardening.)

"Those grains went into bread and cereal, food that could fill a person up."

David's perception of farming is colored by his lifelong experience of food insecurity. Rachel has never gone hungry, but she also wants more than what her mother gave her.

Rachel hasn't shot a coyote since the time she mistook David for one.

Besides, coyotes eat woodchucks, which eat her gardens.

Rachel doesn't necessarily see the value in gardening things you can't eat, like flowers and decorative gourds, but she understands the value of money. As long as people want to pay her for them, she'll sell them.

stretching boards help prepare animal skins for sale

Hunting and trapping connect Margo to her late grandfather as well as to the land and the river. In addition, they connect her to Fishbone and her new community.

To be free, Margo has to learn to follow the rules: there are rules about when and rules about who can hunt. There are even rules about how to hunt. If she follows these rules she can ignore the rest of society's rules.

Potawatomi gardens connect Rachel to her own past as well as the broken tradition of the land. In addition, they connect her to George and to George's land.

When Margo learns she can sell muskrat skins to Fishbone for money, her plan to live the way she wants begins to feel safer and more possible.

Margo justifies liberating food from gardens when her need is great.

Margo has a lot of trauma around deer hunting

110

Destruction of

Authenticity: the barn represents the last vestige of a vanishing past, the idealization of farm life, and the old community's collective soul.

Many generations of Harlands used the barn to facilitate farm labor. They also worked to keep the barn in usable condition.

In contrast, Milton converted his family's historic barn into a bar and grill. He also wants to preserve history (in a museum) but embraces change. He hopes the converted barn will nourish the community, just on two different levels from its original purpose.

The Oldest Barn in the Township

George's no-account brother Johnny has a long history of statuatory rape of local teen girls, including April May's daughters, in this barn. Rachel's mother murders him in the barn after catching him assaulting 14-year-old Rachel. April May watches Rachel bury Johnny there. With the barn's destruction, Johnny and his crimes become, like the old ways the barn represented, ancient history. **Now George and Rachel, no longer bound by the past, are free to think of farming in different ways in the future.**

bonus destruction/ foreshadowing: Todd throws a pumpkin through the window of George's house.

Accidental: David loves the barn and knows better than to smoke there. He didn't mean to start a fire.

A public loss: although George and Rachel are the only people whose lives are truly affected by the barn, it holds symbolic value for the entire community and many people mourn its destruction.

Beloved Icons

Authenticity: Margo's grandfather used this work vessel to fish and check traps. After Old Man Murray dies, the boat represents Margo's good relationship with her grandfather, but after Bernard dies, the boat represents Margo's escape from the Murrays.

In contrast: Mike, who works for the power company and doesn't know how to fish, is building a bigger boat inside his house. He is part of the new, domesticated world that will supplant the wilderness. Margo's survival skills are a luxurious goal for him. He hopes to learn them, someday.

The River Rose, a Small Teak Boat

History repeats: Billy stole the boat once before, when their grandfather first gave it to Margo, but Cal made him give it back. That time he returned it full of snakes. He doesn't even want it anymore, he just wants her not to have it, and he knows she will steal it back if he doesn't eradicate it. He's already robbed Margo of her father.

After being chainsawed to kindling, *The River Rose* is reduced to ashes, just like the barn. Its destruction is just another in a long series of painful losses Margo endures throughout her journey. **No longer "stuck on the Stark," she is free to explore new rivers.**

Intentional: Cousin Billy chops the boat to kindling for the sole purpose of keeping Margo from having it.

A private loss: although Margo inherited the boat from her grandfather, her cousin destroys it out of anger and jealousy, and none of Grandpa Murray's descendents join Margo in feeling sorrow over the loss of this piece of history that connected them to him. The teens using its remains for firewood do not even recognize its significance or their role in its demise.

The Meaning of Home

What she had

tomatoes symbolize the beginning of Rachel's domestication

- Margo
- The Glutton
- outsider*
- small gardens
- privacy

*Outside status, for Rachel, is a plus, at least to begin with. It gives her the freedom to behave shockingly and anti-socially and be excused for it.

the destruction of the baby chair symbolizes the end of Margo's childhood

- Murrays
- Murrayville
- belonging*
- The Stark River
- baked goods

*Belonging, for Margo, has some negatives, including putting up with her cousins' nonsense and a great sense of loss when family betrays her.

What she's lost

revenge is a roadkill woodchuck in Billy's Camaro

isolation

Rachel has lived her entire life separated from the community by virtue of Margo's eccentricity, but, having known no other way of existing, it seems natural and agreeable to her to be alone and without friends. It's difficult to convince her she needs other people, or should trust them, or even reveal her weaknesses.

vulnerability

Given her parents' status among the Murrays, Margo has always been vulnerable, but she accepts her cousins' behavior as the normal way of relating to family. Her trust is eroded away as each of her champions proves mortal and flawed, until she at last determines to become completely self-reliant so she can live alone.

What she's gained

Seeking emergency medical care for David

security

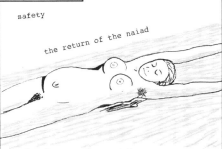

safety

the return of the naiad

family•dream gardens•
supportive community

baby•The Glutton•
supportive community

The Future

From the ashes of a historic barn, new possibilities arise: the strengthening of three marriages; a safe, sane, loving home and family for David; fresh perspectives on making a living growing crops on farmland. In support of George, Parks and Milton can reconnect with the land, while Steve will find a more civic minded way of uplifting the community.

"She was thinking that if George died in his sleep, she could walk down the hall...and wake David...and when she told him what they were going to do next, then she would know."

"George thought that a boy who knew regret might listen to the kind of stories Old Harold used to tell.... George would tell David that if this place was going to survive, the farmers needed a new way of seeing."

protecting David

creating intentional family

the desired connection to the land has been cemented

David's first meal in forever

embracing the ways of the past and mixing them with modern thought to generate prosperity for the future

---

From the run-down scraps of Smoke's life, Margo can build the sanctuary for which she has been searching. His homemade houseboat, formerly known as the *Pride and Joy*, now *The Glutton*, provides shelter; his large, misandrist dog, Nightmare, protects her from rapists; his advice and his association with Fishbone has provided her with ways to make a living.

"She had given the baby every opportunity to leave, but it had stayed, and she would not let it die now.... Margo would do at least as good a job as one of those wolves who raised human children. She could do as good a job as her own mother—and she would not abandon her child."

"She felt the baby startle at her contact with the river, had felt it jostle as she began to swim, and then the baby relaxed. As Margo floated, the baby floated with her."

collecting knowledge from the past to ensure security in the future

the essential connection to the river has been assured

The Glutton, a homemade houseboat

achieving harmony

protecting Rachel

Notes

Page numbers derived from the first edition hardcovers of *Q Road* (Scribner's, 2002) (QR) and *Once Upon a River* (Norton, 2011) (OUAR).

Title Page

"At the eastern edge . . ." (QR 1)
"The Stark River flowed . . ." (OUAR 15)

WILD

"The mystery of her face . . ." (QR 8)
"Whenever she was standing . . ." (QR 3)
"David knew she worked hard . . ." (QR 4)
"Her body in twilight . . ." (QR 82)

CHILD!

"Nobody ever expected her . . ." (OUAR 23)
"Margo learned that when . . ." (OUAR 15)
"'You're so lovely,' he whispered . . ." (OUAR 22)
"'I've never shot like that . . .'" (OUAR 19)

Roots

"Are you sure you're . . ." (QR 23)
"When you think about . . ." (QR 66)
"If men could feel . . ." (QR 24)
"I thought I could . . ." (QR 25)
"I would have given anything . . ." (OUAR 285)
"I know I didn't . . ." (OUAR 287)
"Don't you ever forget . . ." (OUAR 36)
"You think before you shoot . . ." (OUAR 39)
"You look like an angel . . ." (OUAR 36)
"Like all the farmers . . ." (QR 182)
"I admired the Old Man . . ." (OUAR 42)

The Land

"She rubbed her hip and belly . . ." (QR 84)
"I wish I didn't . . ." (QR 263)

Structure

"For the Indian hunter . . ." (OUAR 239)
"Did you ever hear about . . ." (OUAR 97)

"Good" Guys. Sex. Consent?

"He didn't want to think . . ." (QR 82)
"She had nowhere else to . . ." (OUAR 83)
"She did not know . . ." (OUAR 84)
"She was surprised . . ." (OUAR 136)

Gardening vs Hunting

"Those grains went into . . ." (QR 3)

The Future

"She was thinking that . . ." (QR 253)
"George thought that . . ." (QR 258)
"She had given the baby every . . ." (OUAR 330)
"She felt the baby . . ." (OUAR 346)

PART 2
Teaching Essays

Kalamazoo County

Nurturing a Community of Readers

MARSHA MEYER

When I invited Bonnie Jo Campbell to our book group, the Mavens, we filled the table with plenty of homemade cookies and our notebooks with questions. We weren't paying her, and she was taking time from writing award-winning fiction to meet with us. *Once Upon a River* had just come out, and there was going to be a movie. Fortunately, we only live about twenty minutes from Bonnie's home. When she came to the door, she apologized for her straw- and mud-caked boots. She had just come from the vet castrating Don Quixote, her beloved donkey, and didn't have time to change. After being introduced, she asked everyone in the room to talk about themselves, inquiring how they ran their organic farm, what was their favorite book to teach, what books had sparked our juiciest discussions. She shared passages from her book, her writing process, what childhood experiences and landscapes had influenced her writing, what drew her to rivers. With Campbell, you not only become a fan, you become a lifelong friend. It's true that not all communities have a Bonnie Jo Campbell living down the street, but many villages and cities have writers who live within driving distance. Inviting local authors to a book group is just one way to nurture a community of readers.

I have been a public librarian for over forty years, most recently at the Portage District Library south of Kalamazoo, Michigan. As a teacher and librarian, I am a book pusher. My mission is to lure readers and nonreaders of all ages to a variety of genres, topics, diverse cultures and writing styles. We want people to be addicted to reading, to stretch their perspective sometimes beyond their comfort zone. We want them to recognize their ability to think through rough times, create beautiful art, listen deeply to those with different views, and explore wherever their curiosity takes them. We want them to know they are not alone. Rudine Sims Bishop, renowned scholar of multicultural children's literature, observed, "Literature transforms human experience and reflects it back to us, and in that reflection we can see our own lives and experiences as part of the larger human experience. Reading, then, becomes a means of self-affirmation, and readers often seek their mirrors in books" (ix). Being a librarian is much more than shelving books and reading novels. It's about knowing area residents, showcasing their talents and stories.

An effective way to personalize and humanize the relationship between writer and reader is to invite authors to read their work. Author readings, especially in libraries, can be intimidating to some people who think they will be too scholarly. They're afraid they won't know what to say, especially if they haven't read the book or feel shy about asking what could be a dumb question. Campbell and many other authors are not only entertaining storytellers and language maestros, but they have also been teachers in college classrooms and writing workshops. They understand that many people don't analyze tropes, denouement, or foreshadowing. They want to know where the stories and characters come from, if they are autobiographical, and what discoveries the writer made while researching and writing their work. They wonder why they chose to write their novel in verse, what is creative nonfiction, if the characters directed the action or were forged from a preconceived outline. They are curious to know why someone decides to be a writer and if she can make a living at it. They ask Campbell if she grew up being as self-sufficient as Margo in *Once Upon a River* and Rachel in *Q Road*, as well as where she learned so much about the flow of a river, how to shoot an acorn from across a field, and live off the land. Meeting and reading about people who grew up with similar insecurities or lack of opportunities encourages reluctant readers to find solace in someone like themselves and feel less marginalized. It can create a reading culture where book discussions are prevalent not only in homes and libraries but in prisons, juvenile homes, senior living centers, grocery-store parking lots, and coffee shops.

Author visits can be rewarding to writers as well. Writing is a solitary task. Live input from a nonacademic readership can be helpful and energizing. Writers want to find out if their work touched their readers, if the plot and characters, the language and setting drew them in and sparked empathy. At author readings, writers appreciate a bookseller selling their books and the opportunity to sign copies and talk with their readers. Authors are generous, but they do need to make a living. Their time and expertise deserve to be paid for beyond cookies and gas money. At Kalamazoo events, our three independent bookstores often sell Campbell's books. This not only shows the mutual support between authors and booksellers—it also nurtures the overall community because it personalizes the relationships between bookseller, reader, and writer.

Reading Together

In 1998, Nancy Pearl, librarian at the Seattle Public Library, created a community reading program called "If All of Seattle Read the Same Book." She describes the reasons behind the program: "I have for a long time felt our society is becoming more and more fractured and divisive. . . . If you give people a good book to talk about, you can build a community out of a diverse group. A common language grows out of it" (qtd. in Simpson). John Cole describes how such programs, now commonly called "One Book One Community"—with one book read by a city, university, state, or other group—have since exploded in popularity. One Book One Community events introduce a broad range of people to books, authors, and issues they might not have had the opportunity or inkling to experience. Reading the same book can encourage collaborations between unexpected or little-known local organizations. Librarians can reach out to numerous groups: social service and arts organizations, colleges, senior living complexes, bookstores, secondary and elementary schools, churches, businesses, neighborhood centers, and libraries of all sizes. As a result, teachers, librarians, and experts in various fields guide exploration into hot topics, historical events, and the power of language and provide the general public an opportunity to share their own stories and experiences.

The Kalamazoo Public Library's One Book program, called Reading Together, has invited nationally known authors such as Kareem Abdul-Jabbar and James McBride. The library draws funding from the city as well as outside grants, local businesses, and nonprofits such as the Friends of Kalamazoo Public Library. A steering committee composed of librarians, high school teachers, Western Michigan University and Kalamazoo College instructors, and local government representatives plans and implements panel discussions, book talks, lectures on associated topics, and programs at local museums. For instance, when Tim O'Brien's *The Things We Carried* was chosen in 2006, veterans from the Vietnam War shared their stories at the Air Zoo Aerospace & Science Museum in Kalamazoo, which houses planes and historical information from early flight to 1990. Another book discussion each year pairs a high school English class with residents of a senior living facility. The possibilities for pairing diverse groups are endless.

Not every community has the resources to bring in big-name authors. Fortunately, Kalamazoo is chock full of excellent novelists, poets, short story and creative nonfiction writers. We have a university, a prestigious college, and a vibrant community college with published and award-winning writers who are invested in fostering readers not only for their work but other authors as well. If you don't have authors in your village or town, there are writers within your state. In Michigan, the Michigan Center for the Book was created by the Library of Michigan to promote an awareness of books, reading, literacy, authors, and Michigan's rich literary heritage. The Center offers grants for books and author visits to libraries and schools. Other states have similar programs through their state libraries and humanities councils. Meeting an author and reading about characters rooted in readers' experiences and who come from their neck of the woods personalizes authors and their stories.

Providing book-centered programs in different locations can make reading a social event. Some ideas include holding book discussions outside the library: international mystery book discussions at local restaurants offering international cuisine, science fiction/fantasy novels made into movies at a theater followed by viewing the film, mother/daughter book-related teas at Victorian B&B's, art-themed book discussions held at an art museum featuring a collection of the featured artist or art movement. In Kalamazoo, I've attended author readings at the Kalamazoo Art Center, the downtown Methodist church, and Bell's Brewery. In 2015, Campbell celebrated the publication of *Mothers, Tell Your Daughters* at Old Dog Tavern, and the book paired perfectly with a lager.

A Community of Readers

The individual impact of being in the same room with an author (even on Zoom) can be profound. The same is true discussing your favorite books with other bibliophiles. One of our most popular programs at Portage

District Library was our annual "What Some Are Reading" event. We invited area book groups to share what books sparked the liveliest discussions. We asked a local author, a literature professor from Western Michigan University, and owners of our independent bookstores to reveal their top ten titles of the year and why. The discussions went on well past library closing hours. Afterwards, some book groups decided to have a joint meeting once a year to discuss a book both groups loved.

I have experienced many events that affirmed the power of language and its capacity to nurture a community of understanding. The closing reading of our first Kalamazoo Poetry Festival featured local poets representing the Hispanic American Council, Kalamazoo Gay and Lesbian Resource Center, Ministry with Community, the Black Arts & Cultural Center, the Book Arts Center, and the leaders of workshops held the previous week, including Campbell and other local writers. We inquired if our interpreter for the deaf had a student who would like to read a poem. A middle schooler stepped in front of over one hundred people and signed a poem he wrote as the interpreter read it. It brought the audience to silence, then to their feet.

Schools can also be effective locations for connecting readers to authors. The teacher can encourage students to reach out to the author. "Author Invitation" makes an interesting option for an assignment. The students can then arrange the visit, prepare the author for the reading, handle introductions, and write thank-you notes. Libraries working with teachers can help offer space, funding, and grant options for the author lectures that match the curriculum, and include the entire family to take part in hearing and talking with an author. Libraries can also purchase or loan extra copies of the book to supplement the school library. The librarian who has ongoing relationships with high school teachers can be a powerful resource.

Along with libraries and schools, independent bookstores help knit communities together and nurture a reading culture. They know what new authors or topics will be hot, when authors are coming out with a new title, and who is willing to offer a reading or craft talk. Gloria Tiller, owner of Kazoo Books, tells me that she just wants people to read. She feels that a community of readers understand more of the world, whether they read a book featuring food from Provence or a novel about a young woman experiencing the lush beauty and harsh lessons of the Kalamazoo River. Similarly, Joanna Parzakonis aims to heighten a reading culture and the joy of reading. According to the website of her stores Bookbug and This Is a Bookstore, and evidenced by their many author readings, their mission centers on "lifting the voices and art of those especially who experience cultural and economic marginalization." Dean Margaret Hauck, owner of Michigan News Agency, is another huge promoter of reading local authors. She shared with me that her vision for the Kalamazoo community and Michigan News Agency is to encourage this community to become enlightened, diverse, and resilient. The partnership with her friends in Southwest Michigan and our outstanding local authors enables her and the Michigan News Agency to encourage local authors and readers and to bring the world to Kalamazoo.

Sometimes during those events, readers make unexpected connections with visiting authors. After a large public reading and talk featuring author Jeffrey Eugenides, a local teen told the story of being invited to a talk session with her teacher and a small group of teens after the presentation in the auditorium. During that discussion, she shared an observation about a chapter title. Eugenides responded that he had never noticed the coincidence she pointed out and that she was the first to bring it up. The student was thrilled, and this exchange helped her to realize that finding meaning in a work of literature is not a matter of right or wrong. By speaking with an author about his intent, she learned to embrace the idea that reading is a process filled with discovery and each reader's observations are valid.

Author visits not only nurture a reading community but also help foster empathy and develop curious and open minds. The most popular programs I've planned and implemented didn't have to do with audience numbers. More importantly, they revealed to the participants something about themselves and expanded the world they thought they knew.

Works Cited

Bishop, Rudine Sims. "Mirrors, Windows, and Sliding Glass Doors." *Perspectives*, vol. 6, no. 3, 1990, pp. ix–xi.

Cole, John Y. "One Book Projects Grow in Popularity." *Library of Congress Information Bulletin*, vol. 65, no. 1, 2006, www.loc.gov/loc/lcib/0601/cfb.html.

"Mission and Vision." This Is a Bookstore & Bookbug, www.bookbugkalamazoo.com/mission-vision.

Simpson, Erin J. "One City, One Book: Creating Conversation." *Books Make a Difference*, March/April 2013, booksmakeadifference.com/onecityonebook/.

Entering the Current

Connecting High School Readers with Once Upon a River

BECKY COOPER

We all know the signs: from the overt (heavy sighing, eye-rolling, audible grumbling) to the subtle (dwindling smiles, missing dead-lines, waiting for someone else to speak). The students let us know when we've lost them. "Will this be on the test?" When I hear this question, I know it may be time to try something else.

I teach for the Academically Talented Youth Program (ATYP) in the office of Pre-College Programming at Western Michigan University, which provides an advanced and accelerated experience for middle and high school students who exhibit as highly gifted in math and/or language arts. After taking the SAT or ACT exam offered through Northwestern University's Midwest Academic Talent Search, they are invited to join us through qualifying scores. The program draws from more than ten counties in Southwest Michigan and allows students to remain enrolled and connected with their local district—an adaptation inspired by similar initiatives at Johns Hopkins. One year of ATYP English serves as the equivalent of two years of honors English at a regular high school, and the students in our program prove highly motivated. The first two years require a portfolio of each student's writing to be submitted. Before revisions, they will write upwards of 200 pages for each class. In year three, they are invited to take our AP English course, where along with rigorous weekly writing responses, notebook writing, practice essays, and practice exams, they will sit for both AP Literature and Language exams in May.

This generation knows all about testing. It seems they are constantly prepping for tests both at their regular schools and for us—all the time.

Many of my colleagues share my concern about whether students are gaining a deep love for literature through our current educational models. They're motivated to pass the test—and while it's my job to guide them through two "high-stakes" exams, I'm motivated to teach them about what literature can do. It's easy to lose sight of the greater purpose of literature to connect with other human beings and understand or empathize better with their struggles, to engage with the author's opinions so they may craft more well-informed opinions of their own, to understand the cyclical nature of history and their position within their own current historical context. With this focus in mind, I assign a creative final project to inspire students to discover how they may experience an author's work in more meaningful ways that traditional exams simply cannot achieve—in ways that promise more of a lasting impact.

In our program, the student population does not yet reflect the full diversity of our community. We have students who tend to come from middle to higher socioeconomic backgrounds, who are generally white. We have students who come from Asian, Indian, and Middle Eastern families, but fewer from Indigenous, Latinx, or African American households. Only a handful of our students experience financial hardship. Our reading selections should broaden the context for students as they encounter a character whose life may be very different from their own—and while some students recognize aspects of their lives on the page, their classmates may be noticing the ways their particular privilege has discouraged them from expanding their worldview. For these students, limited experiences present a hurdle to connection. The stories we read together provide a bridge to begin relating to others, to build stronger bonds in the classroom, and to prepare them for greater involvement in the world today.

Bonnie Jo Campbell's *Once Upon a River* provides opportunities for us to discuss interstices of gender, violence, and class structure. This particular text also allows our students to contemplate a piece set very close to home. They know this landscape—Comstock and Kalamazoo are next-door neighbors, and the Kalamazoo River, the main stage for Margo's journey, flows through both communities. In an interview for *The Rumpus* in 2017, Catherine Eaton asks Campbell about writing "Nature" as a character. The author replies:

> I love investigating the natural world, and I find a lot of truths there, truths about survival and beauty.... Mostly the natural land-

scapes work as a sounding board for my characters, so they can understand themselves, and it acts as a mirror in which we readers see ourselves. The natural world is the place into which all my characters have to situate themselves in order to be who they really are, and that makes my rural fiction feel different from a lot of urban fiction . . . maybe nature also works as a metaphor for whatever emotional troubles my characters have to negotiate. I'm interested in my characters as survivors, and maybe that works best when the old-fashioned notion of humans surviving in wilderness is not too far away. ("The Rumpus Interview")

In my classroom, we wonder and discuss how some of us consciously or unconsciously judge protagonists who live in a more rural area as opposed to the city or suburbs. As one may imagine, this conversation provides an opportunity to explore the ways we may feel divorced from or connected to nature, as Campbell describes earlier, and to further unpack and examine how we may need to engage more deliberately in anti-classism.

As we begin reading about Margo and the ways her family navigates class divides, we reflect upon how this story occurring in the 1970s still invites us to notice attitudes and prejudices that persist today. While considering this specific concern with my students, I think about Paul Gorski's statement in his blog post "The Question of Class" for the Southern Poverty Law Center's Teaching Tolerance project (now called Learning for Justice):

> The question, of course, for any educator of privilege committed to educational equity is this: Do we choose to study supposed cultures or mindsets of poverty because doing so doesn't require an examination of our own class-based prejudices? By avoiding that question, we also avoid the messy, painful work of analyzing how classism pervades our classrooms and schools, never moving forward toward an authentic understanding of poverty, class and education.

I find this point essential to consider while working through any texts that address socioeconomic issues. Gorski's thoughts have helped me to frame and better understand what lies at the heart of *Once Upon a River*, as well as the work we undertake as educators. As students note how their experiences differ from Margo's, they observe that Margo knows infinitely more about survival than they do. They marvel at her ability to survive on her own on the river. They confess that they have little, if any, practical knowledge to equip them for such circumstances. It's humbling—and I notice a few students recalibrating some previously held opinions.

As we read on, I also notice how students grow to respect Margo's strength and appreciate her dedication to her singular purpose. During one class conversation, I ask them why the relationship with Michael doesn't work out—would he not provide a less chaotic life? Would he not support her in furthering her formal education? They say she is not interested in being controlled. Michael wants to fix her. And he comes across as paternalistic in their eyes. Even though he appears as a source for potential stability, one student tells me, "That would be a *no*." Here, they display their understanding of "benevolent" sexism and note that Margo is still on her quest to find her mother. They tell me that the quest is stronger than her feelings for Michael. At this point, I feel they are ready to start contemplating how they would like to approach their individual projects.

Inviting each student to choose a nontraditional approach such as poetry, sculpture, drawing, or painting to analyze Campbell's novel gives them multiple paths toward deeper reflection and allows them to feel more personally drawn to the material. According to secondary education instructors Nancy Bailey and Kristen Carroll, "Multimodal communication and representation, including film, written scripts, comic strips, music, and photography, encourage students to carefully select information from the research they want to communicate and to analyze it in ways that they may not if they are merely reporting it in a traditional format" (82). Allowing students to direct their exploration in ways that encourage more complex thinking guarantees not only sustained interest but also a richer understanding of the multiple meanings a text may reveal to them through a nonlinear approach.

Sounding the Depths

On a nuts-and-bolts level, we all use these strategies in our classrooms: pair/share writings, small group projects, and large group discussions. *Once Upon a River* lands at the end of the year for us, so students feel comfortable with all of these activities. And because we have discussed different literary lenses (historical, Marxist, feminist, postcolonialist, gender/queer, psychoanalytical, and critical race theory, to name a few), they find themselves better able to situate the concerns of main characters like Margo. They have the language to begin their critical analysis.

After we've had those weighty, authentic discussions using the literary lenses mentioned earlier, I tell the students that we won't be writing another essay for this novel. Sometimes this announcement is met with cheers, and sometimes they shoot dubious looks my way; no matter the initial response, I talk transparently about *why*. We spend most of our year in the practice of writing essays to earn a certain score on an exam. This time, taking cues from forward-thinking teachers, I share with the class that they will have more freedom to connect with the text on a personally significant level. Celebrated educator Tom Romano states in his influential book *Blending Genre, Altering Style: Writing Multigenre Papers*:

> I revel in seeing human minds at work. There is not right or wrong about this. It is simply remarkable to see people making meaning, regardless of their age and the meaning they make. We teachers—if we are paying attention to those whom we teach and expecting more of them than rudimentary thinking and memorization—see this common miracle of sense making all the time . . . the most significant learning comes when students launch their own dive and teach the teacher. (172)

Romano conveys the joy of the endeavor at hand. And I am reminded to share with the individuals in our classroom that they possess knowledge, experience, ability, and insight that will not only benefit their peers but their instructor as well. I let them know I'm excited to see their growth and anticipating how I will grow along with them. Our project invites all of us to move from the abstract to the concrete, from the monotony of test-taking to an expansion of empathy.

We read over the parameters together, and then I provide time for questions and clarifications. The prompt reads as follows:

> *First*: After contemplation of Campbell's novel, think about what resonated with you the most. What elements or scenes continue to occupy your imagination? What do you want to comment upon, explore further, or investigate more deeply?

Next: Choose an artistic medium that you enjoy. Craft an artistic response to Campbell's novel using the medium of your choice: painting, photography, film, poetry, sculpture, collage, music, etc. If your project gets more complicated than usual for one person (such as a short film) and you wish to have *one* partner, consult with me and it's likely you will get the green light!

Last: Write a couple of paragraphs explaining your project to the reader—point out the specific ways you feel you have successfully captured the element of Campbell's work you sought to respond to. You will be graded upon completion and presentation during our last day of class.

Some students feel elated by the options before them, while others seem to prefer the safety net of a more structured and traditional assignment. It's important to let them know that we are not judging the art itself; we are evaluating their level of effort and engagement. For emphasis, I might show them the limits of my own drawing skills on the board, encouraging their laughter: "Maybe this isn't the medium for me. I'll find something that would allow me to better express myself." I also write this question on the board: "Do we have to present our work?" The answer: "Yes. Each of us will gain from what you share. *You* will grow from investing yourself in your project and allowing us to see how this novel has made an impact on you." I tell them that taking chances may feel scary at first, but ultimately, they will feel excited. To illustrate and inspire, I might show them a few examples from previous students.

At this point, I emphasize how this project can provide a way for us to show our empathy, to be vulnerable, and to feel heard, but we will need to create an atmosphere in our room that makes people feel safe to explore difficult subjects. As we follow Margo's journey through multiple traumas and her quest to find her mother, students connect with her plight while contemplating the extremity of her situation. Because of the sensitivity of the material, some instructors may feel that providing a trigger warning is appropriate, especially for high-school-aged students. Prior to reading the novel, our class discusses the concept of trigger warnings and the debate over whether or not they prove useful. I find that students appreciate the invitation to address this issue in a scholarly way, which enables them to delve into a more in-depth debate as they feel less fear of judgment from their peers. Sometimes the structure of an academic dialogue, with its understood norms, provides a sense of security as we approach topics that may cause discomfort in some students.

To begin, I share some relatively recent findings. In *Scholarship of Teaching and Learning in Psychology*, Guy Boysen explores the research on trauma as it applies to the topic of trigger warnings actually helping students in psychology courses. He invites teachers to consider the following observation:

> The decision to give or not give trigger warnings in class represents a pedagogical choice that can be informed by research evidence. Clinical research supports the basic phenomenon of trauma-based triggers of distress, and students with documented PTSD diagnoses could request trigger warnings as an accommodation for a disability. With such an accommodation, students may be able to reduce distress and increase performance by controlling exposure and arousal. These points are well grounded in empirical research. (171)

Boysen's article offers a thorough examination of the kinds of questions teachers in any field should investigate concerning trauma, supported by research, before making their decision. Benjamin Bellet, Payton Jones, and Richard McNally expand upon the conversation, adding this caution: "The question of whether trigger warnings are beneficial or harmful for trauma survivors is an important one. However, because trigger warnings are now applied to a broad range of content in many different settings, another important question is whether they foster attitudes that undermine resilience in people who have not—or not yet—experienced trauma" (135). The arguments against trigger warnings include the concern that students may view themselves as more vulnerable than they are, and that this perception will hinder their classroom participation and lead toward censorship. Bellet et al. conclude that trigger warnings may not serve the purpose of generating resilience and, in fact, may actively increase anxiety for some students.

Our class examines the dialogue that emerges between these articles' findings as applied to a broader range of the population, and we note how both studies agree that more research is needed. Taking both articles into consideration, I ask students to share their thoughts. From this conversation, we strive to build a consensus about how we prefer to move forward and deal with some of the topics that Campbell's novel explores that students may not have discussed in a public space before: issues of socioeconomic class, molestation, rape, death of a parent, abandonment, sexual autonomy, revenge, gun violence . . . to name a few. By approaching concerns via the debate on trigger warnings and our subsequent community-building, I've noticed that students respond intellectually, personally, and emotionally. We relate to one another as *people*.

I recently asked former students to share with me their thoughts about our process in order to gauge how accurately I have been evaluating their sense of security and freedom while exploring *Once Upon a River*. One student reports:

> English was a safe space for me, where an openly collaborative and creative environment was encouraged and nurtured. Discussions about works being explored in class were commonplace, and with each conversation, Ms. Cooper took these ideas and brought them to life. This helped us understand complex topics such as the American Dream in present-day society and guided us through the process of analyzing them through a personal lens. Her class has had a truly profound impact on me, and with each step of the way, I felt supported and valued.

Another young man writes:

> I feel there were several things that went a long way to make the class feel like a safe environment. Reading the book at the end of the year allowed the class to develop a positive culture where students felt comfortable enough to discuss the sensitive content of the novel. Ms. Cooper's upfront addressing of the subject matter profoundly helped to facilitate discussion. By providing content warnings prior to assigning the reading, she demonstrated a considerate attitude and circumvented an issue of the class sitting silently, with no student wanting to be the first to broach a topic. Finally, the use of an artistic final project rather than a purely academic one set a focus on the human aspect of the novel and magnified my engagement with the reading. Writing a paper would have invited me to focus on a piece of symbolism while ignoring the broader issues Campbell highlights in the story.

And last, this young woman shares her thoughts on the experience, as a person who has been through trauma like Margo's:

> I loved reading that book so much. I went through a sexual assault issue when I was younger and parts of that book made me emotional when we talked in class, but the support I felt from you and my classmates made it feel good to talk about. I felt like I was being actually listened to. As a class we created an area where everyone was able to be heard without judgement and I haven't experienced anything that felt the same since.

Reading the Water

By encouraging students' creativity alongside critical exploration, I noticed sustained interest and much greater appreciation of the literature. Their written self-reflections articulate what they wished to explore, and whether they feel they were successful. When students present their work to their classmates, they invite one another to see what matters to them. It's thrilling to witness how thoughtfully students throw themselves into this entire process—and how receptive they are to one another's experiences.

In what follows are several student examples. The first is a student response, followed by her poem:

> I wrote a poem about Margo and my interpretation of her story. It discusses the contrasting ideas outlined above, for as I read the story, Margo became an enigma to me. Despite the trauma she has faced, she does what she must do to survive, even though this only damages her further at times. Margo inspires me and reminds me of myself and I hoped to communicate this feeling through my poem.

> Margo
> sweet, bruised fruit
> forbidden
> from leaving the river
> she hangs delicately
> over the water
> or does she crouch?

balanced, ready to
pounce?
a young enigma
I see myself in her
as she sees her green eyes
in the face of a
familiar current
fearless fire doused
by cruel men
she bites back
harder
until she breaks
the bonds of reckless
control
she rests her soft chin
on the gate, a golden
barrier, gleaming, let her
into the clean air and
the dry earth
let her live like me

One young person revealed that he was not a good ally to a friend when she needed him. He states in his reflection how the poem he wrote responds to incidents he witnessed at school involving the sexual harassment his friend experienced. He did not speak up in her defense, and he felt guilty for not standing up for her, for fear of becoming a target as well. It was clear that reading about the many ways Margo suffered from the toxic elements of her community helped this student to recognize the damage that was being inflicted upon the lives of the people he was close to; he found himself better able to identify such elements as unacceptable; and he could examine his own complicity. It seemed as though the rest of the class appreciated his candor.

Another student interviewed several friends to discover that not only had they all experienced sexual harassment, but many had also experienced it *that day*. At school. He explained how this made him keenly aware of how differently he moves through the world than his friends do. One shared concerns about navigating sexual autonomy, and another spoke about privilege and consent. The young woman who shared that she had been abused sang to us. Her voice brought the entire room to tears in gratitude and respect for her strength.

One student shared her thoughts on an encounter Margo has with one of the deer in the novel. She writes: "The reflection of Margo in the animal's eye portrays the connection the young girl feels to female deer. She shares an identity of vulnerability with the creature, which translates through the eye of the animal."

Some students spent their time imagining what it was like to be Margo: What would she choose to wear? What would a map of her surroundings look like? With this idea in mind, one student reflects:

> I sought to understand the specific geographic location of Campbell's project, seeing as [it] played a significant role in shaping the story. Thus, I began by evaluating which parts of Campbell's Stark River were fictional and which portions are based off a real river.

Reflection of Margo in a deer's eye (student art, pencil), by Eva Bugnaski

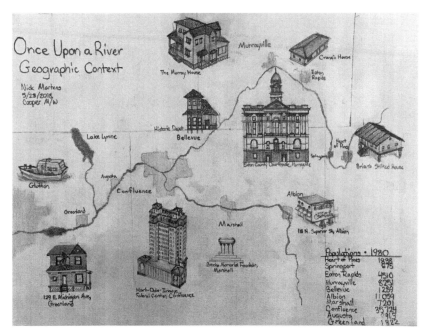

Once Upon a River Geographic Context (student art, pencil), by Nick Martens

If Margo danced, how would she move? Using her own body to express how she imagines Margo might feel, this student had a partner film her while dancing in the woods:

> As the person in the pictures, I tried to embody Margo and present her innermost thoughts through poses that relay to the audience not only her struggles and emotional turmoil, but also her strength in being able to overcome tragedy. Although Margo does not recognize herself as valuable beyond her physical properties, her mindset and the way in which she perceives herself changes throughout her journey, and my partner and I used the photographs to illustrate this progression.

Unusual choices such as painting the novel's cover art onto a jacket or applying tarot cards to Margo's journey surprised me. The films students made were lovely and thoughtful, as one student demonstrates through her writing:

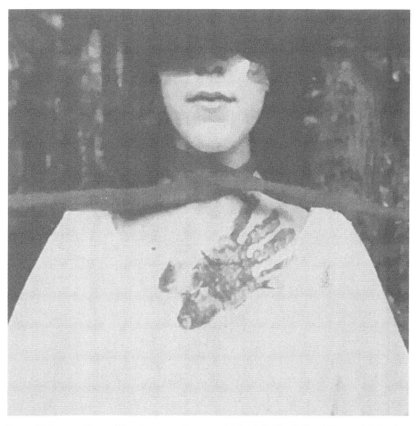

Bust of Margo with scarf (student art, photograph), by Julia Rudlaf and Emma Michaels

Wading up and down the cool stream with pants pulled above our knees, Campbell's character came alive in a way text on a page cannot fully capture. Like Margo, we watched birds dive into the water, fish swim off the banks, and even a doe leap up the riverbank. . . . Discussing *Once Upon a River* while out in the Michigan woods during our project resulted in both a film and a better understanding of the inspiration behind the novel and reasons Campbell writes passionately about the river.

Several students tried their hand at watercolor, with impressive results. The following student, who made an entire journal, states:

Margo dancing (student art, photograph), by Julia Rudlaf and
Emma Michaels

These faces are all rough ideas of characters within the book. In close
proximity, with a general layering of watercolors, I believe they display the layers of different sexual experiences and assaults Margo
has been through and the journey she has made as a person.

It might be easy to forget that, along with our students, we educators
also benefit from this period of growth. With every tough question asked,
I consider my own answers, observations, and paradigm. Since starting
this project in 2015, I have noticed that my students tend to reflect and
respond along traditional gender lines—more than I thought they might.
Many of the young women relate to the harassment and assault Margo
goes through, while most of the young men feel shocked by the ubiquity

Journal of Margo's journey (student art, watercolor and ink), by Hanna Glass-Chapman

of their experiences. I anticipate a day when this will be different. Simply based on the power of their connections, their testimonies, and their growing empathy, I feel hopeful. Every spring I look forward to this time, just to see what each new group will reveal about themselves—about all of our lives together.

Bringing the Craft Home

Creating a space in our classrooms that invites challenging discussions while encouraging compassion requires intentionality. We have the opportunity to show our students that becoming aware of our implicit biases and then examining them allows us to grow. For students who have experienced being "othered," finding representation in the text empowers them. Even for those already doing this work, seeking out training in this area helps our staff to avoid blunders and missteps. For example, our staff have taken advantage of anti-racism workshops and other programs offered by ERACCE: Eliminating Racism and Creating/Celebrating Equity. The Arcus Center for Social Justice Leadership at Kalamazoo College hosts similar workshops and events. Many groups provide information, resources, and support to people in the community seeking to educate themselves. There may be organizations in your area that offer similar opportunities. Over the course of the school year, our reading list strives to provide the basis for a greater awareness and understanding of the authors' projects and our own, real-world connections. But first we have to show them how to dive in.

I remind myself to model, coach, listen, and then listen some more. When seeking the resources and guidance of our university's office of diversity and inclusion, we show them we care and use their help—through coalition. This is how educators can model for our students on a real-world level. By doing so, we will be able to better provide a space for students to work out what they see happening in the text and how it relates to concerns we see in the world around us. Emphasizing the importance of building real relationships and noting real-world relevance remains essential.

Students want to make a difference, and they value the ways we help them to kindle their fire. We can assist them by looking for chances to be more involved. One such opportunity presented itself in the fall of 2020, when our class was invited to tour a traveling art exhibit, "Black Refractions: Highlights from The Studio Museum in Harlem" at the Kalamazoo Art Institute, one of the few fortunate places where the show appeared. Brent Harris, a Kalamazoo artist featured in the accompanying local exhibit, agreed to take us on a personalized exploration, complete with guided questions and considerable discussion. The students expressed a deep appreciation for this opportunity and for Harris's work. I asked them to create a poem or reflection based on one of the art pieces that affected them the most in order to collect and send their responses to the artist as a thank-you—so he could see the level at which the students were listening and absorbing what he had to say in conjunction with the impact of the art itself.

This kind of collaboration allows students to directly connect with artists, to learn from the people who make meaning of life through their art while they demonstrate to the artist how their work impacts their audience. After the visit, one student wrote:

> If Mr. Harris hadn't led our tour and told us about the different pieces, but especially his, I wouldn't have enjoyed the experience as much. I left the exhibit feeling smarter just by hearing the ideas from my classmates and the guide. This whole encounter was very enriching, enjoyable, and impressive.

Many students echoed this sentiment and thought more about representation in art, expressing interest in future opportunities to connect with local artists and activists. In light of this successful venture, I felt energized to seek even more ways for students to move toward the world outside of the classroom. Because I had been using Campbell's novel to initiate greater community connections for the past several years, I'd begun seeking and discovering the many potential workshops and coalitions Kalamazoo has to offer; this collaboration with Brent Harris and the Kalamazoo Art Institute serves as a recent example of how multigenre projects inspire students to write personal reflections that will provide a meaningful mirror of their growth as human beings.

When possible, by selecting a local author like Bonnie Jo Campbell, educators can start the work closer to home. The next time my class reads *Once Upon a River*, I will ask them to consider ways they might take what they learn out into our community. This may include engaging with local literacy groups; attending reading series provided by local universities, community colleges, and public libraries; or researching opportunities for community activism. For example, Campbell's novel, as a work that centers nature, allows us to discuss the condition of the Kalamazoo River and the history of its pollution. Even though my students are still in high school, they will find that their voices and efforts have power. They can research local environmental care efforts, such as the Kalamazoo River Watershed Council, and then direct their energies toward whatever level of civic involvement proves possible for them. After personally connecting with the text, they are excited to move outward, to engage with the greater human current.

The multigenre approach is not a new idea—many of us use it to some degree with various texts in our classes. But this approach proves especially rewarding to use with *Once Upon a River* because the novel covers such intense issues that students find themselves more likely to delve profoundly into their projects. They have more space to experiment, to discover, and then, they are more apt to share authentically of themselves and what they have learned from Margo's journey. Allowing them autonomy through the selection of their medium and content with an emphasis upon personal connection, we allow their learning to become more meaningful to them. If we can create ways for students to connect more deeply with their communities, we will set them on a lifelong path of civic involvement. Every year I ask my students if I should keep Campbell's novel on the syllabus. Overwhelmingly, they answer, "Yes."

Works Cited

Bailey, Nancy M., and Kristen M. Carroll. "Motivating Students' Research Skills and Interests through a Multimodal, Multigenre Research Project." *English Journal*, vol. 99, no. 6, 2010, pp. 78–85.

Bellet, Benjamin W., et al. "Trigger Warning: Empirical Evidence Ahead." *Journal of Behavior Therapy and Experimental Psychiatry*, vol. 61, 2018, pp. 134–41.

Boysen, Guy A. "Evidence-Based Answers to Questions about Trigger Warnings for Clinically-Based Distress: A Review for Teachers." *Scholarship of Teaching and Learning in Psychology*, vol. 3, no. 2, 2017, pp. 163–77.

Campbell, Bonnie Jo. *Once Upon a River*. Norton, 2011.

———. "The Rumpus Interview with Bonnie Jo Campbell." Interview by Catherine Eaton. *The Rumpus*, 17 Mar. 2017, https://therumpus .net/2017/03/the-rumpus-interview-with-bonnie-jo-campbell/.

Gorski, Paul. "The Question of Class." *Teaching Tolerance*, no. 31, Spring 2007, https://www.tolerance.org/magazine/spring-2007/the-ques tion-of-class.

Romano, Tom. *Blending Genre, Altering Style: Writing Multigenre Papers*. Boynton/Cook, 2000.

Fiction Friction

Teaching Chronic and Acute Conflict in
Bonnie Jo Campbell's Short Fiction

RS DEEREN

In May 1997, McComb Elementary School in Caro, Michigan, hosted its annual Young Author's Day: the culminating celebration of student brainstorming, writing, and illustrating. I was eight years old and had written a story entitled "The Dragon Slayer." It was eighteen sentences long. Set in a forest, the story follows a boy fleeing a two-headed dragon. Along the way, he runs into an old man and then a girl who, upon learning why the boy is running, flee with him. The trio run and run until they encounter a knight in shining armor who, instead of running, "went to the dragon and took his sword and slayed the dragon. The End." The story won that year's "McCombacott Award"—our version of the Caldecott Medal—for illustration. It did not place in the best storytelling category, the pun name of which I no longer remember.

There are some aspects to "The Dragon Slayer" that, in terms of conflict, work: there is a clear threat in the form of a two-headed dragon; that threat is immediate and present throughout the story; and, finally, the knight is the means used to resolve the conflict by eliminating the threat. The list of story elements that don't work so well, or are completely absent, is much longer. Of interest, however, is the ending: the knight slays the dragon. The End. Stripped down to bare elements of conflict—good vs. evil; us vs. them—eight-year-old me showed some working knowledge. There was a clear, acute conflict here: characters faced an issue they needed to overcome, and they overcame it.[1] However, once the dragon was slain, there was nothing for the trio to run from, nothing for the knight to slay, nothing to continue the story, and nothing left for readers to mull over. The story lacked chronic conflict. That is, the story lacked both complex issues that contextualize a character's in/ability to navigate acute conflict, and issues that influence how readers engage with this navigation.[2] The shape of "The Dragon Slayer" is a straight line from the dragon (evil) to the knight (good). The acute conflict is that straight line: "Go Do X," with "X" being "Slay the Dragon." How is the dragon slain? By finding a knight in shining armor. Writers need acute conflict because it gives the characters something to do and keeps the story moving forward. At the same time, readers desire acute conflict because seeing the characters doing something in a scene captures their attention and keeps them reading to find out *if* and *how* the characters triumph.

On the other hand, chronic conflicts are the detours, roadblocks, and parameters that complicate the straight line for the characters as well as the world of the story. Examples of this could be: What if the old man limped, or the dragon was the last of its kind? How would these long-standing issues impact the story, making overcoming the acute conflict more challenging or complicated? Writers need chronic conflict because it allows them to draft insightful stories with complex characters juggling numerous issues. This benefits readers who look for whether the characters *can* or *should* triumph, over both the immediate acute and lingering chronic conflicts. Writers rub acute and chronic conflicts against each other, causing friction that raises the stakes for characters and the tension for readers, creating endings that keep readers engaged long after the final sentence.[3]

For beginning creative writers looking to study the uses of conflict as a tool for both plot progression and character development, Bonnie Jo Campbell's short fiction exemplifies the friction between acute and chronic conflicts. In *American Salvage* (2009) and *Mothers, Tell Your Daughters* (2015), Campbell's characters face an array of acute conflicts while simultaneously dealing with chronic conflicts. In "The Trespasser," the opening story of *American Salvage*, acute conflict is immediately present: someone has broken into a family's cottage; there is fire damage and garbage everywhere. A disastrous mess, but nothing that can't be repaired or replaced. A girl slips through the back door unnoticed. She must escape before she's discovered, and she does. The End. Left at just this, there isn't much story. However, along with acute conflict, there is chronic conflict to rub against it. The tinfoil, Sudafed packages, and destroyed stove depict a methamphetamine lab. The family, along with readers, sees the graphic impact of two major chronic conflicts, addiction and poverty, as they journey throughout the cottage. Likewise, in "Sleepover," the opening piece in *Mothers, Tell Your Daughters*, readers witness more characters slipping through the back door. Here, two teenage boys make out with two girls. When the sisters' mother comes home, the boys flee. Again, a straight line: flee from danger. The End. Before the boys escape, though, one of them divulges the boys' fantasy of "the perfect girl": a combination of the narrator's head and her sister's body (13). Here, the misogyny becomes the chronic conflict that can influence how readers interpret the story.

In terms of reading for craft, using chronic conflict to contextualize acute conflict allows creative-writing students to engage with narrative endings on a level beyond "Slay the dragon. The End." In "The Trespasser," the daughter has nightmares. After seeing the destruction in the cottage, especially the bloodstained mattress, she sees herself on that mattress, the blood her own (*American Salvage* 4). In "Sleepover," the sisters watch *Frankenstein*, the boys' "perfect girl" remark still fresh as the sisters witness "the men band together to kill the monster" (*Mothers* 14). In *Craft in the Real World*, Matthew Salesses states that "fiction does not exist in a vacuum," and characters have "context" assigned to them by real-world aspects such as race, class, gender, etc. (59). Identifying this real-world context while reading will help beginning creative writers understand how chronic conflict complicates an ending. Now, instead of a story about a clandestine romance, "Sleepover" becomes a tug of war between the boys' objectifying fantasy and the narrator initially taking this fantasy as a compliment. Furthermore, the boys say something harmful but make a successful escape from any repercussions. With both story endings, a major question is: "will the characters overcome X?" The acute conflict answers this question: yes. With the presence of the chronic conflict, however, readers have many questions: What does it mean for the girls to watch *Frankenstein* after being told about the boys' fantasy? What lasting impact does the bloodstained mattress have on the daughter in "The Trespasser?" How will this impact the characters? Who learns what, if anything?

In this chapter, I show how chronic conflict has dual roles in fiction: complicating the previously established acute conflicts, and developing more dynamic and intriguing characters. Rather than simply complicating one acute conflict, scenes in Campbell's stories allow for multiple conflicts to rub against each other. Furthermore, these conflicts have varying levels of urgency, resulting in some acute conflicts being more pressing and others needing more effort to navigate. By using pre-reading questions in my classes, I prime new creative writers to read with attention to craft. With post-reading exercises, I offer writers a chance to draft, and then complicate, different types of conflict.

The "What" of Story: Acute Conflict and Characters in Action

Here is an idea: a story about marriage. Consider Campbell's "Bringing Belle Home," a story about buff Thomssen and wan Belle, both addicts, both trying to balance their own traumas against the long, troubled history they have with each other. After weeks of estrangement, they run into each other at a bar. They get mad—and physical—until someone calls the police. Now let's ruin it. A story about marriage: Spouses talk to each other. We learn they fight often. The husband wants one thing; the wife doesn't. They talk about the good times and argue about the bad. Then, she shares some new information. Now they have something new to discuss. They talk and talk, maybe yell, until . . . they talk about something new. Throughout this talking, the writer neglects setting, characterization, scene, etc. We have nothing but placeholders, existing nowhere, talking about an idea. The story was left behind in favor of an idea: what is marriage? Heather Sellers has a word on ideas—namely, they "can potentially be bad for writers" (Sellers 154). Many times, new students of creative writing have great ideas, but lack practice in identifying, and thus engaging with, craft elements. As such, their stories become talking-heads drafts that revolve around the idea the writer wants to convey while other narrative elements go by the wayside. As Sellers states, the idea is "dead on arrival" because the draft grew out of thought, not imagery (155).

I help students see that stories are more than ideas by highlighting conflict in scene. A place to start is seeing, even listing, what characters are doing in scene. Whether it is a dragon, a break-in at a family cottage, or a girl's make-out partner trying to escape her mother, acute conflict is the tangible problem characters face within the confines of the story; it is the "What" of fiction. To avoid meaningless back-and-forth, Benjamin Percy states, bluntly, in *Thrill Me: Essays on Fiction*, "if you must have a protracted verbal exchange, then, damn it, give your characters something to do" (24). Like Sellers's call for imagery, when characters do something, somewhere, other than talk, readers are engaged and more likely to read on.

In "Playhouse," the protagonist, Janie, visits her brother after a three-week absence. She's been nauseous this whole time and hopes her brother, Steve, might know why. Janie doesn't remember much from her previous visit: there was a party, the two fought, and she drank heavily. When I teach this story, I ask students to list information that may imply something is off from Janie's normal day-to-day. This listing primes student readers to look for potential conflict. Janie initially faces two acute conflicts: she is sick, but she must confront Steve, with whom she's recently fought, to find out why (*Mothers* 15). In the house, Janie's stomach churns at the smell of bratwurst. She "wants to ask about food poisoning, but [doesn't] want to start on something negative," so she accepts a glass of wine hoping it will settle her stomach (17). In the navigation of acute conflicts, Janie chooses to avoid being negative with Steve despite her own health. This shows a hierarchy of conflict—what Percy calls "urgency." For Percy, a story has a "narrative goal" spanning from the first page to the last as the story's "higher-order goal" (21). These goals are the straight line of acute conflict: do the thing. For Janie, it is finding out why she is sick. However, stories are more than a straight line; they are not just a boy running from a dragon. Before a character can attend to their higher-order goal, and before they can overcome the main acute conflict, they must deal with more urgent conflict. Percy describes "lower-order goals" that drive individual scenes, benchmarks on the path to accomplishing higher-order goals (23). Janie puts her illness aside because avoiding a fight is more urgent. With the nausea, wine, and no resolution to their fight, the story presents another lower-order goal: Steve asks Janie to help him assemble a plastic playhouse for his daughter, Pinky. Janie agrees and, in doing so, she is injured when Steve drives a screw into her arm.

I also teach my students to look for road signs in the story that signal potential conflict. Students who can identify those signals—who are not simply reading for plot—have the opportunity to improve their own writing. In "Bringing Belle Home," Thomssen enters his regular bar and, initially, is glad his estranged wife, Belle, isn't around "to complicate things" (*American Salvage* 92). Students come to understand that this is a road sign signaling a forthcoming conflict. Now, instead of a story about a man at a bar, beginning creative writers can focus on what Campbell might do to "complicate things." Enter Belle—thin, sockless in winter, roots grown out, still married to Thomssen but flirting with the bartender. Thomssen watches Belle, thinking about their history: the violence she endured at the hands of her father; Thomssen's guilt for not saving her; their fraught marriage. This whole time, he's staring at her. She doesn't like this, letting him know by chucking an ashtray at him. This opens the door for Thomssen to reconnect with Belle, a lower-order goal, by offering her twenty dollars. He knows she needs the money. When she takes it, he grabs her wrist: "Let go," she says. "Talk to me," he replies (98). This physical altercation presents an urgent acute conflict for Belle: get free of Thomssen. She screams and bites him. The grab also highlights an acute conflict Thomssen faces on his path towards bringing Belle home: he wants her to talk to him, and he achieves this through coercion and force. Belle asks Thomssen what he wants, and he replies with his main acute conflict: "Please, Belle, come home with me" (99). The back half of the story shows the two positioning around this conflict. Belle tells him why they can't be happy together—addiction. Thomssen counters that they "need each other," "belong together," can change by loving each other enough (99–100).

With characters now established within the confines of acute conflict, I encourage students to focus on seeing how characters navigate said conflicts. This gives teachers an opportunity to show how conflict informs characterization. Percy calls the undertaking of a task a "metaphoric backdrop [to] enhance characterization," and describes the notion of "avoidance" in stretches of dialogue where characters avoid what they should be talking about (26). In "Playhouse," Steve tackles his work with blinders on. He screws the playhouse's roof down and when this injures Janie, Steve asks if the screw went through the roof but doesn't ask about his sister's arm. When the two reminisce about their childhood playhouse, Steve has fond memories, but Janie divulges that she warded off a sexual assault in the playhouse by squeezing the attacker's privates "until he howled," a solution Steve found funny, a notion Janie only "kind of" agrees with (*Mothers* 22). Rather than discuss Janie's sickness, their fight, or sexual assault, the siblings avoid heavy topics.

This avoidance is a choice, and I ask students what it tells them about Janie. Often, they respond that Janie has a history of adopting Steve's opinions instead of fighting with him, even when doing so erases her experiences or displaces her needs. In "Bringing Belle Home," Thomssen's initial acute conflict is to get Belle to talk to him as a first step to getting her to come home. Readers who focus on craft can look for how he goes about accomplishing this. As stated earlier, he knows Belle needs money, so he offers her twenty dollars to bait her over to his table (*American Salvage*

98). Knowing that she never tips bartenders, he still tells her to do so and says nothing as she pockets the change after buying herself a beer and him a double shot. It's a short moment, but my students begin to understand more about these two based on how they go about getting what they want. They learn that Belle needs Thomssen for financial support, but more importantly, they learn that Thomssen knows how to control and manipulate Belle.

Stripping these interactions down to their parts leaves Janie and Steve as fighting siblings and Belle and Thomssen as troubled spouses. Acute conflicts can be overcome, as they are merely tasks: assemble the playhouse, get the screw out of Janie's arm, make Belle talk to Thomssen, make Thomssen release Belle. Once these narrative chores are accomplished, the characters are free to tackle their main acute conflicts, but again, on their own, this won't make for a sustainable story: Janie wants to know why she is sick and eventually sees a doctor; Thomssen wants Belle to come home and he convinces her. The "What?" of these stories has been established, but for them to stand as dynamic stories with equally dynamic characters, they need to answer the "So What?" question; the means should complicate the ends for these characters, making them engaging for readers and helpful for creative-writing students. In short, these acute conflicts need to rub against chronic conflict.

The "So What" of a Story: Complication through Chronic Conflict

The previously mentioned stories, on acute conflict alone, could probably be told—like my second-grade story, "The Dragon Slayer"—in about eighteen sentences, but readers wouldn't get much satisfaction from them. The boy in "The Dragon Slayer" is a narrative placeholder, something for the dragon to chase and nothing more. Without chronic conflict, Janie, Steve, Belle, and Thomssen are placeholders too. Whether it is a long-standing issue that actively hinders a character, such as addiction or disability, or it is a set of circumstances that define the world the characters live in, like poverty or misogyny, chronic conflict influences how readers interpret the actions and choices of characters in their undertaking of the acute conflict. Secondly, chronic conflict presents more questions than answers. This elevates Campbell's readers from reading to see what happens next to reading as a mode of questioning, of asking "So what?" and applying answers learned from reading how the characters navigate both types of conflict. Janie doesn't want to fight with Steve, doesn't want to be a "drama queen" (*Mothers* 33). Why is she like this? As shown, it's keeping her from overcoming her acute conflict: finding out why she is sick. Belle is an addict, and Thomssen is a "mean fucking drunk" (*American Salvage* 99). How does knowing this about them elevate the already tense exchange where he clutches her wrist? Finally, what does this say about the world Campbell writes about?

In *The Practice of Creative Writing*, Heather Sellers describes how "layering" can raise tension in a draft. Her examples include layering images, relationships, and, like Percy, layering dialogue with action (237–40). To keep readers from growing "bored at best," Sellers shows that layering complicates what is happening on the page (238). Applying this to Campbell's work, when Janie walks past the pink peonies at the beginning of "Playhouse," it serves as vivid setting, though not much else. Layering this image with Janie learning that she was raped by those same flowers turns the image of peaceful color into something heinous (*Mothers* 32). Likewise, readers see Thomssen as a hulking figure, but this on its own is merely a characteristic. However, layered with how fragile Belle is, his heft becomes something violent and dangerous (*American Salvage* 98). Going beyond these types of layering, I offer layering types of conflict. Unlike levels of urgency Percy describes and the acute conflicts writers have characters juggle, the chronic conflict looms over the whole story. As a teaching tool, I use this framework: whereas the acute conflict exists in the confines of the story, the chronic conflict was in place before the story started and exists after the last line.

To help beginning creative writers identify chronic conflicts, I ask students to list issues facing characters that cannot be overcome within the confines of the story. Having students, on their own, think of chronic issues they face is helpful here as it primes them to think of how real-world issues inform reading and storytelling. Returning to "Playhouse," alcoholism and anger issues factor predominantly in the siblings' actions. Janie binge-drank at the party; she blacked out, and awoke under a cold shower back home. Since then, she's "been shaky" (*Mothers* 15). Two pages later, she's drinking a glass of wine, even though on hot days, she "prefers mixed drinks . . . or just a few shots" (17–18). Before she and Steve undertake assembling the playhouse, she "drains" her wine and puts the glass where Pinky can't reach it, noting Pinky drinks whatever she can reach (19). Meanwhile, Steve has spent the afternoon and evening drinking. His hands can't stop shaking, and when the drill bit goes into Janie's arm, he states he's too drunk to drive her to the hospital (21). Compounding this, readers learn that Steve needs Janie's help because his ex-wife refuses to be around him and power tools, citing his "inner rage" (18). With these issues now highlighted, my students explore how they impacted the lives of these characters before page one, and also investigate how they inform their actions on the page.

Remembering that the initial, urgent acute conflict of this scene is to assemble the playhouse, the table is set for both conflicts to rub. Janie questions Steve's use of power tools for this chore, but he insists, stating that he wants a secure roof for Pinky. Janie backs off, echoing earlier sentiments of not wanting to fight and be seen as a "drama queen," not wanting to trigger Steve's rage. The tension here rises when Steve drills into Janie's arm. She feels the vibrations throughout herself, worrying the bit has hit bone (20). Throughout this, Steve splits his attention between getting the job done and getting mad at the evening news. Meanwhile, Janie doesn't make any demands of her brother, despite the high urgency of the situation. She asks him multiple times to "back that screw out" rather than confront him directly (20). Once free from the screw, Janie clutches her arm while Steve admires a job well done. When he realizes what's happened, Janie asks if she should go to the hospital. Steve replies that if she does that, she'll "be paying that bill for years" (21). Janie reluctantly agrees, rather than press Steve, and the scene moves to him complaining that Janie should get her "damned GED" (24).

Why do Janie and Steve drink so much? What is the impact of Steve's "inner rage?" Why does the scene unfold like this? Chronic conflict sparks these types of questions, and, through them, the scene evolves beyond merely accomplishing a task. Sellers calls conflicts "cause-and-effect situations" that impact the "direction of the story" (87). This causality is more readily seen in acute conflicts: Janie is sick > Janie seeks advice from Steve > Steve injures Janie > Steve advises Janie against going to the hospital > Janie agrees. Still a straight line on its own. I apply this line to looming chronic conflicts as well to show students another type of causality, one primed with information on who these characters are *before* page one: Steve has inner rage and Janie has a history of adopting his opinions > Janie rarely questions Steve > Steve and Janie drink a lot > Steve injures Janie > Steve advises Janie against going to the hospital > Janie agrees. The scene, of course, ends the same way, but the lesson for students here is to show how chronic conflict offers lenses through which readers can question the unfolding action.

Another option is to make readers aware of chronic conflicts before action. This happens in the slow buildup of "Bringing Belle Home." The story introduces chronic conflict with Thomssen in the first paragraph. When he enters the bar, Thomssen tells readers that he "could resist coming here most days of the week" but rather than face an empty house, he "allowed himself a few hours" at the bar (*American Salvage* 92). The pull between "resist" and "allowed" is telling, especially since Thomssen's drinking is framed as a solution to loneliness. This concession and agreement with oneself about drinking is alcoholic behavior. After settling in his usual spot in the corner and watching Belle enter, readers learn the history between the two. Belle's father was dangerous and "every week or two he lost his temper and whaled on her" (94). Despite this, she bucked his authority and ran away. Twenty years later, she came back into Thomssen's life with rotted teeth, addicted to drugs (96). Now the story has two deeply, chronically conflicted characters, addicts, in a bar, and as stated in the previous section, their interactions have high tension from Belle's first line of dialogue.

So, what can beginning creative writers do with this information to become more craft-focused readers and, thus, grow as writers? According to Sellers, a combination of conflicts is what makes up a scene (87). She distills scene to three "essential ingredients": a ticking clock, an intriguing place, and "two or more characters involved with troubles" (88). "Bringing Belle Home" has addicts in a bar, self-medicating from decades of trauma, and though there isn't an obvious ticking clock in the opening scenes, there is a sense of urgency: Thomssen needs to talk to Belle; Belle doesn't want to talk to him, but she needs money, possibly to fuel her addiction. Framing "characters involved in troubles" with chronic conflict transforms a tense moment into one with contextual, emotional baggage attached to characters involved. When Thomssen grabs Belle's wrist, the layered image of their mismatched sizes already grabs readers. However, now that we know about Belle's abusive father, and about Thomssen's fantasies of beating the father, this moment is heightened. Here, I highlight how the acute conflict rubs against the chronic conflict, and students get to see Thomssen resolve one acute conflict—getting Belle to talk to him—but then question the way he does it, a questioning that arises from chronic conflict. Why would Thomssen think physical force would be a good idea?

He knows Belle's history. Why does Belle keep coming back to him? He has hurt her before.

Learning the circumstances influencing character actions and choices plays into the joy of discovery, one of many reasons people read. Utilizing chronic conflicts blurs the line between good vs. evil, dragon vs. knight. Sometimes, it dissolves that line completely, especially in Campbell's realist stories where life isn't black and white. Steve drinks a lot, which on its own doesn't make him a bad person, but it impacts his family. Pinky drinks whatever she can grab. Janie drinks a lot too, especially around Steve. Their drinking leads to injury and sexual violence for Janie. Thomssen wants to protect Belle, and that on its own is a noble enough goal. Belle lies and steals, and that on its own could make her a villain. However, their respective addictions, and even deeper, the causes of those addictions, bring into question their actions. Is Thomssen a good guy who means well and sometimes fails? Is he just like Belle's father? Is Belle a criminal, an addict, or a victim? These questions, like chronic conflicts, loom over the acute conflicts and exist after the final lines of the stories.

How Does It End? What Does It Mean?

Acute conflict is what happens in a story. Chronic conflict is what a story is "about." When considering the endings of drafts, beginning creative writers who have considered how chronic conflict informs and impedes acute conflict have satisfied their reader's desire to see characters not only in action externally but also internally reconciling who they are, the circumstances they live with, and the urgent matters that face them. Janie learns that her sickness isn't food poisoning, isn't morning sickness, and that her arm will heal, the acute conflict overcome with a trip to the hospital. Janie started the story wanting to avoid fighting with Steve, not wanting to be a "drama queen," and, once she sees the doctor, wants to say that everything leading up to that point has been her fault. However, she begins to question this last bit when she sees parallels between her life and Pinky's. Janie envisions the future Pinky might lead, which draws comparisons to the life Janie currently has. Janie projects as she wonders what is to become of "a girl who loves fun," of the deeper emotional hurt that she feels, and the blame she unjustly places on herself (*Mothers* 36). There is a high level of tension here because of these parallels that Janie is inches away from recognizing as one of her chronic conflicts. Will she see what readers see and stand up to Steve? After

Steve injures Janie and dissuades her from going to the hospital, he asks if it hurts. She says it doesn't (21). By ending the story with Janie stating, "I guess it really does hurt. Now that you mention it," the story achieves an ending that lingers beyond the last line due to the questions it brings up (36). Janie shows signs of recognition, but is she going to be able to overcome a life of capitulation? Can she navigate addiction and male rage in a patriarchal world? Those are the million-dollar questions.

Likewise, in "Bringing Belle Home," the story achieves a frantic ending with a dose of dramatic irony. With Thomssen's higher-order goal to bring Belle home complicated by a more urgent acute conflict—getting arrested—readers see that, in a sense, Thomssen has failed to overcome the main acute conflict: he won't be bringing Belle home. However, as the police lead him out of the bar, he yells instructions to Belle on how to break into his house, which is also hers. This shifts the onus of overcoming the acute conflict onto Belle who, thanks to Thomssen's instructions, has the means to do it. Having known her most of his life, Thomssen is certain Belle can make her way to and into the house, effectively overcoming the acute conflict. However, with the chronic conflict of addiction, the final paragraph complicates the action. Yes, Belle will get inside and keep herself warm with whatever is "within easy reach." She will smoke Thomssen's cigarettes curled up on his couch "like a member of a doomed species," taking the "easy comfort" that comes without too much work (*American Salvage* 106). She will not, however, address the issues that keep her vulnerable to harm: she will not plastic the window to "keep the snow and cold from rushing in after her" (106). With the final line, the chronic conflict brings up more questions than answers: Can Belle overcome her addiction? Can Thomssen? In the bar, Thomssen said he wanted them to be happy—what does that mean for two addicts?

Run, Slay, Both, Or Neither: Contextualizing Conflict

"The Dragon Slayer" sits on what I call my "Greatest Hits Bookshelf" along with *American Salvage, Mothers, Tell Your Daughters,* and various literary magazines I've published in. Part of this is, admittedly, nostalgia, but I feel it's important for writers to remember where they entered the writing world and what reading has helped inspire and shape their work. This also works as a metaphor for individual drafts. Beginning writers enter with an idea and maybe even a loose trajectory for a draft. However, if they stick with just an idea, they risk preaching to readers, at best. At worst, they may never find the ending to their draft. As writing teachers, we see students excited about their ideas and we hear students groan about reading lists. I tell students we aren't writers unless we are readers first. Reading Campbell's work with the intention of seeing how acute and chronic conflicts push plots and complicate characters is a good way to help students recognize practical writing choices they can use to turn their ideas into engaging drafts. Additionally, reading with intention, looking for where chronic conflicts contextualize acute conflicts can help students enhance their critiques for their fellow writers. If they want their boy to flee from the dragon, rock on, but once they begin to complicate the escape, they'll have a draft that engages their readers. Maybe the boy doesn't escape the dragon, or maybe he didn't need to run in the first place.

Notes

1. For my definition of "acute conflict," I draw from Benjamin Percy, who describes conflict as "obstacles" that impede a character's journey (28, 83, 97), and Heather Sellers, who defines conflict as "essential 'what happens' moments . . . with implications for the character" (86–87).
2. For my definition of "chronic conflict," I expand on Matthew Salesses's framing of conflict, which he argues "presents a worldview" based on the context of the character's race, gender, sexuality, ability, socioeconomic status, etc. My use of "chronic conflict" describes both the aspects of a character, such as being an addict, and the larger context in which a character lives, such as being a woman in a misogynistic society.
3. In contemporary western discourse, definitions of conflict focus on overt conflict arising when an external force directly opposes a character's internal "desire." Percy describes this opposition as tension-raising "obstacles in the way of that desire" (97), while Sellers describes it as "the blow-by-blow account" of narrative (86). For this chapter, I use the term "rub" as it relates to subtle friction. Rather than an overt, violent "blow" or clash between the internal and external, acute and chronic conflicts are constantly in contact, influencing character actions and informing readers of broader contexts beyond plot progression.

Works Cited

Campbell, Bonnie Jo. *American Salvage*. Wayne State UP, 2009.

———. *Mothers, Tell Your Daughters*. Norton, 2015.

Percy, Benjamin. *Thrill Me: Essays on Fiction*. Graywolf Press, 2016.

Salesses, Matthew. *Craft in the Real World: Rethinking Fiction Writing and Workshopping*. e-book, Catapult, 2021.

Schultz, John. *Writing from Start to Finish: The "Story Workshop" Basic Forms Rhetoric-Reader*. Boynton/Cook, 1988.

Sellers, Heather. *The Practice of Creative Writing: A Guide for Students*, 3rd ed. Bedford/St. Martin's, 2017.

The Expatriate Midwesterner

Teaching Bonnie Jo Campbell to Second Language Writing Students

DOUG SHELDON

When teaching Midwestern literature, one is obliged to do some myth-busting. The Midwest transcends flatness and corn, factories and office parks, white and male. When many of my students arrive, they have preconceived notions about what the Midwest is and is not. Movies from *Superman* to *Star Trek* portray the Midwest as a corn-fed and cow-bred center of American blandness. It is a place where Clark Kent and James T. Kirk must escape from, fleeing to big cities back east or, in the case of the latter, another planet entirely. The rise of for-profit recruiting programs embedded on university campuses has yielded another perspective that aids in Midwestern myth-busting: the temporary, international Midwesterner. These programs recruit learners from non-English-speaking nations with the goal of matriculating the student into a four-year collegiate program, mostly in the STEM fields. If these students do not meet minimum standardized test scores (e.g., TOEFL, IELTS), they start in sheltered English as a Second Language (ESL) coursework. Then they advance to the course at hand: the first of a two-tier First Year Writing (FYW) course aimed at genre production, essay essentials, and best practices for academic writing. In English Language Learner (ELL) composition classes at my institution, students complete four major writing projects over the course of a sixteen-week semester, including a writer's introduction, a rhetorical analysis, a multimodal rhetorical analysis, and a final reflective project. The project described in this essay is part of the multimodal rhetorical analysis, in which students view several types of text (short story, novel, graphic novel) in order to think critically and write essays in a second language, as well as to produce critical responses to multimodal texts as individuals and in groups.

One of my main goals for a composition course is to get students to discuss the role of place in their education. When they arrive, they have not been able to ask two essential questions: Why did I choose the Midwest? And am I now a Midwesterner, even if I will return home? The expat-Midwesterner has the unique position of balancing on a transnational fulcrum. On one end is their homeland, safe and secure, questions and answers only in their mother tongue. On the other end, the Midwest, vast and unknown, with English speedily demanding their attention. Why, then, choose Bonnie Jo Campbell's work, chiefly *Once Upon a River*, to teach to these students? Because much like Margo, who fled the now-eroded comforts of home, the international Midwesterner is on a river of their own, alone in a wash of faces and experiences that can confound and shock. Margo's journey to discovery is not unlike their own. Dangers lurk in a land they have never navigated solo, and sometimes those designated to protect them on said journey have neglected or abandoned them, or been relieved of that duty. As an ELL instructor and Midwestern scholar, I find myself obliged to provide texts to students that connect them with characters on similar journeys. While they will likely not face the same adversities as Campbell's characters, molding a classroom around interrogation of personal adversity steadies their legs a bit as they navigate the rapids of their new Midwestern life.

When working with international English speakers, recognizing the level of English usage in their home nation is of paramount importance. This usage diagram consists of three main circles:

1. Inner circle: Nations in which English is the predominant spoken and written language of communication by its citizenry, i.e., the United States, England, and Australia.
2. Outer circle: Nations in which English is used as a communication tool but is not a dominant communication force within the culture.
3. Expanding circle: Nations in which English is expanding to communities but is not a dominant linguistic force in the nation. (Adapted from Jenkins 12)

So what does this mean for FYW professors? Most students in international recruited programs are from the expanding circle and the outer circle of these language groups, so in teaching ELL composition, we must be mindful to give up-to-date English language usage. At the University of Illinois, Chicago (UIC), a large urban university where language diversity is an ever-expanding component of student populations, I encounter bilingual students who have been raised in the United States as well as international students who are coming directly from non-inner-circle nations, and these populations make up a larger proportion of our students. However, in the courses that I teach, students are recruited directly from nations that are predominantly within the outer and expanding circles of English language production. Students from these nations are classified as English language learners, and thus they require specialized assessment techniques and focused writing practice to apply their implicit knowledge of English writing, with explicit lessons on skills yet to be developed, as recommended by Rod Ellis.

Methodology and Pedagogy

The methodology applied to this type of course focuses on using "authentic text," meaning text written in English for an English-reading audience. The class operates on a sociocognitive approach to second language learning, which, according to Dwight Atkinson, views English as working both in the mind and in the world and implies that thought cannot be separated from action in second language production. Therefore, using English-language short stories, novels, and comics allows ELL students to view English in action, as it is produced and read by proficient users of the language. Bonnie Jo Campbell's work is highly effective in this process. Since many of these students have come specifically to the Midwest and have chosen to study among other local and transplant Midwesterners, Campbell's work provides authentic speech conversations and other language uses that could be encountered outside of the writing classroom. Her short story "Family Reunion" and its expanded version, the novel *Once Upon a River*, deliver students authentic Midwestern interactions and cultural identifiers. For the graphic-novel portion of the assignment, Monica Friedman's graphic interpretations of Campbell's work add a multimodality that eases linguistic comprehension of texts and the writing/revision process. Since the first five weeks of the course can be spent acclimating students to English composition essentials, such as summary, quotation/paraphrase, and essay elements, reading a novel like *Once Upon a River* can not only stabilize the craft of essay writing but also give time for group discussion about their own journeys of linguistic and cultural acclimation.

So, how can this stabilization process be achieved to reach international Midwesterners? What kinds of teaching perspectives are required? According to Ulla Conner and William Rozycki, a class designed for ELL students who have enrolled in other academic majors requires texts to act in an intercultural rhetorical context and stimulate writing skills that will move beyond the classroom setting. Furthermore, as Leora Freedman argues, working with trained close-reading contexts best supports the student retention of content. Implementing a sociocognitive perspective also allows for what Haydee Daguay-James and Ferdinand Bulusan describe as "written metacognition," in which teachers set goals for students to revisit their readings and annotations with projects that would best allow for linguistic and skill acquisition (28). The activities that follow adopt an instructor awareness of metacognition and reflection as essential to student retention of content. They also show how literature can model elaborative processes and stimulate rhetorical awareness of choice when it comes to comprehending process-based writing assignments.

In sum, these allow for the use of Midwestern literature of place to stabilize a cultural context for the international learner and provide a stable environment for student comprehension and absorption of methods. Campbell's texts illuminate gender, sexuality, economic, and civic realities of Midwestern culture, making it prime content for critical analysis to spur reading and writing. Looking to the character of Marylou/Margo (the character's name changes between "Family Reunion" and *Once Upon a River*) and her relationships with the men in her life—her caring, yet stern, father; her abusive uncle; the cadre of other characters whose apologisms allow for toxic relationships to fester under the surface of the placid-looking Midwestern landscape—encourage students to interrogate their own journeys as students and language learners. Who has protected them? Who has abandoned them? Who has prevented them or encouraged them on their travels down their rivers? Campbell's attunement to nature and Margo's voyage in *Once Upon a River* complement the international Midwesterner on their expressive path to navigate their collegiate career, and this can be measured in writing projects aimed at this goal.

Building from Text to Multimodality

We begin this unit by reading "Family Reunion," in which Marylou, a young rural Midwesterner, exacts revenge on an abusive family member. We then witness the evolution of Marylou into Margo in Campbell's novel *Once Upon a River*, where we get an expanded examination of family and its relation to landscape, abuse, and Midwesterness. And finally, we use a digital cartoon version of "Family Reunion" by Monica Friedman, who has illustrated the emasculation scene in comic-book-style panels. This multimodal conception, including the editing of text and the addition of other modes of enhancement, gives ELL readers a sociocognitive opportunity to use multiple mediums as tools for comprehension. The graphic panels ease the vacillation between first and second languages and aid the learner in expressing analytical conclusions.

This series of readings is accompanied with in-class reviews and discussions of major topics within the novel, which encompasses the first five or so weeks of the course and includes three required office-hour meetings with the me. The students form reading groups of three and sign up on a table posted to the Learning Management System (LMS) through Google Docs. During these meetings students must have their annotated texts and a laptop or phone to access blog posts. We hold these little reading groups to iron out any language and comprehension issues or clarify cultural misunderstandings of "Family Reunion" and *Once Upon a River*. The meetings usually last about 45 minutes and replace a lecture day. For the final meeting, students are given the following sections from Campbell's story and novel in combination with Friedman's cartoon.

Teaching second language learners requires me to be mindful of the complex thinking processes in which the learner will absorb textual content. Saying "it's harder" is obvious, but when one considers that the student is reading text in an additional language, processing its meaning in that additional language, then negotiating that meaning with their first-language mental processes, we can see that textual analysis forms a multi-tiered language system. To tackle these hurdles, I use a reading methodology that focuses on paragraph, to page, to chapter in a deductive method, which allows for the learner to reason with the text and establish a relationship to the content being analyzed (Ferris and Hedgcock 147). The text, ultimately, becomes a negotiable object. Assigning a short story or a maximum of two chapters from a novel at a time, I ask the students to provide a mini-summary (one to two sentences in length) of each paragraph (counting dialogue sections as paragraphs) in an LMS blog post, which will round out to about 500 words. They are assigned a daily partner who responds to that post in 150 words, finding at least three agreements and three disagreements to the original post. The original poster replies, defending their choices and giving a metacognitive approach to the comprehension of the text. In such assignments, students are encouraged to shift from summary into comprehension of theme/meaning/message and apply that skill to other assignments and even other classes (Nielsen 8). For the purposes of this unit, students examine how a text changes through expansion and the addition of multimodal concepts (modes: linguistic, aural, visual, spatial, gestural) can enhance or detract from our comprehension of a text. They are given a six-panel comic representation of Campbell's "Family Reunion" and a video lecture posted to the LMS titled "Multimodality, Comic Books, and Comprehension." In this lecture I define multimodality and describe how we will apply it to a reading project based on multiple modes of comprehension.

Multimodal Rhetorical Response

The multimodal rhetorical response/analysis is a comparative study where students examine versions of a text, in both traditional textual and multimodal forms, to produce a written response showing how different modalities alter, clarify, or uphold the communicative subjects within a reading. Students are given three "crossover" examples of texts from each of the versions of Campbell's work. While the scene is graphic in nature, it is not a horror show. Although this is the most direct translation from the short story to the novel, in that it depicts an act of emasculating revenge, students are advised of graphic violence but usually have little problem and have mentioned seeing far worse content in movies.

Comparative Textual Analysis

The project begins with a comparative analysis of the two versions from "Family Reunion" (FR) and *Once Upon a River* (OUAR). Items for this comparison include, but are not limited to, the following questions designed to help an ELL with language comparable to what they have already learned in this class or previous classes:

1. *Tense*: What does examining the differences in tense between FR and OUAR accomplish for an international reader?

Students discuss the length of the two works. The relatively short length of FR lends itself to being told in the present tense for a sense of immediacy or urgency, as we are experiencing the events with Marylou in real time. Whereas in OUAR, we are getting past tense, an immersion in a memory that reflects on past deeds. Recognizing these items is important for working with the paragraph-to-page analysis (Ferris and Hedgcock 147). I use these moments for students to do meta-reflection on their own writing processes and how they wish to communicate in assignments: as urgency or as memory (see précis project and meta-reflections). The meta-reflection focuses on the student's own past writing in the course. They can analyze the urgency reflected in their papers if they use the present or past tense. They relay information on what, depending on their intentions, would be most authentic to their prompts and subjects. Many times, students struggle with this. They feel as though they are not able to identify with the "expert writer" as an expat student. According to Stephen Krashen, there is an affective filter that can apply itself when a challenge is seen as insurmountable. However, allowing students to vocalize their ideas in small groups with me during office hours helps alleviate hesitation.

1. *Word/phrase choices*: Beyond tense, the revised sentences from OUAR contain many alterations from the original. For example:

"Marylou moves the tip of her rifle down to Cal's hand" (FR 83).

"Margo aimed the muzzle of her rifle down at Cal's hand" (OUAR 47).

Students examine and propose reasons, beyond tense, why Campbell may have made certain choices. Switching the verb phrase "moves the tip" to the verb "aimed" might be a signifier of Margo's preparedness and knowledge of hunting. Using the specific word for the specific action enhances our experience within this past-tense novel and allows for a rhetorical acceptance of Margo's abilities.

1. *Elaboration*: How can seeing elaborative edits in action aid in understanding paragraph use?

One of the most challenging conceits in any FYW course is getting students to elaborate on a concept. Using Campbell's edits between the story and the novel, we can study firsthand how to lengthen work without overwriting. Here are the texts side by side:

> The shout of her rifle is followed by a splash of blood on the shed wall and one last horseshoe clink from the pit. Cal's mouth is open in a scream, but in a pitch discernable only by hunting dogs. Marylou grasps the branch above with her free hand to keep herself from falling. The weight of the .22 in the other keeps her from floating up. She closes her eyes to lengthen that perfect terrible moment and hold off the next, when the air will fill with voices. (FR 83)

> The shout of her rifle was followed by a splash of Murray blood on the shed's white wall. She kept her arm steady though the shot, did not blink, and heard one last horseshoe clink from the pit. Cal's mouth was open in a scream, but it must have been a pitch discernable only by hunting dogs. Margo grasped the branch above with her free hand to steady herself. She gripped the rifle firmly in the other. She closed her eyes to lengthen that perfect and terrible moment and hold off the next, when the air would fill with voices. (OUAR 47–48)

Here is where I have students discuss the elaborative nature of adjectives and compound nouns. We then look at how Campbell elaborates the OUAR edit with "a splash of Murray blood on the shed's white wall." What appears simple is the addition of "white" to the shed wall in OUAR. Red blood would show most prominently on a wall that was white, as if Margo is leaving an epitaph to elaborate her crack-shot skill. Students discuss how the blood might be mistaken for something else on a wall of any other color, but on the white wall it would be unmistakable. Students learn how to use adjectives/adjectivals correctly and effectively in their writing. The more complex addition of compounding the noun from "blood" in FR to "Murray blood" in OUAR aids again in rhetorical specificity. Students discuss why Campbell would differentiate between the family to whom the blood belongs. Since Margo is a Crane, and Cal is a

Murray, they have some familial relation, yet it might be that Campbell wants us to see the blood as a symbol of their blood feud. A reader can interpret that Margo does not see herself as attached to that family and is, literally, severing a connective tissue. Close analysis aids in paragraph comprehension and allows students to see how subtle elaborative changes can aid readers rhetorically in understanding the writer's ethos, and can deliver written authority to the textual context.

Multimodal Analysis

Now that the students have completed a textual comparative analysis to the two versions of this scene, I add the multimodal presentation of the story by Monica Friedman. When I informally survey the students, often close to 75 percent of them have never read a comic book. Remediation on the reading of comics is a must so they know how to analyze this new kind of text. First, we review the modes for analysis and comic-book elements. In the Vox.com article "How to Read a Comic Book: Appreciating the Story behind the Art," Alex Abad-Santos includes a visual breakdown of how to read a comic book, defines key terms, and provides the following instructions:

> Comic books have a form and their own language to refer to that form. . . . Pages are meant to be read from left to right and in a "z-like" pattern—you read the rows as they're tiered and make your way down a page. Each page consists of panels—single illustrations, usually sequential, that tell the story. And the space that separates each panel is known as the gutter. . . . While stuff like the gutter and the size of a panel or what a panel's border or frame looks like might seem like tiny details, they're actually places where comic book artists are weaving in important concepts and making deliberate decisions.

To flesh out Friedman's multimodal adaptations of Campbell's most expressive and communicative passages, students use the terminology from Abad-Santos's article in communion with modalities defined by the University of Michigan's Digital Rhetoric Collaborative: linguistic, visual, aural, spatial, and gestural. The synthesis of comic-book terminology with these modes allows students to actualize intentions in a multimodal text and analyze the choices made by author(s) to represent rhetorical authenticity. Shoshana Folman and Ulla Connor suggest that this would allow the ELL learner to better comprehend the intercultural methodology of using Midwestern literature to rhetorically acculturate the second language culture into which they have matriculated. Explicit collaborative multicultural analysis, in combination with implicit skills used, provides multimodal comprehension of metacognition to be applied in larger rhetorical writing projects.

In the following figures, we see panels 2 and 9, respectively, from Monica Friedman's graphic adaptation of Campbell's writing. In this panel, the use of black frames presents a stark visual mode. Friedman adds a caged-in feeling, contrasted with the blank white space, which echoes Marylou's free feelings in the wilderness. The spatial placement of narrative text vs. dialogue moves the reader's eye quickly between time and space to elaborate the trauma that sets in from Cal's monstrous act. The combination of these items delivers a sense of isolation and preservation in combination with Campbell's creation of scene. We see how Marylou/Margo feels strung up like the trophy buck, a utilitarian object to be used and discarded.

In this panel, the overlapping visuals of the scope and the "target" in the panel put us in Marylou's mind; the white barn becomes part of the scenery, like a can placed on a fence in OUAR. The rhetorical choice to leave the actual shot out of the visual is a powerful way to end. We know he is losing that part of him, like he stole a part of Marylou, and Friedman choosing to leave it out is still a rhetorical, visual choice. This omission

Panel 2 from "Family Reunion," by Monica Friedman, 2017

She watches her uncle, drunk, peeing on the side of the shed where he raped her. Marylou is a dead shot. She never misses.

Panel 6 from "Family Reunion," by Monica Friedman, 2017

mirrors Campbell's use of silence and echo to engage the reader with Marylou/Margo and her act of revenge, ending her silence and taking her place as a hunter for survival.

With the rhetorical analysis charting and annotating complete, each three-person group produces a rhetorical précis, or summary of rhetorical elements, present in the reading of the three texts. While this is usually intended for a textual reading, I have altered it from its original form to fit the multimodal rhetorical analysis. A précis, according to Margaret Woodworth, will follow this form:

1. Name of author[s], [optional: a phrase describing author], genre and title of work, date in parentheses (additional publishing information in parentheses or note); a rhetorically accurate verb (such as "assert," "argue," "suggest," "imply," "claim," etc.); and a THAT clause containing the major assertion (thesis statement) of the work.
2. An explanation of how the author develops and/or supports the thesis, usually in chronological order.
3. A statement of the author's apparent purpose, followed by an "in order" phrase.
4. A description of the intended audience and/or the relationship the author establishes with the audience. (167)

However, for the purposes of teaching literary work to the ELL student, I have made certain amendments to make it a six-sentence paragraph, which includes these:

1a. What multimodal items were most prevalent in this work beyond text and how did they influence your reading *after* seeing the comic?
4a. What was most challenging about this reading unit, using three texts, and what steps would you take to improve your comprehension (based on our lesson documents)?

The précis measures several items a student would need in the first tier of the first-year writing course. First, it measures comprehension. Have they read the text and do they understand the contexts discussed throughout the class? Second, it measures their understanding of multimodality and the parts of a comic book. The use of modes and modal rhetoric to analyze texts can act as a checklist for inclusion in their own future writing projects. Third, it measures cross-textual rhetorical understanding. In this assignment, students are afforded the opportunity to move beyond simple comparative analysis and use different versions of text to adopt revision as a rhetorical act to elaborate argumentative analyses.

Conclusions and Pedagogical Implications

After implementing the preceding methods and textual analyses, I consider a few questions: Did I help "myth-bust" the Midwest? Did the implementation of multiple versions of a literary text aid the international Midwesterner and English language learner in the comprehension of their own metacognitive processes? Were the skills taught acquired though sociocognitive methods? While the answers to the questions will be individualized to the courses in which they were implemented, a general answer can be applied. In a sheltered ELL composition course (pedagogically speaking, "sheltered" refers to a course designed specifically for additional language learners), the revisions of written language provide metacognitive awareness of elaboration within their own paragraphs. The implementations of deductive paragraph analysis in combination with a review of students' past drafts encourages engagement with how writing shifts from draft one to the final submission. This can be done by assigning a reflective essay to be reviewed during a one-on-one or small group session where the student defends their choices and explains their own rhetorical processes (more elaboration practice). I can then bring Campbell's texts back to the discussion and ask the following questions:

1. How did the examination of the textual differences raise your awareness of elaborative edits?
2. How did you implement the rhetorical items listed in your précis activity when performing your revisions?
3. What will you use in future writing projects to achieve your rhetorical goals?

The ELL learner benefits greatly from the ability to articulate successes/frustrations with the learning process, as it can ease the multilingual negotiations taking place during their writing projects. This linguistic and rhetorical examination also applies a sense of sociocognitive awareness in that the instructional method is designed not only to move them beyond the formations of "clear" paragraphs but also to enhance the use of communicative language in their daily lives. Now that students have navigated through one set of obstacles, their writing becomes a vessel that carries them to the next series of readings and assignments. It is a referent, an addition to the legend on the map of their writing voyage, and, like Marylou/Margo, they might just learn something about the complex harshness and beauty of their world. And my hope is that they might also desire to read more literature of their adopted home region.

Works Cited

Abad-Santos, Alex. "How to Read a Comic Book: Appreciating the Story behind the Art." *Vox*, 25 Feb. 2015, www.vox.com/2015/2/25/8101837/ody-c-comic-book-panels.

Atkinson, Dwight. "A Sociocognitive Approach to Second Language Acquisition: How Mind, Body, and World Work Together in Learning Additional Languages." *Alternative Approaches to Second Language Acquisition*. Routledge, 2011, pp. 143–66.

Campbell, Bonnie Jo. "Family Reunion." *American Salvage*. Wayne State UP, 2009, pp. 73–83.

———. *Once Upon a River*. Norton, 2011.

Connor, Ulla, and William Rozycki. "ESP and Intercultural Rhetoric." *The Handbook of English for Specific Purposes*, edited by Brian Partridge and Sue Starfield. Wiley, 2012, pp. 427–43.

Daguay-James, Haydee, and Ferdinand Bulusan. "Metacognitive Strategies on Reading English Texts of ESL Freshmen: A Sequential Explanatory Mixed Design." *TESOL International Journal*, vol. 15, no. 1, 2020, pp. 20–30.

Ellis, Rod. "Modelling Learning Difficulty and Second Language Proficiency: The Differential Contributions of Implicit and Explicit Knowledge." *Applied Linguistics*, vol. 27, no. 3, 2006, pp. 431–63.

Ferris, Dana R., and John Hedgcock. *Teaching L2 Composition*. Routledge, 2013.

Folman, Shoshana, and Ulla Connor. "Writing from Sources in Two Cultural Contexts." *Writing in Context(s)*, vol. 15, 2005, pp. 165–84.

Freedman, Leora. "Using Close Reading as a Course Theme in a Multilingual Disciplinary Classroom." *Reading in a Foreign Language*, vol. 27, no. 2, 2015, pp. 262–71.

Friedman, Monica. "Family Reunion." *Qwertyvsdvorak*, 17 Nov. 2017, qwertyvsdvorak.com/2017/11/17/family-reunion/.

Jenkins, Jennifer. *Global Englishes*. Routledge, 2015.

Krashen, Stephen D. *Principles and Practice in Second Language Acquisition*, 3rd ed. Phoenix ELT, 1995.

"Modes." *Digital Rhetoric Collaborative*. Gayle Morris Sweetland Center for Writing, University of Michigan, 23 Apr. 2015, webservices.itcs.umich.edu/mediawiki/DigitalRhetoricCollaborative/index.php/Modes.

Nielsen, Danielle. "Interdisciplinary Themes and Metacognition in the First-Year Writing Classroom." *CEA Forum*, vol. 48, no. 2, 2019, pp. 3–36. *ERIC*, www.cea-web.org.

Woodworth, Margaret K. "The Rhetorical Précis." *Rhetoric Review*, vol. 7, no. 1, 1988, pp. 156–64.

American Weirdos on Parade

*Reader-Response Journals and "The Smallest
Man in the World"*

JENNY ROBERTSON

I remember how I felt returning from a semester studying conservation in Tanzania: noticing the strange ubiquity of carpets, the sterile hospital atmosphere of American supermarkets, the monstrous wastefulness of our garbage. Many aspects of my home culture seemed suddenly unfamiliar and nonsensical. While a doctoral student I was fortunate to teach at the University of Louisiana at Lafayette, a southern public research institution with a diverse student body. Thirty-five percent of those enrolled are students of color, and many are first-generation students, children of immigrants, and international students from, at last count, seventy-three countries. In Spring 2019, I taught a sophomore-level English elective on contemporary global short fiction that included authors from over twenty countries and six continents. I grouped our assigned stories under three headings: People and Other Wild Creatures; Migration; and Time, Memory, and Tradition. Under each heading, an assortment of stories spoke to these themes and also related in interesting ways to one another. The syllabus was heavily weighted toward stories from non-U.S. authors.

I chose Bonnie Jo Campbell's story "The Smallest Man in the World," published in 1999 as part of her award-winning collection *Women & Other Animals*, as one of the few representing American fiction. In this story set in a generic American bar, an emotionally stunted town beauty falls in love at first sight with a drunk and somewhat boorish little person performer, in town with a traveling circus. Much as I experienced life after my college semester abroad in Tanzania, my students arriving at Campbell's American story were like travelers returning home after a long absence. They were astute observers of her cultural critique, noting issues of empathy, surface vs. depth, and individuals' relative value. While many of these observations arose in class discussion, their most thoughtful insights were preserved in journal entries. This essay will focus on the role of reader-response journals in a global short fiction course, through the filter of student responses to Campbell's story "The Smallest Man in the World," beginning with a course overview and segueing into student writing.

The Course

I assigned two required texts for this course, both anthologies: *The Art of the Story: An International Anthology of Contemporary Short Stories*, edited by Daniel Halpern, and *Flash Fiction International: Very Short Stories from Around the World*, edited by James Thomas, Robert Shapard, and Christopher Merrill. In addition, I chose supplemental short stories to fit the themes of the course. Choosing the few representatives from my home country was the most difficult part of building the syllabus. In the end, I noted some similarities in the stories that I picked. All of them, in one way or another, questioned the idea and ideals of America: what and who Americans are; who gets to be included in that designation; what our values are and how we enforce them; as well as cultural particularities of America, past and present, including public spectacle, commerce, and celebrity.

While I could easily fill a four-year series of American fiction courses with my favorite works, here are some that made the cut. The people of a rural American town stone a woman to death in Shirley Jackson's "The Lottery." Mrs. Shortley and Mrs. McIntyre conspire to murder and drive off the hardworking refugee family that threatens their racial pecking order in Flannery O'Connor's "The Displaced Person." In Ray Bradbury's "June 2001—And the Moon Be Still as Bright," the first U.S. colonizers of Mars repeat the cultural and human genocide that marred our own country's history. I included these not-quite-contemporary stories because of their authors' willingness to critique and reject American exceptionalism. I usually began each class with a short lecture, drawing maps and information on the board and giving historical context for the events that arose in each story. Students' clear-eyed understanding of America's fault lines fit into the larger narratives we were exploring in the course: nationalism, transnationalism, migration, belonging, tradition, diversity, and identity.

At first glance, "The Smallest Man in the World" seems to avoid similar kinds of critique. Its narrator, a self-absorbed, self-proclaimed Most Beautiful Woman in the Bar, focuses on surface issues and herself. Lurking below this shiny surface, however, lies a steady drumbeat of American stereotypes, informed by Campbell's time working with the circus selling snow cones. She relayed this experience in a 2012 interview with *TriQuarterly*: "So I told this boyfriend I was going to join the circus, and he said, no you're not, and so I did. We traveled to Tucson and then to LA and then all the way up the coast to Seattle, and then we started working our way back. I made it to Salt Lake City, and then I ended up going back to college after that" ("Bonnie"). Campbell's story set off impassioned class discussion, and my students wrote thoughtful journal entries comparing "The Smallest Man" with other stories from around the world. By this point in the semester my students had read stories in which characters encountered great difficulty: racial profiling, unjust arrest, dictatorial regimes, family rejection, loss of home country, persecution, and death. Our class had engaged in long discussions about stereotypes of race, ethnicity, class, and gender as they appeared in the short fiction we read. Campbell's narrative raised very American ideas of beauty, spectacle, and commerce.

I also chose a flash fiction story to pair with our assigned reading: either I or a student volunteer would read the short piece at the end of class, with time to draw comparisons between the two works. For instance, I paired "An Ugly Man," a flash piece by Marcela Fuentes, with "The Smallest Man," drawing out student discussion on love and its relationship to inner and outer beauty. Whether on the day's main story or the flash pairing, the bulk of our time together was spent in student-driven discussion. I asked many of the questions, but the interests, reactions, and critique of the student readers determined the course of our conversations. Graded assignments included presentations of group work and a final independent project, both of which were lively and illuminating, but the most pedagogically rewarding aspect of the course was collecting the reader-response journals my students used to catalog their reactions over the course of the semester.

While I had assigned journals in classes for years, perhaps instinctively understanding that students needed a place to record responses to their reading, the benefit of reader-response journals is also well supported by scholarship. In "Liberating Students through Reader-Response Pedagogy in the Introductory Literature Course," Lois Tucker provides a good overview of previous work on the subject and advances her own argument on using reader-response journals in courses like mine. Tucker describes four benefits of including this approach in an introductory literary course: increasing student experience of the readings' relevance; spurring active, not passive, engagement with texts; validating students as readers capable of evaluating meaning; and providing students an opportunity to express themselves. Introductory literature courses, often filled with nonmajors fulfilling a graduation requirement, especially benefit from reader-response journals' ability to increase student engagement and agency. As Tucker writes, "For so many, the text and the process has precluded them. They have just been carried along for the ride in previous classroom encounters with literary works, and no one has demonstrated that the students' own experience is germane to the course reading assignments" (200).

My own experience confirmed Tucker's claims, as well as Patricia Prandini Buckler's consideration of reader-response journals as antidotes to student alienation from and frustration with literary studies. I found that reader-response journals gave the students a safe, ungraded place to explore ideas, to draw comparisons between stories, and to try out arguments. Students who already spoke up in class discussion continued to engage with ideas on paper. Students who seldom raised their hands provided insight into their thought processes by communicating with me in the less-intimidating journal format. I appreciated the opportunity to express interest in their thoughts, to be delighted and surprised—and frequently amused—by their reactions, and to witness their growth as readers and writers. This class, especially, learned as a community, and the pairing of class discussion and reader-response journals went a long way toward creating that environment. Students were more confident in their assessment of the stories and came to class more prepared to add their two cents. And I enjoyed seeing the stories anew through their eyes.

Student Responses to "The Smallest Man in the World"

In this section I give a guided tour of Campbell's story, pausing to share and comment on excerpts from student journals, to approximate the individual (and yet, also, group) experience of reader-response journals as tools to evaluate a particular text. At first glance, this story might be expected to represent a very particular reality, not to offer blanket judgment of our modern society. Campbell is known for her portrayals of rural Americans: specifically, a kind of white, rural, poor, rough-living, land-and-tradition-tied American often living on the southwestern badlands of Michigan (think Kalamazoo and its surrounds). But what's particularly interesting to me about this story is its generic setting, especially when set near or against her more regionally specific stories. This "most beautiful woman" is in a bar, a setting so banal it serves as the blank template for a high percentage of American jokes. The first-person narrator calls it her "regular bar" but offers few other details ("The Smallest" 171). It has a jukebox, a polished bar, stools, and tables, but the reader is never told which city, let alone which state, they're in. And, if the narrator's sister can be trusted, it's not a particularly interesting bar: "'Why do you come here?' asks my sister, spinning around once on her barstool. 'There's nothing to do.' She spins again. 'You should tell them to get magnetic darts or something'" (171). Campbell's use of a generic bar setting lifts this story into the realm of American parable, and students understood that she was speaking about general principles they could track in their own lives and communities.

Beauty

Campbell's narrator asserts that she has always been the most beautiful person in her hometown bar, a claim that prompted skepticism among my students. From her opening assertions, the narrator promises to be more memorable than the setting: "Understand that I am not bragging when I say I am the most beautiful woman in the bar. . . . Beauty is not a virtue. And beauty is not in the eye of the beholder. Beauty is a fact like height, or symmetry, or hair color" (171). The narrator judges her beauty in relation to the people around her. Campbell presents her preeminence in this matter as a given, a consistent variable, until the circus comes to town and there are new women—showgirls and outsiders—to consider.

The narrator "proves" her beauty by comparing it to others'. Her first, and most prolonged comparison is with her sister, who has joined her at the bar. Though both women share physical features, "green eyes, high cheekbones, and thick dark hair" (172), the narrator asserts her outer superiority. The sister has, unlike the narrator, a warm and friendly personality, a loving husband, a job in service to the community, and active hobbies and interests. Yet, the narrator says, "it is a puzzle why I am more beautiful than she, perhaps it is because she has developed so many other interests" (172). Each of the narrator's assertions about beauty introduces another question. Is beauty as she presents it a vocation? A lifestyle that one chooses to inhabit in lieu of developing a personality?

My students were not sympathetic to Campbell's narrator, especially as she noted the real power she wielded as a result of her appearance. In support of her assertion that her beauty is a fact, not a perception, the narrator lists examples from her lived experience. She knows that men in the bar will always want to go home with her: "My sister knows that when I get drunk I become friendly, and she knows that men who came into the bar with perfectly nice women, or who have left women as pretty and caring as my sister at home, will risk future happiness in order to spend the night with me" (174). And she is able to solve customers' complaints at her hotel job merely by standing silently in front of them: her beauty stuns them into submission (179). One student brought the narrator's character flaws into conversation with contemporary feminism and, more personally, with individual women's awareness of their own power.

> I focused a lot on the idea of feminism while reading. The narrator was clearly very insecure and lacked heavily on her interactions with other women. . . . It made me think even worse of her. No matter how highly she spoke of herself, she still knew she was not a good person. . . . I think a lot of women are ignorant to their power as women. We are so much more than what meets the eye and truth-fully, I find a joyful personality more attractive than a pretty face. I wish I could talk to the narrator and ask her if she wants to change. If she's interested in being a better person or if she is content with being ugly. (TS)

Journals gave this student an opportunity to advance their own argument for personality's primacy over surface beauty, and even led to an imagined conversation between the student and the character.

This student's journal gestures toward the stark differences between the narrator and her sister. The narrator says of her sister, "She is warm, communicative, and generous, and I am not—just ask any of my three ex-husbands. If you want to know the other difficulties of being close to me, you will have to ask them or her, because I do not intend to enumerate my faults" ("The Smallest" 172). This statement both opens and closes a door to the character's interior life: she admits she has faults but refuses to share them with the reader. Instead, she presents a running commentary on the strength of her beauty in relation to the people who pass through her bar, and past her line of sight. All is well as long as she remains, as the evil queen in Snow White would understand, the fairest of them all. Both characters understand that beauty needs mirrors and constant reassurance that it exists. While one stereotype of beauty is that of confidence, this narrator shows its inherent insecurity, especially when attached to a character who seems unlikable in any other way.

While the narrator seems to accept the tradeoff between looks and personal growth, my students found little merit in this choice, and judged her lacking in comparison with her sister's well-rounded nature.

> Her sister constantly reaches out to her and though the main character loves being in her sister's company, she claims that she doesn't like to talk. Perhaps she has no sense of selflessness because, as she said, everyone has always done everything for her. (JN)

Journal writing provided a home and a method for gathering the insights of close reading. This student used the narrator's own assertions against her, as evidence for the origins of her antisocial behaviors. The narrator's sister has love, connection, community, purpose, vocation, impending motherhood: all things that will last and go forward, bearing fruit. My students notice, in ways the narrator does not, that she's built her life around "looking good," a state that will not improve over time. Just ask the evil queen.

Others

Another theme that Campbell explores—both obliquely and directly—is the appearance of other people. The most beautiful woman spends almost the entire story observing, judging, and giving commentary on the outer surfaces of the other bar patrons. We're told that this is her typical routine: "As usual, I sit at the far end of the bar, on the brass and leather barstool nearest the wall so I can see everyone in the place" ("The Smallest" 172). She judges the regulars, from "the sweaty man who has been coming in for the last few months with his shirt buttons more and more strained" to a woman who "must be seventy, maybe with grandchildren" who "drinks to excess nightly, done up in foundation and blusher" (173), as well as a "pale-skinned couple" who "move in unison, their once-independent bodies working as complementary parts of a whole" (174). In each case, the narrator interprets others' surfaces and presents them as evidence of larger truths. She spends so much time preparing and preserving her own beautiful surface, it seems that level of analysis may be the only one available to her.

She also evaluates the circus folk who have entered the bar. She is especially concerned with the four showgirls. From her corner perch she compares her "natural" beauty with theirs, which she decides is staged: "Though they portray beautiful women, they are not particularly beautiful. Real beauty would be too quiet on the arena floor, and it could not compete with the menagerie of elephants and horseback riders. Beauty cannot transmit over long distances, could not possibly stretch into the upper tiers of a stadium; costumes do a better job than the real thing" (178). This may be a hint about why the narrator so often inhabits a smaller space, where her beauty can have its full impact and she can study its effects.

We had discussed racism and ethnic identity in many of the other stories we read that semester, and my students were interested in the glancing way Campbell included race in this story. When the Smallest Man in the World enters the bar, he is accompanied by "two big men in circus coveralls" (172). They have "identical builds, but one is white with blond hair and slightly crossed eyes, and the other is black and scruffy-headed. Both give the impression that the coveralls are the only clothes they own" (172). This is the only mention of race in the story, with the exception of the narrator describing herself: "My arms stretch out brightly on the bar, my skin a bronze color which makes unclear precisely what my race is. Some people assume I come from an island where all the women are beautiful" (176). These brief asides may not lend themselves to deep analysis, but they do stand as symbols with her themes of beauty and spectacle. In the circus, as the narrator has suggested, surface difference must be exaggerated to read from the high seats: perhaps the circus chose on purpose the contrast of one white/blond man and one black man, both large and dressed identically, against each other and also against the stature of the Smallest Man in the World. And the narrator hints that exoticism, which is a form of rarity and spectacle, is an element of her own beauty. Any deeper issues regarding race in America are glossed over in her telling of the story; she is, as usual, concerned only with matters of surface.

Though the narrator largely avoids issues of race, *otherness* is a major factor in her response to the Smallest Man in the World, whose entrance seems to unlock something in her psyche. He notices the narrator when he looks over the bar patrons: "He holds up his drink in my direction in appreciation of my beauty, and I lift my drink in appreciation of his smallness" (173). He drinks, gets rowdy, attempts to crawl up the show-girls' skirts and is mocked and rejected, and in doing so somehow becomes more and more fascinating to the narrator. My students were perplexed by the main character's reaction to this performance:

> What intrigued me in this story was the narrator's perception of her own beauty and the way she saw those she considered "different." She singled both herself and the smallest man in the world out because she believed they were both very different from everyone else. She saw herself as extremely beautiful, and she saw the man as extremely small. How would this create such a "bond" between the two? It is almost as if she's being extremely judgmental of those who she does not see as special. She's very assuming about everything in this sto-ry, which kind of bothered me about her. She assumed every man would want to go home with her, and she assumed that she had her pick of the place. She had no regard for personality, which she even admitted to lacking, but rather focused on looks of everyone at the bar. (EG)

Reader-response journals allow students to posit their own questions about texts, and then to answer them, backing up their ideas with evidence and hypotheses. Reading their entries, I was very much aware of witness-ing thoughts in motion: elements of an argument being tried out in a less formal manner than they might be in an academic paper. While I often reminded students that these entries were low-pressure environments (shared only with me, not their classmates; ungraded except for length and adherence to due date; places to record their informal thoughts), per-haps I was tricking them into trusting themselves. In these entries they were doing the work of thinking through argument, a process integral to their final papers, contributions to class discussion, and overall sense of our class readings' relations to one another.

Some students were skeptical about the narrator's intentions, seeing just another surface judgment in her interest in the Smallest Man, though others saw a necessary evolution in her sense of self, and a breakthrough to a new way of seeing:

> Beauty is not as the narrator thinks, and I think she sees this in the smallest man in the world. She reinterprets what beauty is through her interactions with him. Beauty then becomes about all the parts being in the right place. Smallness is equated with beauty, to be small is to hide imperfections, and this is beauty. I think it is important then when the narrator reminds us that she cares more of her physical beauty than her mental health. Why does the author tell us this? In the narrator's efforts to preserve the outside of herself, i.e. her body, she has neglected that which is of equal if not more importance, i.e. her mind. What then, is the significance of the smallest man in the world? In him is the potential for her to admire something other than herself. In him is the opportunity for her to hide her imperfections as she develops her mind. All he must do is jump, for beauty cannot acquire perfection without another. (CB)

This student, a philosophy major, brought questions and training from other disciplines to his evaluation of this short story. I noted that most students confidently asserted their knowledge from both real-world experience and previous study in their journals. Their connections were thoughtful and, to me as their teacher, interesting and often surprising, offering me new ways to look at a text.

Noting the sweaty man's awkward reaction to her beauty, the narrator remarks that "his body has recently become a stranger to him. I tend my own body with such care that I cannot imagine losing touch with it—I am far more likely to lose my mind, something nobody notices" ("The Smallest" 174–75). My students were, as I mentioned before, not especially empathetic toward the narrator's problems, perhaps with this exception. This observation by the narrator invited them to question how often they'd misjudged others based on how good-looking they seemed, or how often they'd been judged by the same standards. One student wrote about the human tendency to obsess about physical presentation:

The world we live in today is filled with imitations and copycats. We are given what makes someone physically beautiful and if we don't portray that description, we try our best to do so. Most guys don't go to the gym because it's healthy for their bodies, they go because they want an attractive body. Women see celebrities with big breasts and big butts and want to imitate them because that's a modern day description of what beauty is. We as a society hide behind masks not realizing the face underneath is probably a million times more beautiful than the people we pretended to be. (DF)

Though I never asked them, I wondered how often students surprised themselves with their own journal entries. I could certainly track their thoughts as they developed on the page, through stages of initial observation and reaction (positive, negative, or confused), through questions, trial assertions, and, more often than not, a solid landing. I could feel their increasing trust in their own powers of deduction. After writing these entries, these students could, when asked, easily answer what they thought about a story, and why.

Watching the Smallest Man grow increasingly drunk and out of control, the narrator begins to fantasize about a future in which they are a couple: "I wonder if the Smallest Man in the World thinks about growing the way I think about growing less beautiful. Perhaps he and I could live together, drink less, entertain in our home. . . . Along the stairway leading to our bedroom, beside the studio shots of our children, would hang photos of our old deformed selves" ("The Smallest" 179). Here is one student's response to this imaginary future:

The main character of this story has one characteristic that others seem to use to define her entire existence: her beauty. She has always lived with this label, as we see through her flashback of her winning a high school beauty pageant. I found it interesting when she mentioned that the creator of beauty pageants is P.T. Barnum, a man who founded a large and successful circus. This ties into the way she views beauty as similar to an abnormality, something that people pay to see. Beauty to her warrants the same reaction as someone with a third limb, or conjoined twins. I don't think that she's being completely arrogant when she says that she is the most beautiful woman. When she fantasizes about what life would be like with the Smallest Man in the World, she says that pictures of their old deformed selves will hang along the stairway. This makes it obvious that to her, being beautiful is like being a freak of nature. It's a burden to her. (JN)

The narrator expresses her desire to escape the "trap" of beauty, imagining a life in which she can move without concern for how she looks. However, we are very quickly led to question her sincerity.

> You might suggest that if I genuinely look forward to growing plain, I should skip the facials, the weekly manicures and the constant touch-ups for my auburn highlights; I should let my hair hang in an easy style like my sister's, or cut it short and convenient as the showgirls have done. Well, you may as well suggest to a tall man that he slump; for me to neglect my beauty now would feel like a denial of the facts. ("The Smallest" 179)

She undermines her own argument when she says to let go of her beauty routines now would be ludicrous. She doesn't know who she is without her beauty and the power and complication it gives to her daily life. It's a given, a gift or curse, but she's also anxious about its disappearance. She's never expanded her sense of self or the world beyond this identity, even though she seems to know other possibilities are out there (first, in the descriptions comparing her and her sister, and then, one by one, in her judgments of the "regular" bar patrons and the circus performers). But she stubbornly refuses to consider an expansion of her own world.

The Beautiful Circus

My students were skeptical of the narrator's constant claims to extreme beauty and loath to grant her the special status she believed it granted her. What exactly is the difference between the bar's regulars and the outsiders who are just traveling through? Between the beautiful and the ordinary? The grotesque, strange, and special—and the boring? What is the difference between those who are born with their uniqueness and those who have to paint it on? Her assertion of supreme beauty places her squarely in the canon of American showmanship: in this country people are always shouting about being the best and most beautiful, strangest, or toughest. And in this country people pay money to witness those making these claims, whether or not they're true.

The narrator is fascinated with spectacle and oddities. She tells the reader she attends the circus whenever it comes through town and visits county-fair sideshows: "This July I traveled thirty miles and paid two dollars each to see the world's smallest horse, the fattest pig, the longest alligator. You must take for granted that they really are the longest, the smallest, and the fattest. Who is to say that the posted weight, height, or length is even honest? Who is in charge of freak show weights and measures?" (177). And with this confession, the speaker is revealed, as my students had suspected, to be an unreliable narrator. We have to take her word that she is the most beautiful woman in the bar.

The narrator's assertion that her beauty is a fact, not something she has any control over or has to work for, is contradicted by her vision of herself as a circus performer who paints her features for maximum effect:

> When I fix my face in the morning, it sometimes occurs to me to make myself up as a clown by lipsticking a massive smile onto my cheeks. Or exaggerating the sadness by painting a frown and a few shiny tears. I have heard that each circus clown must register a face with the national clown organization. Maybe women should have to do that, for we are famous for reproducing the full lips and long curving eyebrows of teenage runway models; perhaps women could be forced to be themselves, the way my sister is herself. (175)

This conflation and comparison between circus and regulars, beautiful women and clowns, shows some slippage in the differences and hierarchies the narrator lives her life by. Campbell accentuates this effect. By the end of the story, the regulars have been transformed into weirdos on parade too: even the nondescript pale-skinned couple morphs into Siamese twins. And the narrator's own self-image has slipped. Or else it has always been this mix of spectacle and strangeness. As one student wrote,

> A key point in the story I picked up on is the part where the most beautiful woman mentions clown school. Every clown must submit their own ID picture however, each face submitted must be different. We should be more like the clowns that embrace what makes us different. The most beautiful woman in the bar saw that the smallest

man in the world was unique. Ultimately, the same very thing that made him different than most men is the same thing that attracted her to him. (DF)

Perhaps the most beautiful woman, deep down, doesn't believe she's that special. And perhaps she is drawn to what seems to her to be more authentic uniqueness in the form of the Smallest Man, who can't hide his difference with makeup or highlights, who makes his living by monetizing the attraction the country has for seeing a spectacle.

My students note the very American willingness to be defined by stereotypes in our discussions of "The Smallest Man in the World." Freaks and beauty queens, cowboys and Indians. Paul Bunyan, Lake Wobegon, and a million other myths. So many cardboard cutouts float around this relatively young country's landscape they're like funhouse mirrors: you almost can't see who you are as an individual because they keep distorting your vision. Campbell's contemporary fable of shallowness lays bare the consequences of embracing the warped vision those mirrors reflect. My students recoiled at the confessions of the narrator, though she was calm in her telling, and, for all we could tell, honest in her narrative. These people are caricatures, seen from the outside, just as they'd be in a joke about stock characters walking into a bar. And the tragedy of the main character is that she's taken that dehumanizing outside view as her inner self-image. She is "the most beautiful woman in the bar" and perhaps that's all she'll ever be, even and especially to herself. And yet, if there's hope for the narrator, it has arrived in the person of the Smallest Man in the World, whether or not they escape to build a life together.

Conclusion

Teaching global literature is a worthy end in itself: it expands our understanding of the world, offers an opportunity to add historical and cultural context, increases empathy, and reinforces our common humanity. An unexpected benefit to this course, as it was with my own experience studying abroad, was the way studying fiction from other countries changed our understanding of our own. This productive disorientation—seeing one's home from the outside—was most productively captured in my students' reader-response journals. Their entries served as markers of their travels, and as resting places where they could make sense of the evolution of their thoughts.

I echo Lois Tucker's advocacy for using reader-response journals in introductory literature courses. This assignment empowered my students as readers, engaged them intellectually and personally, increased their participation in class discussion, and generated intuitive and creative connections between texts. At the end of the course, one of my global short fiction students told me that this assignment convinced him to change his major and work toward a future in writing for film. He read twice the recommended stories in our assigned anthology because he delighted in the process of writing about creative works. Many other students remarked how much they'd enjoyed the course and how much they'd miss it. I suspect a major aspect of their enjoyment arose from their own efforts on the page. After a semester of writing these journal entries, they appeared confident in their ability to encounter new texts, to interrogate them and filter them through their own experiences, and to offer valuable commentary. I felt honored to witness their reactions to the texts they were reading in real time, and to watch many of these one-page entries develop into insightful final projects and papers. And to travel with them, via the short story, all around the world and back home again.

Note

*   The author wishes to thank her students in ENGL 210–World of Contemporary Short Stories, which she taught in Spring 2019 at the University of Louisiana at Lafayette. Thanks especially to Chandler Burks, Darrel Francis III, Emily Gomez, Jenny Nguyen, and Tylar Sanchez, who gave their permission to be quoted in this chapter.

Works Cited

Buckler, Patricia Prandini. "Combining Personal and Textual Experience: A Reader Response Approach to Teaching American Literature." *Practicing Theory in Introductory College Literature Courses*, edited by James M. Cahalan and David B. Downing. NCTE, 1991, pp. 36–46.

Campbell, Bonnie Jo. "Bonnie Jo Campbell: Interview." Interview by Matt Carmichael. *TriQuarterly*, 30 July 2012, www.triquarterly .org/interviews/bonnie-jo-campbell-interview.

———. "The Smallest Man in the World." *Women & Other Animals*. 1999. Scribner's, 2002, pp. 171–80.

Tucker, Lois. "Liberating Students through Reader-Response Pedagogy in the Introductory Literature Course." *Teaching English in the Two-Year College*, vol. 28, no. 2, 2020, pp. 199–206.

APPENDIX
Teaching Activities

Introduction

As the contributors to *Michigan Salvage* make clear, Bonnie Jo Campbell's fiction is accessible to a diverse cross-section of readers. Campbell herself widens this interest by participating in readings and workshops all over the country, in settings from university creative-writing classes and local libraries to churches and beer halls. The activities that follow are designed to underscore this book's value to teachers of all kinds, facilitating rich interactions with Campbell's fiction within a variety of settings and among a wide swath of readers. These activities showcase practical ways to engage readers in multiple learning environments. The section opens with a public librarian's advice on how to plan and implement an author visit, which will be valuable to anyone looking to coordinate an event for their library, book club, or other community space (including classrooms!). The remainder of the activities offer specific strategies related to the chapters in this book. "Research and Writing" prompts readers to explore the rich histories and geographies evoked in Campbell's work. "Discussion" features questions and classroom activities designed to get students talking, thinking, and actively engaging in the fiction. "Creative" highlights varied and inventive approaches that inspire students in a range of classrooms, including introductory creative-writing courses, high school language-arts classes, and college literature courses.

While these activities are geared toward specific stories and novels, they engage central concerns in Campbell's fiction and, as teachers will find, can be adapted and reshaped for other texts as well as a variety of learning environments.

List of Activities

1. Planning and Implementing an Author Visit

Research & Writing

2. Where You At? A Bioregional Report
3. What's Your Indigenous Narrative?
4. Histories of Drugs and Alcohol

Discussion

5. Mothers, Daughters, and Rape Culture
6. Choices and Circumstances
7. Thousands of Smaller Messes
8. Slowing Down on Short Short Stories
9. Multimodal Analysis

Creative

10. Harnessing the Power of Celebrity
11. How to Complicate a How-To
12. What Do You See?
13. Lit-Crit Collage: Stories in Pictures in Stories

1. Planning and Implementing an Author Visit

MARSHA MEYER

This guide to planning an author visit is geared toward public libraries, but it could be adapted for classrooms, bookstores, or book clubs. It addresses the many details and contingencies that arise while planning and preparing for author visits. For further suggestions, contact the American Library Association, your state's Center for the Book, or state and local humanities councils.

Process

1. Seek suggestions for speakers from a committee of library staff, teachers, and collaborating organizations. Start preparing at least six months ahead of time. Many authors schedule visits twelve months ahead, and popular authors as much as two years in advance. Nearby colleges are other sources for affordable and insightful speakers.

2. Define the audience and determine the type of programs you want to include in the visit (e.g., craft talks, speaker panel, school visits, evening interview or lecture, reception, book signing). Make sure your locations are adequate for the size of audience. Select several authors and possible dates, as the first choice might not be available at the time desired. Prepare a timeline detailing preparation for the visit and a date range for the visit.

3. Select a speaker, then contact the author or their publisher. Check the author's website for contact information. The publisher or booking agent will need details such as the date and location of the visit, audience and type of program, and a contact name and phone number. Independent bookstores can help you contact publishers and find out if and when that speaker will be in your area.

4. Compile a detailed budget, which should include the honorarium, transportation, hotel and meal costs, reception food, location fees, and sound systems. Funds can come from local and state humanities grants, collaborations with area organizations, and library friends groups.

5. Confirm details in writing (your library or local government may require a contract). Include the speaker's fee, arrangements, accommodations, and a detailed timeline. A week prior, call to confirm the visit and ask about any audio-visual needs, as well as meal and housing arrangements.

6. Make all local arrangements. Arrange for a book sale with a local bookstore. Develop and implement a publicity plan. Be sure to notify local radio stations, newspapers, and magazines as well as churches, businesses, schools, libraries, and book groups. Partner organizations can help with fundraising, publicity, transportation, donating locations, printing programs, and other details.

7. Display the author's work before the visit and offer programs featuring it. Include biographical information in the library newsletter, website, and program flyers. Ask the publisher's marketing department for free posters or flyers, or create your own materials to distribute.

8. Confirm local arrangements. Distribute a final itinerary the week before the visit to ensure a smoothly run event. Several days before the event, check on room setup and remind drivers or hosts. Be sure the introduction for the author is written and have a check in hand to pay them.

9. After the event, write thank-you notes. Send to the author and booking agent as well as volunteers, the source of books, and others who helped make the visit a success.

10. Evaluate the program. Make notes of lessons learned. Review attendance numbers, response to publicity, and reactions to the program. This follow-up will help you plan your next author event.

2. Where You At? A Bioregional Report

JEFFREY INSKO

This research and writing assignment offers students the opportunity to become more familiar with the geographical spaces they inhabit, to get to know them in a way that most of our social lives are structured (water comes from a faucet, food comes from the store) to prevent us from knowing. The scope and scale of this project can vary, from a brief in-class report to a longer research essay. It is inspired by the "Bioregional Quiz" developed by Leonard Charles, Jim Dodge, Lynn Milliman, and Victoria Stockley and published in *Coevolution Quarterly* in 1981. The quiz posed a series of questions to test one's local knowledge: Where does your garbage go? How long is the growing season where you live? What species have become extinct in your area?

This activity encourages students to seek answers to such questions and, perhaps, cultivate the kind of deep knowledge of and attachment to a place experienced by characters like Margo in *Once Upon a River*.

Process

1. Students select a natural feature of the area in which they live: a lake, river, stream, or watershed, a forest or open space, a native species of flora or fauna.

2. Students research the history of the feature they have selected in order to analyze the changes to that feature over time. This research will likely focus upon questions of land use, changing landscapes, pollution and environmental damage, migratory patterns, disruptions, and extinctions.

3. Students produce a report of their findings. Reports could take many forms: formal essays, oral and/or multi-media presentations, mapping projects, even personal essays that examine students' personal relations to the feature they have chosen in light of their discoveries.

3. What's Your Indigenous Narrative?

HEATHER A. HOWARD-BOBIWASH

This activity facilitates the personal development of productive representational practices in relation to Indigenous peoples and places. Students engage in a process of researching, creating, and sharing an accurate and respectful story about a place, item, practice, or person already a part of their everyday lives. The exercise encourages critical thinking about how portrayals and/or silenced absences of Indigeneity are all around us, produce social norms, have real consequences for Indigenous persons and communities, and are integrated with how Michigander and American identities are constructed. This activity picks up on a central theme in *Once Upon a River* about how our environment shapes who we are. It is aimed at empowering students to understand how Indigeneity exists in their environments and orients them in their relationships to the places they live, work, and play.

Prompt

- Begin by viewing the world around you with conscious attention to see if you can spot representations of Indigeneity. List them. Your list might include Indigenous names of places, products (e.g., cars), animals, plants, foods, or clothing, and you might also find references to Indigeneity in group activities (e.g., school sports), transportation, architecture, symbols, seasonal pursuits, and holidays, or even people in your family tree. If you don't see anything in your daily life that reflects some aspect of Indigeneity, pick the land you stand on.

- Choose one element on your list to be the focus of the story you will tell. Research it, asking questions like: Why does this have this name? Who is represented by or in this item, place, or name? How have I come to be located where I am in relation to or in contact with this place, person, item? What has changed over time? How does the future look for this item, place, person? How does my journey continue alongside?

- Use Indigenous resources to answer these questions (or even to initiate your observations in the first step). The resources listed below can be visited online or in person, and you could also seek out Indigenous community resources and institutions near where you live, where sources have been assembled in anticipation of your questions. Some of these questions are personally reflective, and some may require you to start conversations in your family, neighborhood, school, or community.
- Tell the story of your engagement with the steps of this process. This can take any form of expression that best suits you—an essay, a short story, a blog post, an art piece, or a poem—but it should be prepared as though you will present it to an audience of Indigenous people.
- Share your story with others and keep the conversation going!

Additional Resources

In addition to the resources cited in "Mothers, Daughters, and Rape Culture in *Mothers, Tell Your Daughters*," the following can be used as starting points for research.

American Indians at the University of Michigan, umich.edu/~aium /about.html

Anishinabek: The People of this Place, Grand Rapids Public Museum, www .grpm.org/anishinabek/

Center for Native American Studies, Northern Michigan University, www.nmu.edu/nativeamericanstudies/

Great Lakes Indian Fish and Wildlife Commission, glifwc.org/

Land Acknowledgment, Kalamazoo College, land.kzoo.edu/

Land Grant Universities, www.landgrabu.org/

Michigan History Center, content.govdelivery.com/accounts/MIDNR /bulletins/2a566db

The National Native American Boarding School Healing Coalition, boardingschoolhealing.org/curriculum/

Native American Material, Clarke Historical Library, Central Michigan University, www.cmich.edu/library/clarke/ResearchResources /Native_American_Material/Pages/default.aspx

Native American Studies Research Guide, Michigan State University Library, libguides.lib.msu.edu/nativeamericans

North American Indian Association of Detroit, naiadetroit.org/

"What It Means to Be a Chippewa," Central Michigan University, https://
www.cmich.edu/offices-departments/native-american-programs
/what-it-means-to-be-chippewa
Tribal Colleges, tribalcollegejournal.org/map-of-tribal-colleges/
Ziibiwing Center of Anishinabe Culture and Lifeways, www.sagchip.org
/ziibiwing/index.htm

4. Histories of Drugs and Alcohol

ELLEN LANSKY

These writing prompts encourage students to think through the culture of drugs and alcohol in Campbell's story "Playhouse." By considering the lines between use and abuse, as well as the histories and behaviors that have developed throughout aspects of American life, students will achieve a more complete and complex understanding of the story, not to mention the world around them.

Prompts

- Investigate the scholarship on date rape, especially as it considers the influence of alcohol and binge drinking. Find some examples from local, regional, or national news. What happens to the female victims of date rape? What is the fate of the male perpetrators? How does the influence of alcohol affect women differently than men in these cases? How are bystanders treated? Write about the ways Campbell represents these dynamics in "Playhouse." Consider the extent to which Campbell tells a standard story as opposed to the ways she puts a different spin on the narrative.
- In "Playhouse," Pinky's mom, a character known as The Bitch, "lost her custody rights when she was convicted of cooking meth" (18). Research the history of "cooking meth" in rural/small-town America, particularly in areas such as Campbell's fictional Michigan. Seek out a memoir such as Carl Hart's *High Price* and write about how it illuminates drug use, addiction, and drug policy, especially as they affect vulnerable families and communities (such as working-class or poor white people in Michigan).
- In "Playhouse," Steve's "Summer Solstice" party takes a dark turn when Janie takes a bottle of tequila "down by the peonies" and Steve tells his friends to "go down and harass [her]" (26). This prompt has two parts. First, investigate the Summer Solstice and who celebrates it. What are some typical activities at Summer Solstice celebrations? Second, look into the history of tequila. What are its origins, and

how/when did it become a mainstream (or white, working-class) American party drink? What do you make of the fact that Steve, his friends, and his sister do not seem to be particularly invested in celebrating the Summer Solstice (as a traditional event), nor do they seem to have any particular cultural connection to tequila?

5. Mothers, Daughters, and Rape Culture

LAURA FINE

In this debate over a story from Campbell's *Mothers, Tell Your Daughters*, students consider how characters understand, resist, or reinscribe elements of their culture. By participating in this debate, students practice critically reading texts and integrating cultural analysis into arguments. While this debate is focused on the story "Tell Yourself," it could be expanded to include other Campbell stories and novels that display elements and outcomes of rape culture in American life.

Process

1. Introduce the central question of the debate and separate students into four groups.
    1.1 Resolved: The mother in "Tell Yourself" accurately gauges the danger rape culture poses to her daughter.
    1.2. Groups 1 and 3: Agree, with textual evidence and own analysis. (Pro)
    1.3. Groups 2 and 4: Disagree, with textual evidence and own analysis. (Con)
2. Groups meet for fifteen minutes to find evidence and develop analysis for their assigned position. Appoint someone to present ideas to class. Prepare to take notes on effective arguments made on each side.
3. Group 1 speaker (Pro) lays out group's arguments to class.
4. Group 2 speaker (Con) lays out group's arguments to class.
5. Groups meet briefly to determine quick response to other group's points (new ideas only—not points already covered in previous speech).
6. Group spokespersons give final responses to the class.
    [Repeat steps 3–6 with Groups 3–4.]
7. Open the floor for general discussion.

6. Choices and Circumstances

CHARLES CUNNINGHAM

This discussion prompt engages a central characteristic of Campbell's fiction, concern for people that mainstream America (if there is such a thing) might regard as failures: the working poor, drug addicts, and those who live on society's margins for a variety of other reasons. *American Salvage* invites its readers to see these people not simply as objects of scorn or pity, but as human beings who lead deep and complex lives, both emotionally and intellectually. In doing so, the stories also beg us to try to understand how their characters came to live on the margins.

Process

1. Ask students to consider this proposition: people make their own choices in life, but not in circumstances or conditions they choose. Those conditions would include their family backgrounds, where and when they were born, and the things that happen to them in life over which they have no control. Our lives are lived in this interaction—this dialectic—between choices and circumstances.

2. Note that this proposition can be an excellent framework for discussing the characters in individual stories. For example, the "hunter" in "The Inventor, 1972" is obviously a victim of circumstances that are historical, familial, and cultural. Including a year in the title points us toward this kind of analysis.

3. Choose another story from *American Salvage* and analyze the dialectic between choices and circumstances confronted by one or more of its characters. In this conversation, the larger goal will be to follow through with what Campbell seems to want us to do: develop an understanding of human suffering and triumph in a way that isn't mediated by pernicious pop-culture expectations.

7. Thousands of Smaller Messes

GARTH SABO

In "World of Gas," Campbell's protagonist Susan reflects that "Every man wanted to be a hot-headed Bruce Willis character, fighting against the evil foreign enemy while despising the domestic bureaucracy. Men wanted to focus on just one big thing, leaving the thousands of smaller messes for the women around them to clean up" (34–35). In this activity, students are prompted to work creatively to find ways to make these "thousands of smaller messes" an object of narrative interest, followed by a reflection on the ways that Campbell's writing aims to accomplish something similar.

Process

1. Students freewrite their response to the following prompt (5 min.): "If you had to go a month without your phone, what would you find most difficult?" Encourage them to write descriptively about the elements of their current routine that would be disrupted by this outage. Consider their emotional reliance on the device, as well as how they use their phones to maintain relationships. What would take more time without their phones? What would be impossible?

2. Students freewrite again, this time from the opposite perspective: "What would be better or easier if you relied less on your device?" If time allows, consider reading the last paragraph of "World of Gas" aloud to spark their thinking. Don't be afraid to contradict elements of their first freewrite: In what ways does their phone hamper their relationships with others? What would they have more time for or be able to do differently if their phone use was disrupted?

3. Students share their thoughts by reading or summarizing what they have written. Emphasize ways that each contribution adds nuance to the overall picture of technological reliance the group is creating together. If possible, point out the number of students who used their phones or another device in order to participate in the activity.

4. Point out that the details that the group emphasized correspond to what Campbell describes as "the domestic bureaucracy," which she contrasts with big-budget Hollywood blockbusters. Ask students to identify any media (movies, television, books, comics, etc.) that have addressed the role of phones in our daily lives. As examples are suggested, ask students to provide a brief summary of each media item. Note which items depict technological reliance in spectacular terms versus those that seem to take a more mundane approach. If they struggle to think of examples, ask them why this universal experience seems to be so difficult to bring to life for an audience.

5. Turn the conversation outward. Why is it so much easier to "focus on just one big thing" instead of "the thousands of smaller messes" that Campbell finds so interesting? Do they see any examples elsewhere in Campbell's writing where she tries to make these issues the center of the story she's telling? Where does she seem successful? What would it take for a book, film, television show, etc., to be able to address this topic in a way that is entertaining?

8. Slowing Down on Short Short Stories

ALEJANDRA ORTEGA

Bonnie Jo Campbell often conveys a lot of information about a character's life in a short amount of time. Sometimes, the brevity of the story can make it easy to read too quickly. This activity encourages students to take their time reading two stories, and the act of slowing down not only facilitates critical reading skills but also encourages students to examine how the author engages with larger contexts and themes. While these particular stories from *American Salvage* facilitate a discussion on gendered violence produced by patriarchal capitalism, this approach could be adapted to understanding the conceptual investments in other story pairings.

Process

1. Divide the class in half. Assign one half of the class "The Trespasser" and the other "The Solutions to Brian's Problem." (Although the class may be assigned to read both short stories, students will only need to complete this activity for one of them.)
2. Individually, students read their assigned story carefully and select one quotation that they believe best represents the titular character. Ask them to prepare one or two detailed sentences explaining why they chose that quotation.
3. In story groups, discuss the selected quotations and assigned stories more generally. Students should not only share their thoughts with their classmates but also consider different perspectives while engaging with Campbell's style and form. Ask the two groups to rank their top three quotations.
4. As a class, a volunteer from each group shares their group's top three quotations, explaining why they serve as a representation of their short story's titular character.
5. Broaden the discussion to consider how the selected quotations not only characterize those specific characters but also engage with concerns of gendered violence.

9. Multimodal Analysis

DOUG SHELDON

This activity is based on the development of a single scene in Campbell's short story "Family Reunion," the novel *Once Upon a River*, and Monica Friedman's comic adaptation of "Family Reunion": Marylou/Margo's revenge against her abusive uncle. By comparing these three versions, students develop a more complete understanding of multimodality by thinking through the relationship between visual and linguistic modes. This activity leads to the rhetorical précis described in Sheldon's chapter.

Process

1. Review multimodal and comic book terminology using these sources:

   Abad-Santos, Alex. "How to Read a Comic Book: Appreciating the Story behind the Art." *Vox*, 25 Feb. 2015, www.vox .com/2015/2/25/8101837/ody-c-comic-book-panels.

   "Modes." Digital Rhetoric Collaborative. Gayle Morris Sweetland Center for Writing, U of Michigan, 23 April 2015, http:// webservices.itcs.umich.edu/mediawiki/DigitalRhetoric Collaborative/index.php/Modes.

2. Show students a sample comic page. Ask students to describe it using Abad-Santos's comic terms and identify at least two modes that are active in the sample.

3. Provide handout with three versions of Marylou/Margo's revenge (or show on projector).

4. In small groups, students perform a multimodal analysis of the text, explaining how multimodality and the elements of a comic work in tandem to elaborate Campbell's writing. What enhancements are made? What pathos and ethos are shared or amplified in the transfer process? Encourage students to compare and contrast the different delivery methods in visual form, such as a Venn diagram.

5. Either discuss as a class or ask students to upload their comparisons. Note the use of multimodal and comic book terminology along with the ways they address the crucial changes between the modes of delivery of the text.

10. Harnessing the Power of Celebrity

JENNY ROBERTSON

This creative-writing activity encourages writers to harness the power of celebrity, as seen in "The Smallest Man in the World" with the appearances of P.T. Barnum, Hank Williams, and Helen of Troy. Whether you mention Elvis, Prince, or the Notorious RBG, famous folks serve as talismans of culture, and when they appear in a work of fiction they bring along all the issues, intensity, and cultural associations encoded in their names. This activity is adapted from Campbell's own exercise, which Robertson experienced during her low-residency MFA at Pacific University.

Prompt

+ Choose a character attribute that has a lot of weight and stereotypes attached to it. Campbell chose "beauty" for "The Smallest Man in the World," but you could pick "intelligence," "patriotism," "popularity," or any of a million other descriptors. Freewrite a quick paragraph describing someone who seems to epitomize this attribute. What environment would they feel most comfortable in? What do they love about the way they are? What do they hate about the way they are seen by others?

+ Pick one to three celebrities who are somehow linked with the character attribute you've chosen. They can represent the stereotypes attached to that attribute or stand for its exact opposite.

+ Write a scene in which your character is at first very happily living out a typical day, then upend those expectations. Write 1–2 pages (a piece of flash fiction or the beginnings of a longer story) and find ways to include your celebrities. Make it uncomfortable. Make it funny. Make us care about the character and their suddenly disturbed world.

11. How to Complicate a How-To

RS DEEREN

In this early-stage writing exercise, students draft a How-To Guide for something they know how to do well. It doesn't matter what the task is; what matters is that the task requires multiple involved steps that the writer must take their readers through. In this activity, writers will see how a skill that is second nature to them is still very involved, requiring the ability to accomplish many steps before completion of the task. These steps are all moments that can be impacted by a Chronic Conflict. This exercise was adapted from John Schultz's *Story Workshop*.

Process

1. Project a sample How-To on the board or make it available online.
2. Individually, students write out a step-by-step How-To Guide of something they know how to do. Each student's How-To should have at least five steps.
3. In groups, students share their How-To's. After each student, group members respond with what drew their attention as well as questions they have about how to accomplish the task. Inevitably, the writer has left out or forgotten a step. Sharers write down the questions their peers bring up.
4. On their own, students go back to each step and list two or three ways in which steps can be complicated. Finally, have students share, either to groups or the class, a couple of steps and ways in which they could render those steps with more nuance.
5. As homework, students choose two complications and rewrite their How-To's with these complications in mind. Frame the task as the Acute Conflict and the complications of each step as the Chronic Conflicts.

12. What Do You See?

BECKY COOPER

In this companion activity for the artistic project described in Cooper's chapter, students prepare to create their own piece of art by engaging in directed contemplation of an artwork and an artist's reflection. The instructor's role in this activity is to play the "guide by the side," helping discussions along only as needed, mainly encouraging students to showcase their findings. By engaging with previous student projects, students will feel inspired to push themselves into a potentially more satisfying exploration of the text, to try a radically different approach, to experiment with their methods—most importantly, to enjoy this opportunity to see what they can create.

While this project is geared toward Campbell's novel *Once Upon a River*, it could be adapted to nearly any fictional text for which you will ask students to create an artistic response. If you do not have previous student projects, there are bounteous examples online of art-inspired art, many of which include artist's commentary or interviews.

Process

1. Divide students into small discussion groups with notebooks ready. Distribute samples from previous student projects. Give one project to each group, but hold on to the artist reflection for later.
2. Students should sit with the work for at least three minutes: "Observe it. Think about it. Notice the artist's choices." Next, ask them to write down what they feel the artist wanted to convey: What connections do they see at play with this project and the original text? How, specifically, is the artist conveying their understanding or connection with the text? What creative details do they notice? What surprises, confounds, or intrigues them?
3. Group members share their thoughts with each other. What similarities and differences do they notice in their responses to the artwork? What can they extrapolate from this comparison?

4. At this point, share the artist's reflection with the small group. What does the artist reveal in their reflection that the group noticed or did not notice? What did they observe in the artwork that perhaps the artist didn't comment upon? What do they extrapolate from this round?

5. Groups share their artwork and observations with another group or the larger class. What meanings do they identify within the sample artwork? What connections do they see to *Once Upon a River*?

6. Turn the conversation toward the art that students will create. How does this make them think about their upcoming projects? After seeing these pieces of art, what do they think might be possible for themselves? How does this give them permission to experiment?

13. Lit-Crit Collage: Stories in Pictures in Stories

MONICA FRIEDMAN

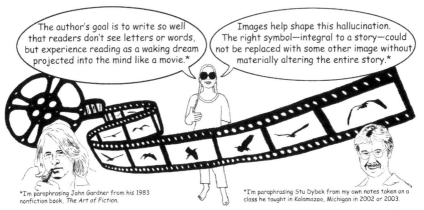

In *Q Road*, some of the most potent images used to spirit readers to a particular place and time include pumpkins, woolly bears, birds, and George Harland's barn. For *Once Upon a River*, we could list herons, deer, guns, and boats. These are short lists. If you want to break these novels down to their visual elements, you could go page by page and pull out many potent and meaningful images: Aunt Joanna's cinnamon bread, George's grandfather's picture of Mary O'Kearsy.

fig 1. This collage of powerful, recurring images summarizes chapter 1 of *Q Road* and creates a picture of autumn in rural Michigan.

In literary writing, images are chosen because they have meanings to the author, who uses the characters to assign further meaning. As a reader, you add another layer, filtering the images through your own knowledge. Consider, for example, a pair of gym shoes. You likely have a picture in your head of "gym shoes," but that image probably changes if I call them sneakers, sneaks, trainers, kicks, tennies, feet whips, running shoes, Nikes, Air Jordans, creps, Scooby Doos, tekkies, and so forth. Their meaning might depend on whether you were an athlete who saw gym shoes as performance enhancers, a mall-walking grandma who appreciated them for restoring her mobility, or a kid who's been wearing hard leather dress shoes all day and recognizes gym shoes as a hallmark of freedom and comfort.

To a collector, gym shoes might represent status. To an image-conscious teen, they might mean acceptance, but to another teen they could indicate conformity. To me, as a gender non-conforming child in the '80s, they meant secretly and subversively asserting my identity. In literary critism, we must employ all our knowledge sources to tease out meaning and intention.

Let's visualize one take on one recurring image from *Q Road*: PUMPKINS!

I'm free associating: listing whatever concepts come to mind when I think about pumpkins. Some are personal; others general, but none are universal, and they're my associations, so none of them can be "wrong."

Devil's Night

going out and actually smashing pumpkins

the band Smashing Pumpkins

being a teenager

holiday spirit

The Pumpkin King

weird nasty candy pumpkins

costumes

friends

The Headless Horseman

spooky

so hard to carve when you're a kid

plastic pumpkins for candy collecting

Halloween

aesthetic

ew, guts

fire

candles

candy

kids

scary movies

jack-o-lanterns

pumpkin carving

trick or treat

roasting pumpkin seeds

in Arizona, you can't carve a pumpkin more than 2 days before Halloween or it will rot and attract ants

creepy

orange

savory dishes

teaching my stepkids how to carve pumpkins

pumpkin juice

heartburn

mom hiding pumpkin in weird food where it doesn't belong like pancakes and kreplach

winning second place in a pumpkin carving contest

canned pumpkin

roasting pumpkins

pumpkin spice

whipped cream

pie

pie as a vehicle for whipped cream

"I never sat on a pumpkin!"

illumination

nostalgia

family

Cinderella's carriage

Thanksgiving

tradition

punkin'

turnip

corn maze

baking all day

food coma

pilgrims

Tisquantum

decorative

pumpkin trebuchet

cider

tiny ornamental pumpkins

American myths and legends

visiting a pumpkin patch

farm stands

treatment of indigenous Americans

lies my teachers taught

my stepson picking a weirdly shaped green pumpkin because he felt sorry for it

farms and gardens

Wampanoag

autumn

three sisters

seasonal

harvest festivals

Sukkot

gourds and squash

Potawatomi gardens

new world foods

All Souls'

Day of the Dead

Samhain

food that lasts all winter

native ways of knowing

pick your own

the dying of the light

honor box

Brian and Kelly's Pumpkin and Christmas Tree Farm

fig 2. Generating a word cloud, such as this figure depicting multiple layers of meaning around the concept of "pumpkins," allows you to see many possible interpretations of any symbol.

If you encounter a symbol that seems important, but you don't have many associations with the image, do more research, including asking other people about their associations. We don't all have the same experiences! I can't tell you how many times a student came to me, mystified about a piece of literature, because they didn't have any context for one important symbol. Once they understood the imagery, their entire perception of the story changed. If you don't want to talk to humans, ask Google. Learn the history of the symbol, what it does in real life, how other writers discuss it in literature. Find out if it appears in old myths, common dream motifs, classical painting, how and why it is important to others.

Every one of those meanings and associations with pumpkin imagery is valid (for me). Now I figure out which ones seem valid for the characters in the story. As I work, I also see how characters may have associations that don't appear in my chart.

You can create similar charts for any symbols based on the information in the book, or you can identify which of your ideas would resonate with a character.

Rachel

farmstand
food
money
gardens
growing
survival

April May

nostalgia
tradition
family
regret
aesthetics
holiday spirit

Nicole

appearances
conformity
smashing pumpkins
fear
nostalgia

fig 3. Comparing how the same image resonates for three different characters.

In *Q Road*, carving pumpkins probably was not an important part of Rachel's childhood; farm stands hold larger meaning for her, and pumpkins mean food and money and a connection to her ancestry. April May and Nicole both have nostalgic associations with pumpkins, but while April May wants them to summon the holiday spirit, perhaps in regard to family traditions, memories, and regret over her inability to protect her daughters from a sexual predator, Nicole's desire to carve pumpkins has a more idiosyncratic motivation—her obsession with appearance—but is overwhelmed by her own rage and disappointment about married life.

Fleshed out with citations and examples from the text, this could be an entire paper (or comic book) on what the image of the pumpkin means to these three characters and how it is integral to the message of the nove

You can also do this work in the opposite direction. Recreate elements of a character, setting, or scene, by identifying images the text associates with your target, to assemble a different picture of what the author is expressing.

dad's coat
mom's coat
warmth
Margo vs Clothing
comfort
dad's workshirt
men's clothes
vs
dad's jeans
women's clothes
nudity (skinny dipping) i
first and last chapter

In *Once Upon a River*, why does Margo feel more comfortable in her father's clothes? Why does she choose Michael's clothes over his ex-wife's? How does her mother's coat make her feel? How is skinny dipping associated with freedom? How are men's clothes associated with safety?

fig 4. Questioning how different images resonate for the same character.

Think of literary criticsm as telling your own story about a story

Now that you have chosen your images and settled on their meaning (your thesis)
COLLAGE TIME!

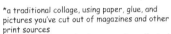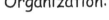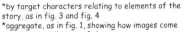

This can be:

*a traditional collage, using paper, glue, and pictures you've cut out of magazines and other print sources
*a digital collage, using images you've collected online and assembled in Photoshop
*a handmade collage or comic, using your own art, either irl or digitally
*a word collage, like the word cloud in fig.2, but more focused, or arranged as a poem
any visual method you prefer: a diorama, found objects in a shadowbox, shapes cut from plain paper, origami, cross stitch, memes, photos of your cat wearing different hats....

Organization:

*by target characters relating to elements of the story, as in fig. 3 and fig. 4
*aggregate, as in fig. 1, showing how images come together to tell parts of the story
*thematic, by grouping images from the entire story together in ways they don't appear in the book
*linear, to denote the passage of time and demonstrate a story's point or goal
anything really, as long as you can explain it. This is a creative exercise. Don't let me squash your vision. The point is to look at literature from a different perspective, based on images rather than words

*If you're visually impaired, don't connect with words and images, or are a rebel seeking a challenge, you could do this assignment as a playlist, a menu, or some other intepretation that appeals to the senses. Collage is a big umbrella.

Method: Choose the topic of your collage. Will you focus on a single character or image, relationships between characters or images, a scene, a theme? Anything aspect of the story is fair game, as long as you have something to say about its meaning, why the author put it there, and what you as a reader got out of it. Consider how to share your perspective visually. Gather your images. Arrange them in whatever way makes sense to you. If it helps, add text to explain your reasoning for each choice: quotes from the original source, your own summarization, citations from other texts, whatever words fit with your images to tell your story. If your collages are small—3 or 4 elements each—make 3 or 4 different ones. When you're finished, your collages should visually present the same information as a paper on the same topic would, and can even serve as the outline for a text-based assignment.

Bonus Activity: retell an entire story using only emojis. Share your work in small groups. Can your group guess your story? Or, you can all create your own interpretation of the same story and compare. Discuss how you chose symbols to represent concepts, how your choices affect the story's meaning, and other ways you could have expressed the same concepts.

Contributors

Becky Cooper is the English chair and AP instructor for the Academically Talented Youth Program at Western Michigan University in Kalamazoo, where she also teaches courses for the Lee Honors College. As of 2022, she has received the Significant Educator Honor through the Kalamazoo Area Math and Science Center twenty times since 2005, and the Significant Educator Award for Excellence in Education in Kalamazoo County eighteen times since 2006. She holds an MFA from Western Michigan University, and she is presently working on two young-adult novel ideas and seeking publication for her manuscript *How the Body Learns to Float*.

Charles Cunningham is professor of English at Eastern Michigan University, where he teaches and writes about U.S. literature and culture. His work has appeared in *Works and Days*, *Reconstruction*, *Cultural Logic*, and the *Journal of Narrative Theory*. He is also active in his faculty union, the EMU-AAUP.

RS Deeren is assistant professor of English and fiction at Austin Peay State University. His debut collection of short stories, *Enough to Lose*, is forthcoming from Wayne State University Press. He is anthologized in *Tales of Two Americas: Stories of Inequality in a Divided Nation*, edited by John Freeman. Deeren earned his PhD from the University of Wisconsin-Milwaukee and holds an MFA from Columbia College Chicago. Before moving to Middle Tennessee, he worked as a line cook, landscaper, lumberjack, and bank teller in the rural Thumb Region of Michigan.

Lisa DuRose is an English faculty member at Inver Hills Community College in Minnesota, where she teaches courses in composition, the novel, and the short story. She has published essays in the *Journal of College and Character*, the *Wallace Stevens Journal*, and *Prospects: An Annual of American Cultural Studies*, and her work on Bonnie Jo Campbell has appeared in *Midwestern Miscellany*, *Rain Taxi*, and Macmillan Learning. She is currently preparing a biography of Campbell.

Laura Fine grew up in Michigan and Minnesota and is now professor of English and department chair at Meredith College in Raleigh, North Carolina. She teaches American and world literature with research areas of interest in contemporary American female writers and Southern literature. She has published articles on Jhumpa Lahiri, Bonnie Jo Campbell, Jesmyn Ward, Dorothy Allison, Carson McCullers, and Harper Lee in *Biography*, the *Southern Literary Journal*, *Critique*, and the *South Carolina Review*.

Monica Friedman is a writer, illustrator, editor, and educator based out of Tucson, Arizona. A former student of Bonnie Jo Campbell's, she is the creator of four volumes of *Bonnie Jo Campbell Comics* and the author of the contemporary desert fantasy novel *The Hermit* (2016), as well as numerous webcomics and works of short speculative fiction. You can enjoy a wide selection of her original words and images at QWERTYvsDvorak.com.

Heather A. Howard-Bobiwash is associate professor of anthropology at Michigan State University. She studies the social relations through which authoritative knowledge—the knowledge that counts—is constructed and applied in cultural, educational, social service, and healthcare settings. She is interested in cultural change, gender, and the meaning people make from engagements of the past in the present. She has twenty-five years of experience in public education and community-based organizing projects that serve the dual role of strengthening Indigenous self-determination and expanding awareness of Indigenous issues. She has edited four volumes in Indigenous and feminist studies and is published in journals ranging from the *Engaged Scholar Journal* to the *American Anthropologist*.

Jeffrey Insko is professor of English at Oakland University, where he teaches courses in nineteenth-century American literature and culture and the environmental humanities. He is the author of *History, Abolition, and the Ever-Present Now in Antebellum American Writing* (2018). He is currently completing a book titled *Untimely Infrastructures: The 2010 Marshall, Michigan Oil Spill in the Human Epoch*, which is in part an environmental history of the Kalamazoo River.

Ellen Lansky is an English faculty member at Inver Hills Community College in Minnesota, where she teaches composition, literature, and creative writing. Her work on literature and addiction has appeared in *Dionysos*, *English Language Notes*, *Literature and Medicine*, and several anthologies, including *Southern Comforts: Drinking & the U.S. South*

(2020). Her article "All Aboard: Reading, Writing, and Drinking with Ernest Hemingway" appeared in a special issue of *English Language Notes*. She is also a fiction writer, and her novel *Suburban Heathens* was published in 2018.

Marsha Meyer has worked in public libraries for over forty years. During that time, she planned and implemented readings for local and national writers including Maya Angelou, Mark Doty, and Bonnie Jo Campbell. She co-founded the Kalamazoo Poetry Festival, a nonprofit that continues to bring poets from around the United States to the Kalamazoo, Michigan, area and celebrate local poets of all ages. Currently she is a member of the Meet Michigan Authors Collaborative, which hosts Michigan author readings at the Richland Community Library.

Andy Oler wrote *Old-Fashioned Modernism: Rural Masculinity and Midwestern Literature* (2019) and edited *Pieces of the Heartland: Representing Midwestern Places* (2018). His writing has appeared in *Queering the Countryside: New Frontiers in Rural Queer Studies* (2016), *College Literature*, and *MidAmerica*, as well as *Hyped on Melancholy*, *Essay Daily*, and the *New Territory*. He teaches at Embry-Riddle Aeronautical University in Daytona Beach, Florida, and serves as departments editor of the *New Territory*.

Alejandra Ortega is assistant professor of English at the College of DuPage. Her research interests include spatial theory, narratology, and ecocriticism, and her work has been published in *ISLE: Interdisciplinary Studies in Literature and Environment* and *Rhizomes: Cultural Studies in Emerging Knowledge*.

Jenny Robertson holds an MFA in fiction from Pacific University and a PhD in English from the University of Louisiana at Lafayette, where she taught creative writing, American literature, drama, and global short fiction. She was awarded second prize in *Cutthroat*'s Rick DeMarinis short story contest by judge Stuart Dybek, and also received *Gulf Stream Literary Magazine*'s 2020 fiction prize. Her fiction chapbook, *Hard Winter, First Thaw*, was published by Michigan Writers Cooperative Press in 2009, and her poems and stories have appeared in *The Best of Cutthroat*, *Flyway: Journal of Writing & Environment*, *Hypertext Magazine*, *Dislocate*, *Dunes Review*, *South Carolina Review*, and elsewhere. Her debut fiction collection, *Hoist House: A Novella & Stories*, is forthcoming from Cornerstone Press.

Garth Sabo is assistant professor in the Center for Integrative Studies in the Arts and Humanities at Michigan State University, where he teaches courses in Midwestern culture, climate fiction, infrastructure, and the medical humanities. His research focuses on the literature of waste and depictions of identity-as-community to be found in filth and detritus. His work has been published in *Arizona Quarterly* and *Midwestern Miscellany*, as well as in edited volumes on American regional studies and the urban gothic.

Doug Sheldon is senior lecturer and English Language Learner specialist in the Department of English at the University of Illinois, Chicago. His research examines the literary-linguistic dimensions of Midwestern literature in tandem with English and additional language usage. Sheldon's teaching employs literary pedagogy within TESOL instruction for generating multilingual writership. His work has appeared in *Teaching Hemingway and Gender, MidAmerica, Midwestern Miscellany*, and the *Flyover Country Review*.

Ross K. Tangedal is associate professor of English and director of the Cornerstone Press at the University of Wisconsin–Stevens Point, where he specializes in American print and publishing culture. He is the author of *The Preface: American Authorship in the Twentieth Century* (2021) and coeditor of *Editing the Harlem Renaissance* (2021). His articles have been published in multiple journals, including the *Papers of the Bibliographical Society of America, South Atlantic Review*, the *Hemingway Review*, the *F. Scott Fitzgerald Review, Authorship*, and *MidAmerica*, and in numerous essay collections. He serves on the editorial team of the Hemingway Letters Project.